The Culinary Institute of America
Vegetables

RECIPES AND TECHNIQUES FROM
THE WORLD'S PREMIER CULINARY COLLEGE

Over 170 New Delicious, Kitchen-Tested Recipes | 100 Color Photographs
Illustrated Step-by-Step Techniques from the Classrooms of the CIA

Photography by Ben Fink

LEBHAR-FRIEDMAN BOOKS
NEW YORK • CHICAGO • LOS ANGELES • LONDON • PARIS • TOKYO

THE CULINARY INSTITUTE OF AMERICA

President	Dr. Tim Ryan
Vice-President, Continuing Education	Mark Erickson
Director of Intellectual Property	Nathalie Fischer
Managing Editor	Kate McBride
Editorial Project Manager	Mary Donovan
Production Assistant	Patrick Decker
Recipe Testers	Maggie Wheeler
	Lisa Lahey

The Culinary Institute of America would like to thank Michael Pederson,
for his skilled execution and presentation of the recipes and methods for the photographs,
and Thomas Schroeder and family for inviting us into their home for the photography.

Special thanks to Migliorelli Farms in Red Hook, New York for providing
some of the items used in the photography.

LEBHAR-FRIEDMAN BOOKS

A company of Lebhar-Friedman, Inc., 425 Park Avenue, New York, New York 10022

Project Manager	Maria Tufts
Art Director	Kevin Hanek

LIBRARY OF CONGRESS CATALOGING-IN-PUBLICATION DATA

Cataloging-in-publication data for this title is on file with the Library of Congress.

ISBN 0-86730-918-0 | 978-0-86730-918-8

Manufactured in Singapore on acid-free paper

Contents

Entrees   167

Roasted Eggplant Stuffed with Curried Lentils ❀ Spicy Eggplant, Wild Mushroom, and Tomato Casserole ❀ Eggplant Rollatini ❀ Capellini with Grilled Vegetables ❀ Asparagus with Shiitakes, Bowtie Pasta, and Spring Peas ❀ Tortelli with Bitter Greens and Ricotta ❀ Fettuccine with Corn, Squash, Chiles, Crème Fraîche, and Cilantro ❀ Chicken and Vegetable Kebabs ❀ Vegetable Burgers ❀ Eggplant and Havarti Sandwiches ❀ Madeira-Glazed Portobello Steak Sandwiches ❀ Chickpea and Vegetable Tagine ❀ Paella Con Verduras ❀ Artichoke and Spinach Risotto ❀ Roasted Vegetable Pizza ❀ Mu Shu Vegetables ❀ Pork Cutlets with a Wild Mushroom Ragout ❀ Stirfried Garden Vegetables with Marinated Tofu ❀ Tofu and Peas with Cilantro in a Red Curry Sauce ❀ Grilled Halibut with Roasted Red and Yellow Pepper Salad ❀ Spinach and Goat Cheese Quiche ❀ Caramelized Onion Tart ❀ Vegetarian Shepherd's Pie ❀ Spaghetti Squash with Vegetable Ragout ❀ Crepes with Spicy Mushrooms and Chile Cream Sauce ❀ Chiles Rellenos ❀ Chayote and Pineapple Chimichangas ❀ Spring Greens and Cannellini Gratin

Sauces & Relishes   255

Basic Tomato Sauce ❀ Tomato Coulis ❀ Pomarola Tomato Sauce ❀ Tomato-Ginger Coulis ❀ Roasted Red Pepper Puree ❀ Tomatillo Salsa ❀ Blackened Tomato Salsa ❀ Tomato Salsa ❀ Green Papaya Salsa ❀ Chayote-Jícama Salsa ❀ Half-Sour Pickles ❀ Sweet Pickle Chips ❀ Pickled Beets and Onions ❀ Red Onion Marmalade ❀ Roasted Red Pepper and Apricot Relish ❀ Corn Relish ❀ Spicy Mango Chutney ❀ Hazelnut Romesco Sauce ❀ Harissa ❀ Tzatziki Sauce ❀ Mustard ❀ Pesto ❀ Cream Sauce ❀ Mayonnaise ❀ Hollandaise Sauce

INDEX   285

Side Dishes   217

Maple-Glazed Brussels Sprouts with Chestnuts ❀ Brussels Sprouts with Mustard Glaze ❀ Asparagus A La Parrilla ❀ Parmesan-Roasted White Asparagus with White Truffle Oil ❀ Belgian Endive A La Meunière ❀ Maple-Glazed Turnips ❀ Creamed Swiss Chard with Prosciutto ❀ Braised Kale ❀ Braised Red Cabbage ❀ Broccoli in Garlic Sauce ❀ Beet Greens and White Beans Sauté ❀ Zucchini Pancakes ❀ Okra Stewed with Tomatoes ❀ Ratatouille ❀ Roasted Corn Succotash ❀ Zucchini Squash with Tomatoes and Andouille ❀ Sautéed Broccoli Raab with Garlic and Crushed Pepper ❀ Sicilian-Style Spinach ❀ Citrus-Roasted Beets ❀ Hoisin-Caramelized Root Vegetables ❀ Sweet and Sour Green Beans with Water Chestnuts ❀ Winter Squashes Sautéed with Cranberries and Toasted Pecans

Introduction

FEW DECADES AGO, shopping for fresh vegetables meant going to the supermarket to pick up some shrink-wrapped green beans and a head of iceberg lettuce. Oddities like avocados, fresh yams, herbs, or any color pepper other than green were rarely stocked in the bins.

Today, the options are much greater. Exotic mushrooms, Asian and Latin vegetables, white asparagus, a staggering array of chiles and peppers, and even heirloom vegetables are stocked in supermarkets. Whole sections are devoted to organic produce. The changes in our markets were spurred in great part by the foods chefs across the country were featuring on their menus. These very same chefs began to talk more and more about buying directly from farmers, or even working directly with the farmers. Foragers became a legitimate source of wild and found foods.

The demand for the finest and the freshest produce didn't stop at the restaurants, of course. Soon, consumers were clamoring for better, fresher, and more flavorful produce as well. That demand contributed directly to the resurgence of community-sponsored farmers' markets throughout the United States. According to the U.S. Department of Agriculture, there were less than 100 farmers' markets operating in the nation three decades ago. Their first Farmer's Market Directory, published in 1994, listed about 1,755 markets across the nation. The most recent directory, from 2004, shows an increase of over 100 percent and lists over 3,700 markets throughout all fifty states. That number will undoubtedly be much larger when the directory is updated again. In addition to farmer's markets, you can choose to participate in community sponsored agriculture (CSA) or visit markets specializing in organic, heirloom, and no-spray vegetables.

The Culinary Institute of America is committed to working as closely with local growers as it can. We've seen the number of farmers that sell directly to the college swell to over 20. We know that it is the right thing to do, because the vegetables are more flavorful. We believe that preserving traditional foods, including heirloom varieties, is important for reasons both gustatory and environmental.

We sincerely hope that the recipes in this book inspire you to eat more vegetables. Everyone agrees that eating a variety of vegetables is the best way to get the vitamins and minerals you need. The decisions you make about what to buy and where to buy it have implications for your health, the health of your community, and the health of the planet. Find the local markets, the specialty growers, and the stores that carry locally produced foods in your town or neighborhood. Grow your own, if you've got the time and space to do so. Try vegetables that are new to you, or try a familiar vegetable in a new way. Enjoy.

Vegetables 101

 ROM THE FIRST tender pea shoots in spring to the last brilliant orange pumpkins in autumn, vegetables are the cook's harbinger of the changing seasons. When the local crop of asparagus or sweet corn first starts to trickle into the market, we can't wait to get it home. We admire such vegetables for their many culinary virtues: bright colors, distinctive flavors, valuable nutrients, and remarkable versatility. Vegetables can be savored just as they come from the farm, or they can be prepared using virtually any cooking method. Enjoy them on their own or incorporated into soups, appetizers, salads, side dishes, and main courses.

You can let the vegetable stand alone or choose from myriad seasonings and garnishes. Simple steamed broccoli, for example, is tender and sweet. Drizzle it with olive oil and a scattering of toasted pine nuts, and you have a completely different dish.

A Vegetable Primer

Vegetables include a number of foods that botanically are classified as fruits. Tomatoes, peppers, squash, and other seed-bearing foods are really fruits. Because these are often used in savory preparations, their culinary application is the guiding principle for listing them here.

The USDA's Dietary Guidelines divides vegetables into five groups: Dark green vegetables, orange vegetables, legumes, starchy vegetables, and other vegetables. Eating a variety of colors—including red cabbage or red bell peppers, yellow sweet corn, white garlic, and deep green spinach— provides a wide array of vitamins, minerals, and phytochemicals, many of which are found in pigments and fiber.

Orange and dark green vegetables are good sources of vitamin C and are high in beta carotene, which the body uses to make vitamin A (the chlorophyll in green vegetables masks the carotenoid pigments). Legumes and dark green vegetables are good sources of folate. Potatoes, avocados, and legumes are also high in potassium.

The Dietary Guidelines recommend 2½ cups of vegetables per day for a 2,000 calorie diet, with the following amounts recommended over the course of a week:

Dark green vegetables *(broccoli, spinach, most greens)*	3 cups/week
Orange vegetables *(carrots, sweet potatoes, pumpkin, winter squash)*	2 cups/week
Legumes *(dried beans, chickpeas, tofu)*	3 cups/week
Starchy vegetables *(corn, white potatoes, green peas)*	3 cups/week
Other vegetables *(tomatoes, cabbage, celery, cucumber, lettuce, onions, peppers, green beans, cauliflower, summer squash)*	6½ cups/week

Most Americans do not eat anywhere near these recommended intakes, with the possible exception of starchy vegetables, specifically potatoes.

SELECTING VEGETABLES

The essential point to remember when choosing vegetables is that they are, in general, highly perishable. The more fresh and appealing a vegetable looks when you buy it (or pick it, if you have a garden), the greater its level of nutrients.

VEGETABLE/FAMILY	REPRESENTATIVE MEMBERS	WHAT TO LOOK FOR	BEST COOKING METHODS
Cabbage family	Bok choy, broccoli, broccoli rabe, Brussels sprouts cauliflower, green/red/savoy/Napa cabbage, kohlrabi	Firm, heavy heads; good color; florets, if any, tightly closed	Boiling, steaming, stir-frying, grilling, braising, stewing
Corn	Yellow, white, and bi-color varieties	Husk firmly attached, kernels plump	Boiling, steaming, roasting, grilling, stewing
Eggplant	Globe, Japanese	Skin firm and glossy, leaves unwilted	Grilling, broiling, roasting, stewing, pan-frying, deep-frying
Greens (leafy)	Arugula, chard, collards, dandelion, kale, mustard, spinach	No wilting or yellowing in leaves, heads heavy for size	Sautéing, stir-frying, steaming, boiling, stewing, braising
Legume family	Green beans, haricots verts, fava beans, garden peas, snow peas, sugar snap peas	Beans and pea pods that are plump, crisp, and evenly colored	Steaming, boiling, sautéing, stir-frying, stewing, braising
Mushroom family	Chanterelle, porcini, morel, portobello, oyster, enoki, shiitake, white; truffles	Caps plump; earthy smell; gills, if any, intact; stems, if any, firmly attached	Sautéing, stir-frying, stewing, braising, grilling, roasting, baking, pan-frying, deep-frying
Onion family (fresh)	Leeks, green onions	Green portions intact and unwilted; bulb firm	Sautéing, grilling, broiling, stewing, braising
Onion family (dried)	Cipollini, red onions, shallots, sweet onions, white onions, yellow onions	Firm and heavy for size, outer layers tight with good color	Sautéing, grilling, broiling, stewing, braising roasting, baking, pan-frying, deep-frying
Pepper family	Bell, chile	Fruit plump, skin glossy and taut	Roasting, grilling, broiling, sautéing, stir-frying, stewing, deep-frying
Roots and tubers	Beets, carrots, parsnips, potatoes, rutabagas, salsify, turnips	Firm and heavy for size, no withering; greens, if attached, unwilted	Boiling, steaming, roasting, baking, sautéing, stir-frying, grilling, broiling, stewing, braising
Squash family (soft-skinned)	Chayote, crookneck, pattypan, yellow, zucchini	Good color, firm, no bruises or soft spots	Sautéing, stir-frying, pan-frying, deep-frying, grilling, broiling, roasting, stewing, braising
Squash family (hard-skinned)	Acorn, butternut, Hubbard, spaghetti, pumpkin	Firm; heavy for size; stem, if any, firmly attached	Boiling, steaming, roasting, baking, sautéing, stewing, braising
Tomatoes	Beefsteak, cherry, currant, pear, plum (Roma)	Good color, heavy for size, skin glossy and intact, slightly yielding when ripe	Sautéing, stir-frying, roasting, grilling, broiling, stewing, braising, simmering

As soon as any vegetable is harvested it begins to undergo significant changes. The more delicate the vegetable, the more dramatic the change. Sweet corn and peas, for instance, begin converting sugars into starch, giving over-the-hill corn and peas a telltale sticky texture and pasty taste. When you consider the time that it takes to get foods from the field to the market, you can see why it is best to shop frequently for vegetables, keep them refrigerated, and cook them within a few days. At some times of the year you may find that frozen vegetables, which are typically processed right in the field upon harvesting, are a good alternative to less-than-ripe fresh produce. Peas, spinach, corn, and green beans are good examples of vegetables that might be best frozen.

Root vegetables (sometimes called winter vegetables) are significantly less perishable and generally can be stored without any marked loss of quality for several weeks or, if carefully handled, even months. Hard-skinned squashes, turnips, carrots, parsnips, and cabbages fall into this category of vegetables. The traditional way to store these vegetables is in a root cellar under a good covering of straw or hay, where they benefit from a constant cool temperature and relatively high humidity. Since most of us don't have root cellars, however, it is best to use them within a week or two of purchase.

If vegetables are sold as organic, they must meet specific guidelines regarding the land they are grown on and the types of fertilizers and other cultivating aids that can be used. Look for the "Organic" symbol on the label or posted near the display.

Some markets offer precut vegetables, which can save on preparation time. When inspecting the package, look for fresh, moist surfaces. Even if the produce is labeled "prewashed," you should rinse it in cool water to refresh it.

Vegetable Cooking Primer

Each vegetable has distinct properties when it is properly cooked. Fully cooked green beans, for example, have a very different texture from fully cooked carrots. Different cooking methods also result in different textures in the finished dish. Stir-fried vegetables may be fairly crisp, while stewed and braised vegetables are often cooked until they nearly fall apart. Personal preference and the cuisine your recipe draws from also influence how you judge doneness.

The most reliable doneness tests for vegetables are taste and touch. Bite into a piece of the vegetable when it is raw, and then again at various points as it cooks. Notice the flavor and texture. If tasting the vegetable isn't practical, pierce it with a knife, fork, or skewer and gauge the resistance it gives. Consider the way you will be using the vegetable to determine the right degree of doneness. Will it be served alone or as part of a complex dish?

Most stand-alone vegetable dishes, whether they are steamed, boiled, sautéed, or grilled, turn out best when the vegetables are cooked just until tender. You should be able to bite into the vegetable easily, but it should still offer a slight resistance.

Stewed and braised vegetables should be fully cooked. Aim to cook vegetables for these dishes until they are completely tender but retain their shape and color. When you boil or steam vegetables for a purée, cook them until they almost fall apart on their own. At this point, they should be easy to push through a sieve or purée in a blender.

In some recipes, vegetables are blanched, not to cook them through but to set their colors, make them easier to peel, or to improve their flavor. Blanched vegetables are boiled very briefly, just long enough to cook the outermost layer, then submerged in cold water to stop the cooking process. The vegetable retains, for the most part, the texture it had when raw. Similarly, vegetables are sometimes boiled, steamed, or roasted to near doneness, then finished in a second step, sometimes using a different technique, such as grilling or sautéing. Boiling or cooking to near doneness is known as parboiling or parcooking.

Vegetables can be the centerpiece of a meal or can be used to add flavor, eye appeal, and texture to meals featuring meat, fish, or poultry. The recipes in this book offer a wide range of choices for those who want to expand their repertoire of vegetable dishes.

DARK GREEN VEGETABLES

Dark green vegetables include most of the crucifers (cabbage family): broccoli, Brussels sprouts, boy choy, kale, and collards. It also includes cooking greens such as Swiss chard and turnip greens, as well as salad greens such as arugula, leaf lettuce, and spinach.

These vegetables are extremely low in calories and fat (usually under 1 gram per serving), and contain generous amounts of fiber, vitamin C, beta carotene, iron, calcium, folate, and vitamin B6. Crucifers, including cabbage and cauliflower (see *Other Vegetables,* page 8) are also high in phytochemicals called glucosinolates, a group that includes indoles, isothiocyanates, and sulforaphane, which are thought to protect against some types of cancer. It is best not to overcook these vegetables: Doing so causes nutrient loss and releases the sulfur-containing phytochemicals that cause their unpleasant aromas. Some of these vegetables, such as kale and Brussels sprouts, are at their best in late fall. Their somewhat pungent flavors mellow after they have been exposed to frost.

ARUGULA has tender leaves with rounded teeth. It has a peppery flavor that becomes more pungent as it ages.

BEET GREENS have flat leaves with red ribs. They're available year-round, but are at their best during summer and early fall. They are generally steamed, sautéed (especially with garlic), or braised.

BOK CHOY has deep green, glossy leaves and green-to-white stems. Its peak season is summer into fall, but it is available year-round. It is usually steamed, braised, or sautéed, but baby bok choy may be served uncooked.

BROCCOLI is dark green, but may have a purple cast. Its peak is summer, though imported broccoli is available year-round. It can be steamed, sautéed, roasted, or pureed. Broccoli stems can toughen; look at the bottoms and choose stalks with little, if any, white core.

BROCCOLI RABE is leafy and green with small florets and stems. Its flavor is slightly sharper than broccoli, its texture chewier. It can be steamed, sautéed, or braised.

BRUSSELS SPROUTS are small, round, and cabbage-shaped. Their peak season is late fall to winter. They can be steamed, boiled, roasted, or sautéed.

COLLARD GREENS have large, flat, rounded leaves. Their peak season is fall. They are generally steamed, sautéed (especially with garlic), or braised.

DANDELION GREENS have narrow leaves with deep teeth on the edges. They are at their best in spring. They are generally steamed, sautéed (especially with garlic), or braised.

ESCAROLE is a lettuce with scalloped edges. It is slightly to very bitter and often is used in soups and stews and as a cooking green.

KALE has ruffled leaves. Its peak season is late fall. It is generally steamed, sautéed (especially with garlic), or braised.

LEAF LETTUCE is a loose-head lettuce with tender leaves that may be tipped with red. It is usually mild, but becomes bitter with age.

MÂCHE is an extremely fragile, perishable salad green sometimes called lamb's ear.

Sam says—
GARDEN
To Cut Food Costs

...ment of Agriculture Washington, D.C.
...e Bulletin on Gardening — *It's food for thought*

MUSTARD GREENS have deeply scalloped, narrow leaves. Their peak season is summer. They are generally steamed, sautéed (especially with garlic), or braised.

ROMAINE LETTUCE grows in a long, cylindrical head. The outer leaves are heavily ribbed; inner leaves are milder and sweeter (the inner leaves are known as the heart).

SPINACH leaves are deep green and may be deeply lobed or flat, depending upon variety. They are available year-round. They can be used raw in salads; when cooked, they are generally steamed, sautéed (especially with garlic), or braised.

SWISS CHARD has deeply lobed, glossy dark green leaves. The stems and ribs may be white, deep ruby, or variegated. The peak season is fall. It is generally steamed, sautéed (especially with garlic), or braised.

TURNIP GREENS have broad, flat, leaves with a coarse texture. Their peak season is summer into fall. They are generally steamed, sautéed (especially with garlic), or braised.

WATERCRESS has rounded scallops on its leaves and a peppery flavor. It is often used in salads and as a garnish.

ORANGE VEGETABLES

Orange vegetables get their coloring from carotenoid pigments; beta carotene is the one the body converts into vitamin A. Their flesh can range in color from deep yellow (such as yams) to dark orange (pumpkin), and their peels can be any color. These vegetables are typically very high in fiber, several of the B vitamins, as well as vitamin C and even E. Some supply iron and magnesium.

Most of these vegetables store well at cool room temperature, though carrots are better refrigerated.

ACORN SQUASH has a very thick skin with deep ridges; it is most often dark green, but orange-skinned varieties are available. It is generally baked, pureed, simmered, glazed with honey or maple syrup, or used to make soups.

BUTTERNUT SQUASH has tan, orange, or light brown skin and an elongated pear shape. It is generally baked, pureed, simmered, glazed with honey or maple syrup, or it can be used to make soups.

PUMPKINS are dark orange with deep ridges. They are generally baked, pureed, simmered, glazed with honey or maple syrup, or used to make soups, pies, or breads.

CARROTS are one of the most popular vegetables. They are available year-round, come in a variety of sizes and shapes, and even in colors other than orange. As they age they become tough, woody, and fibrous. The tops should be cut away before storage to prevent spoilage.

LEGUMES

Although most people think of legumes as dried beans, this group includes thousands of plants: A legume has seed pods that split along both sides when ripe, and legumes are classified by whether these pods are edible. The most common include beans and soybeans, lentils, peanuts, and peas. Fresh beans and peas are sweetest and most tender when they are young. Once picked, their natural sugars begin to convert into starch. Garden peas are especially prone to flavor loss.

Most legumes are a good source of protein—for most of the world, they are the primary source of protein—and contain B vitamins like folate and riboflavin, vitamin E, complex carbohydrates, soluble and insoluble fiber, and minerals such as iron, calcium, and magnesium.

The following fresh legumes have edible pods:

GREEN BEANS are long and slender with an even, matte green color. They peak in mid to late summer, and are available fresh or frozen. Wax beans are yellow and are similar in texture and flavor. Often steamed or sautéed, they can be simmered with ham or bacon as well.

HARICOTS VERTS are smaller and slimmer than regular green beans and have a velvety skin. Their season is the same.

ROMANO BEANS are similar in color to green beans, but they are wider and flatter, with a more developed flavor. Their peak season is mid- to late summer, and they are often braised with ham or bacon.

BURGUNDY BEANS, or purple beans, are similar in shape to green beans; their deep purple to maroon skin turns green as they cook.

The following beans have inedible pods. They are available fresh and dried:

EDAMAME are a type of soybean grown specifically to be harvested when immature. They are higher in protein and fat than other beans, and their protein is complete—that is, it supplies all the essential amino acids in amounts necessary for humans. Edamame can be used like green peas in many dishes or boiled and salted.

FAVA BEANS grow in long, large, pale-green pods. The beans themselves are delicate green and almost kidney shaped. They are at their peak in spring to early summer. They may be cooked and pureed or eaten cold.

FLAGEOLETS grow in green pods; the beans are light green. They are cooked and served whole in side dishes or soups, or braised or pureed.

CRANBERRY BEANS grow in pods that are white with red streaks. The beans are white mottled with red. They are cooked and served whole in side dishes or soups, or braised or pureed.

BLACK-EYED PEAS grow in pods that are green, often mottled with brown. The peas are round and tan with a black "eye." (Peas with a brown "eye" are cowpeas.) Their peak season is throughout summer and into fall. They are cooked and served whole in side dishes or soups, or braised or pureed. Hoppin' John is a well-known dish using black-eyed peas.

LIMA BEANS are the most common shell bean in the United States. They are cooked and served whole in side dishes; they combine with corn kernels to make succotash. Large lima beans are called butter beans; baby lima beans are very mild and tender.

PEAS are also commonly available. Their peak season is early spring to summer. Garden peas, sometimes called *petit pois*, grow in tapered, yet rounded, pods that should "squeak" when rubbed together. The peas are round and light drab green when raw. They can be steamed, stewed, pureed, and used in soups. They supply fiber, thiamin, vitamin C, folate, and iron. Snow peas have flat, edible pods and very small peas. They are usually steamed or stir-fried. Sugar snap peas have edible pods that are deeper green than garden or snow peas; the pods are rounder than snow peas, and the peas are larger. They are steamed or stir-fried.

STARCHY VEGETABLES

Starchy vegetables are usually roots and tubers that serve as nutrient reservoirs for the upper part of a plant. They are rich in carbohydrates, vitamins, and minerals.

Tubers are enlarged, bulbous roots capable of generating a new plant. Potatoes are the most common tuber, but Jerusalem artichokes, jícama, and yams are others.

If leaves are attached to these vegetables, check to see that the greens are fresh; they should not be wilted or discolored. Remove them before storing. Root vegetables should be stored in a cool, dry place, unpeeled. Properly stored they will maintain their quality for several weeks.

BEETS come in a variety of colors and sizes. Red is most common, but pink, purple, golden, white, and chioggia, the red-and-white striped variety, are often available. They peak in summer and early fall. Beets can be used in salads and soups (red beets are classic in borscht), pickled, or roasted.

CELERIAC is related to celery; it is sometimes called celery root. It should feel heavy and firm, and although it is very knobby, the exterior should be free of dents as well as cuts. It is best in fall and winter. It can be served raw in salads or crudités, or cooked in the same manner as potatoes.

JERUSALEM ARTICHOKES aren't from Jerusalem and they aren't related to artichokes. They have a glossy tan or matte brown skin. They are sweet and crisp, and can be eaten raw or cooked. They are at their best from late fall through early spring.

JÍCAMA is usually served raw as part of a crudité platter or in salads, but it can be stir-fried, boiled, or baked. Look for hard, unblemished jícama that are heavy for their size. The smaller ones are generally more tender.

PARSNIPS look something like pale carrots, and have a mild, celery-like aroma. They are available year-round, but supply is lowest in summer. Smaller parsnips are more tender. All parsnips should taper to a slender tip.

RUTABAGA also are called yellow turnips. They are large, round, and usually coated with wax. They are available fresh from late fall through early winter. Because they store well, they can be found all winter long. They are used in soups and as a side dish, often pureed.

TURNIPS are shaped like beets. They are white with a purple blush on the stem end. They are available fresh from late fall through early winter, and throughout winter from storage. Turnip greens are very high in nutrients. If the greens are still attached, remove them and cook them within a day or two.

RADISHES come in many varieties. Globe radishes are the common round red ones with the white flesh, but they may be striped, white, or in specialty colors. Daikon radishes are carrot shaped and milder in flavor. Although they are generally used raw, radishes can be cooked.

SALSIFY, or oyster plant, can be white or black. It is available from fall into winter and is often served creamed.

CORN is technically a grain, but sweet corn and corn kernels are eaten as starchy vegetables. Sweet corn does not keep well; its sugars begin converting to starch immediately after picking, so it should be served as soon as possible after picking.

OTHER VEGETABLES

This catchall category includes crucifers that aren't dark green (such as cauliflower and red cabbage), foods that are botanically considered fruits (tomatoes, peppers, cucumbers, and summer squash), as well as the extensive families of mushrooms and onions. Other vegetables vary considerably in nutrients, seasonality, and keeping qualities.

ARTICHOKES are a member of the thistle family. They come in an array of sizes; the largest ones can be stuffed, medium-sized ones are often served as an appetizer with dipping sauces, and baby artichokes appear in salads and antipasti.

ASPARAGUS is a lily and is distantly related to the onion. It can be steamed, sautéed, or roasted.

AVOCADOS should be ripened at room temperature. Their flesh browns when exposed to air so cut surfaces must be brushed with lemon or lime juice to prevent browning. Haas avocados have a richer flavor than other varieties.

STORAGE TIMES FRESH PRODUCE

ITEM	STORAGE AREA	STORAGE TIME
Avocados	countertop	until ripe
Basil, cilantro, mint, parsley, tarragon	refrigerator	1 week
Broccoli florets	refrigerator	4 days
Cabbage	refrigerator	2 weeks
Carrots, peeled, baby	refrigerator	1 week
Celery	refrigerator	2 weeks
Chives, scallions	refrigerator	1 week
Collard greens, kale, spinach	refrigerator	3–4 days
Eggplant	refrigerator	3–4 days
Ginger	refrigerator	3 weeks
Jalapeño or chipotle peppers	refrigerator	4–5 days
Onions	dry/pantry	3 weeks
Potatoes	dry/pantry	1 month
Salad greens	refrigerator	1–2 days
Tomatoes	countertop	until ripe
Yellow squash, zucchini	refrigerator	4–5 days
White mushrooms	refrigerator	2–3 days

CABBAGE varieties include green, red, Savoy, and napa. All cabbage should feel heavy for its size, and wrapper leaves should be firm.

CAULIFLOWER is at its peak from late summer to fall. It can be served raw as a crudité, pureed, steamed, or roasted.

CELERY is common in salads and crudité, and its cooked applications are numerous.

CUCUMBERS are common in salads and crudité platters, and in salsas and gazpacho. They can be cooked or used in creamed soups. Kirby cucumbers are often pickled. English cucumbers are seedless.

EGGPLANT comes in a range of shapes and sizes, and its skin can range from white to darkest purple. It can be roasted and used in several dishes, braised, grilled, pan-fried, or stewed.

ENDIVE is a family that includes Belgian endive, frisée, and radicchio. These can be used in salads and are delicious braised.

FENNEL, like celery, has a crisp, refreshing texture and a very high water content. It has a subtle anise flavor and can be served raw as part of a crudité platter, braised, or sautéed.

LETTUCES include iceberg, Boston, leaf and oak leaf, and escarole. Although they are usually used in salads, lettuces can be braised. (See also Dark Green Vegetables, page 4.)

MUSHROOMS are a fungus. Some are edible and delicious, others are toxic. If wild mushroom hunting intrigues you, go with a knowledgeable guide, because edible mushrooms often have toxic look-alikes. *Boletus edulis* (sometimes called cèpe or porcini), chanterelles, cremini, morels, portobellos, shiitakes, and truffles are the most common mushrooms. Mushrooms can be sautéed, baked, stuffed as an appetizer, or used in a variety of dishes to add flavor.

The ONION family includes garlic, scallions, leeks, ramps, and shallots, as well as red, Spanish, sweet, yellow, white, pearl, and cippolini onions. Fresh onions, such as scallions and leeks, must be refrigerated; cured or dried onions can be stored in a cool, dry place.

PEPPERS come in two basic types: sweet and chile. Sweet peppers include bell peppers and frying peppers. Bell peppers come in a variety of colors. Chiles come in myriad sizes, shapes, and heat levels, and they can be fresh or dried. As a general rule, smaller, slimmer peppers are hotter than larger ones, but there are exceptions: Habaneros, for example, are round and extremely hot. Wear gloves, wash cutting surfaces and knives, and avoid contact with sensitive tissues when handling these peppers.

SUMMER SQUASH includes pattypan, chayote, crookneck, yellow squash, and zucchini. They are usually steamed, sautéed, or pan-fried. The skin is edible.

TOMATOES are actually berries. Commercially grown tomatoes are picked unripe and allowed to ripen in transit; vine-ripened tomatoes have especially rich flavors and are typically very juicy. The most common tomato varieties include the small cherry, currant, pear, and grape, and come in red or yellow. They peak in mid to late summer, and are usually served fresh in salads or crudité. Plum tomatoes have a greater proportion of flesh to seeds and typically are used in sauces, purees, soups, and cooked dishes. Beefsteak tomatoes and slicing tomatoes typically are used in salads and other uncooked preparations.

Vegetable Cookery

Vegetables are far more important in contemporary menu planning than simply as a side dish meant to "fill up" a plate. They add flavor, color, and texture to any meal, and, more importantly, they provide significant amounts of nutrients, including complex carbohydrates, fiber, vitamins, minerals, antioxidants, and phytochemicals. As eating habits continue to change, reflecting an increasing awareness of the links between diet and health, vegetables are becoming more important.

Vegetable cookery is a true test of your ability to coordinate techniques and raw materials to achieve special flavor and color effects. Proper vegetable cookery calls upon several skills: the ability to purchase foods wisely and to store and handle them properly once purchased; a mastery of the proper techniques for assembling a good mise en place—cleaning, cutting, and trimming; and the ability to combine vegetables appropriately and creatively with other foods to create a pleasing appearance and taste.

GENERAL GUIDELINES

Each vegetable cookery technique produces specific and characteristic results. For example, stirfrying, microwaving, and steaming are often preferred for cooking vegetables that should have a crisp texture and bright color. Boiled vegetables are generally more tender and moist. Baking a vegetable produces a texture that is fluffy, mealy, and dry, with a special "roasted" flavor.

One way to broaden your repertoire of vegetable dishes is to pair a technique with a particular vegetable with which it is not ordinarily associated. For instance, cucumbers, most commonly considered a vegetable to be eaten raw, also may be steamed, sautéed, or even braised. The flavor, texture, and color differences can be quite interesting. Acorn squash does not always have to be baked and glazed with honey; it can be stewed, braised, or prepared in a savory custard. Vegetable cookery can escape the boundaries of "standard" preparations or even personal dislikes.

PURCHASING

To produce the best dishes, you must begin with products of excellent quality. You must be able to evaluate vegetables to determine their freshness and quality. Ideally, the market should serve as your guide. There is no excuse for buying woody broccoli or mealy tomatoes. It almost always is possible to find a better alternative than relying on "standard" vegetable dishes made with less-than-standard ingredients. There are times of the year when the available selection may become slim. Rather than relying on very expensive imported vegetables, you should have the freedom and confidence to use those vegetables that are in season to prepare creative and satisfying dishes.

PROPER HANDLING

Once any vegetable has been harvested it begins to change. Sometimes the change is dramatic and rapid, as is the case for sweet corn or peas—they begin to lose quality, flavor, and texture almost from the moment they are picked. Root vegetables, on the other hand, last over the winter because they lose quality relatively slowly.

VEGETABLE MISE EN PLACE

One way to distinguish a novice from a seasoned chef is the way each approaches the task of cutting vegetables and herbs. The goal is consistency coupled with speed. With continued practice, that goal is attainable by every cook.

To better approach vegetable mise en place:

- *Start by figuring out the proper timing of the work using recipes or your own experience to determine what to prepare ahead of time and what to do at the last minute.*

- *Think out the tasks before beginning the recipe and, wherever possible, double up on prep work. For instance, if you know you'll need garlic in more than one dish, peel and chop the total amount you need for the entire meal.*

- *Arrange the work in a logical flow so that things are positioned within easy reach. This makes the work easier, faster, less wasteful, and more comfortable.*

- *Keep tools and the work surface clean and free of debris. Wipe down knife blades and cutting boards as you work, and especially when you switch from cutting one type of food to another.*

All fresh produce, even if it will be peeled before cutting, must be washed well. Washing removes surface dirt, bacteria, and other contaminants that might otherwise come in contact with cut surfaces by way of your knife or peeler.

PEELING

Vegetables may be peeled in a variety of ways. Not all vegetables require peeling before cooking, but when it is necessary, you should use a tool that evenly and neatly removes the skin without removing too much of the valuable flesh. Rotary peelers are used for thin-skinned vegetables such as carrots, celery, and asparagus. An alternative tool is a paring knife, which is simply scraped across the vegetable's surface to remove a thin layer. Thick-skinned vegetables, such as rutabagas and winter squash, are peeled by cutting away the skin with a chef's knife. Fibrous or tough skins can be removed from broccoli, fennel, and similar vegetables by using a paring knife to trim away the skin; often the skin then can be pulled away after the initial cut by catching it between the flat side of the blade and your thumb and simply pulling it away.

VEGETABLE KNIFE CUTS

The way you cut vegetables determines not only how they will look, but also how they taste and how quickly or slowly they cook.

CHOPPING Coarse chopping is generally used for ingredients that are to be ultimately strained out of the finished dish and discarded or when cutting vegetables that will be puréed. The roots and stem ends must be trimmed and the vegetables peeled as necessary.

The vegetables should be sliced or cut through at nearly regular intervals until the cuts are relatively uniform. You do not have to obtain perfectly neat cuts, but all of the pieces should be roughly the same size.

MINCING Mincing is a very fine cut that is suitable for many vegetables (e.g., onions, garlic, and shallots) and herbs.

Herbs should be rinsed and thoroughly dried before stripping the leaves from their stems. Once rinsed, dried, and stripped, you should gather the leaves in a pile on your cutting board and, with one hand holding them in place, position your knife so that it can slice through the pile and proceed to coarsely chop.

When you have the herbs coarsely chopped, use your fingertips to hold the tip of your knife in contact with the cutting board. While keeping the tip of the blade against the cutting board, lower your knife firmly and rapidly and repeatedly cut through the herbs until the desired fineness is achieved.

SHREDDING OR CHIFFONADE The chiffonade (French for "fine shreds") cut is mainly used for leafy vegetables and herbs, and serves as a garnish or a bed for presenting other ingredients.

When cutting firm heads of greens into shreds or chiffonade, cut out the core. Then, to make it easier to handle the vegetable, you can cut the head into halves or quarters. Large leaves can be cut more easily if you roll the individual leaves into cylinders before cutting. Stack smaller leaves, such as basil, one on top of the other, and then roll them into cylinders and cut. A chef's knife is the best tool to make the very fine, parallel cuts that result in fine shreds without bruising or crushing the greens.

JULIENNE AND BATONNET The julienne and batonnet cuts are long, rectangular in nature, and are seen most prominently in French fries or in a stirfry as a matchstick cut.

To julienne or batonnet a vegetable, rinse, trim, and peel it first. To keep round vegetables from slipping as you work, cut a slice from one side; this cut is sometimes known as a footer. To make very even, exact cuts like those featured in restaurant dishes, you can make additional slices from each side and the ends to make a square or rectangular block with very even sides. If you prefer, though, you can skip this step for a more natural look after the vegetable is cut.

Put the vegetable cut-side down on your work surface and make parallel cuts to produce slices of an even thickness. Stack the slices, align the edges, and make parallel cuts of the same thickness through the stack to produce stick shapes.

DICING The first step in making neat, even cubes or dice is to cut julienne or batonnet as described above. These sticks should be the same width as the cubes or dice you want to make. The recipes in this book call for variously sized dice. Cubes are usually 1 to 1½ inches wide. Large dice are about ¾ inch; medium dice, ½ inch; small dice are ¼ inch, and fine dice, ⅛ inch.

Gather the pieces together so that they are all arranged in a single direction, then cut through them crosswise at evenly spaced intervals to finish cubing or dicing.

SPECIAL TECHNIQUES FOR SPECIFIC VEGETABLES

DICING ONIONS Onions grow in layers, so you need a special approach to cut them into neat, relatively even dice.

Cut onions just before you plan to cook them since their flavor starts to escape once they are cut. First, trim away the roots, leaving the root end of the onion intact, then cut the onion in half from stem end to root end. Peel away the outer layers, discarding both the papery skin and the thin, tough layer just beneath it.

Place an onion half cut-side down on the cutting board. Holding your knife with its blade parallel to the work surface, carefully make 2 or 3 horizontal cuts in the onion, spacing them from ½ inch apart (for coarse dice) to ¼ inch apart (for fine dice). Do not cut all the way through the root end. This will hold the onion layers together for easier, neater dicing.

Make parallel cuts lengthwise with the tip of the knife. Again, do not cut through the root end. Cut the strips crosswise to make dice of the desired size.

An alternative method for slicing or dicing an onion calls for a series of parallel cuts to be made from the root to the stem end, following the natural curve of the onion. After peeling and halving the onion, you can remove the core by cutting a V-shape notch in the root end. Lay the onion on a surface, cut-side down. Hold the knife so that the edge of the blade is at a 90-degree angle to the onion's surface. As you make successive cuts of the required thickness, reposi-

tion the blade to maintain a perpendicular angle with the surface of the onion to produce even strips.

CLEANING LEEKS Leeks are especially prone to catching large amounts of grit and sand between their layers. Any grit should be completely removed by thoroughly rinsing leeks under running water.

First, the leaves should be trimmed to remove the very tough green portion, leaving just the white and light green or yellow portion. Some recipes may indicate that just the white part should be used; the leaves that you trim away can be used to hold herbs and spices tied together in a bouquet garni or added to vegetable broths for more flavor. The leek's roots should be trimmed, with enough of the root left intact to hold the layers together. This will make it easier to cut the leek later. Then water should be run over the leek, while pulling the layers back so that all of the grit can be flushed out.

ROASTING AND PEELING PEPPERS When peppers and chiles are charred over a flame, grilled, roasted, or broiled, not only are the flavors brought out, but the skins are loosened as well. If you have gas burners, hold the peppers over the flame with tongs or a large kitchen fork, turning to char them evenly. If your grill is hot, char the peppers over hot coals or high heat. To roast or broil peppers and chiles in a hot oven or under a broiler, halve them; remove their stems, seeds, and membranes, and place them cut-side down on an oiled sheet pan. Broil or roast until their skin is black and blistered.

Once the entire pepper is evenly charred, transfer it to a paper bag or bowl and close or cover tightly. By the time the pepper is cool enough to handle, about 10 minutes, steam will have loosened the skin enough that it peels away easily. Peel and rub it away with your fingertips or use a paring knife if the skin clings in some places.

SEEDING AND CUTTING PEPPERS A special technique is required when working with sweet peppers to achieve an absolutely even julienne. The pepper's top and bottom are trimmed away. These scraps can be used to prepare coulis or can be finely diced or minced to use in other preparations, such as soups, stuffings, or fillings. Then the seeds and ribs are removed. If necessary, the pepper can be filleted to even the thickness of the flesh and to remove the waxy skin. The prepared pepper is then easy to cut into julienne or other cut.

Chile peppers hold most of their heat in the seeds and ribs. To avoid burning your skin or other sensitive tissues, especially around the eyes, wear rubber gloves when working with very hot peppers. The trimmed and cleaned chile then can be julienned or diced. One word of caution: Thoroughly clean and rinse hands, knives, and all work surfaces after cutting chiles.

PREPARING GARLIC Depending on how it is prepared, garlic contributes distinctly different flavors.

To separate the cloves from an entire head of garlic, wrap the entire head in a clean towel and press down on it firmly with the heel of your hand. To loosen the skin from each clove, place the clove on a cutting board, lay your knife blade flat against it and the heel of your palm on the flat side, and press down lightly on the blade's flat side to crush the garlic clove, breaking the paper. Peel away the skin.

For the best flavor, prepare garlic as close to the time of cooking as possible and cut away any green sprouts in the cloves. Lay the cloves on a cutting board and smash them well, pressing down firmly with the side of your knife blade. Smashing the cloves will ease mincing as well as develop the garlic's flavor to the fullest. Use a rocking motion to chop or mince the garlic to the desired fineness.

To mash garlic, sprinkle roughly chopped garlic with a little salt. Hold your knife so that its blade is nearly flat against the cutting board. Press the flat side of the cutting edge firmly and repeatedly against the garlic dragging it across the board to make a smooth paste.

PREPARING GINGER Sliced ginger is often used to infuse stock soups, broths, and poaching liquids. Thicker pieces hold up well for long simmering, whereas thin slices release flavor quickly in shorter cooking times.

Use a vegetable peeler or a coffee spoon to remove the tan skin of fresh gingerroot, peeling only as much as you will need at a time. Peel off as thin a layer as possible, since much of the flavor of ginger lies just beneath its skin. You will notice, particularly in older ginger, a distinct "grain" that makes it easier to slice cleanly in one direction, producing shreds in the other.

To mince ginger, cut it into thin slices against the grain, then chop it finely as you would garlic. For a moist, fine puree, use a ginger grater, a small ceramic dish lined with tiny points or pyramids, or a flat, file-like metal grater to reduce the fibers of gingerroot into a softer texture.

STRINGING PEAS AND BEANS Snow peas, sugar snap peas, and snap beans usually have a tough string that should be removed before they are cooked and served. This is an easy but time-consuming task. There aren't any special tools to speed the process. The stem end of the pea or bean is snapped and pulled downward toward the tail. The string should pull away easily. The fresher the pea or bean, the easier this process is. This is a very important preparation technique, as it is quite possible for someone to choke on a tough string.

PREPARING ARTICHOKES Artichokes require some special attention before cooking. There are two areas of concern. First, artichokes have sharp barbs on the ends of their leaves that must be removed. Second, they have a tendency to discolor when exposed to air. The barbs are simply snipped away with kitchen scissors. An artichoke's color is kept a pale green by tying a slice of lemon onto the cut surface. Tying artichokes has a secondary benefit—it prevents them from falling apart during cooking and gives this vegetable a neat, compact shape. For more information, see pages 90–91.

WORKING WITH CORN ON THE COB The traditional American way to serve corn is simply boiled, steamed, or roasted on the cob, then swathed in butter. To prepare other corn dishes, such as creamed corn or corncakes, it is necessary to remove the kernels as well as the milk. First, the kernels are scored with a knife to begin to release their juices, or milk, as it is known. Then, the kernels are sliced away and the cob is scraped to express all of the milk.

DRIED VEGETABLES AND FRUITS

Dried vegetables and fruits always have been an important ingredient in most cuisines. Even today, some vegetables and fruits are too perishable to transport great distances or have a very short season. Drying makes foods suitable for long-term storage and concentrates their flavors.

The flavors of dried chiles, mushrooms, tomatoes, and fruits such as apples, cherries, and raisins are intense and distinct. To get the most flavor from dried fruits and vegetables, as well as to improve their texture, recipes may call for them to be rehydrated or "plumped" by letting them soak in a liquid prior to using.

To rehydrate dried vegetables and fruits, place the vegetable or fruit in a bowl or other container. Add enough boiling or very hot liquid (water, wine, fruit juices, or broth) to cover and let the vegetable or fruit steep in the hot water for several minutes, until soft and plumped.

DETERMINING DONENESS AND EVALUATING QUALITY

Vegetables are cooked to produce flavor, texture, and color changes, which make the vegetable easier to chew and digest, as well as improve taste and appearance. Specific techniques are detailed following this general discussion. The success or failure of these preparations depends on cooking the vegetable just to the point of correct doneness. The proper standards of and tests for doneness are reviewed here.

There are distinct differences in how tender a vegetable should be when it is properly cooked. Preferences regarding the correct doneness of certain vegetables may vary from one part of the country to another and from one vegetable to another.

To correctly determine doneness, you should understand the following:

The natural characteristics of the vegetable: Some vegetables should always retain some "bite" (fully cooked but still firm), whereas others are not sufficiently cooked until they are quite tender.

The normal standard of quality for a particular technique: For example, stirfrying vegetables generally results in a very crisp texture, whereas baking or braising produces very tender vegetables.

Regional or cultural preferences regarding doneness: In the South, vegetables are cooked until very tender, often over a long period of time. In Oriental cuisines, vegetables are cooked rapidly so that they retain most of their texture.

The characteristics of a particular vegetable when properly cooked: Winter squash is usually cooked until very tender, whereas green beans, snow peas, and broccoli are usually cooked so that they will retain a significant degree of "bite."

The following tests should be applied, bearing in mind the style of cookery, the vegetable itself, and the desired result:

CHECK THE APPEARANCE The vegetable's appearance often can act as a guide to determining doneness. Blanched and stirfried vegetables should have a vivid color. Spinach, for instance, should be an intense green and have wilted leaves. Sautéed onions become translucent and eventually take on a golden-brown color.

CHECK THE TEXTURE Experience is the best guide. Vegetables that are properly cooked should have the correct degree of bite. Carrots should be tender, but not mushy. Asparagus should be slightly softened, but still firm enough to hold together. Turnips and rutabagas should be quite soft, but should still hold their shape. The best test is to bite into a piece of the vegetable. Vegetables to be pureed should be soft enough to mash easily. To check doneness in vegetables to be pureed, pierce the vegetable with the point of a knife or the tines of a fork. If it is easy to insert, the vegetable is properly cooked.

Note that green vegetables will demonstrate a marked visual difference from one stage of doneness to the next, whereas white and orange vegetables display very little color change from one stage of doneness to the next. Instead, the texture must be checked.

COOKING VEGETABLES IN ADVANCE

Ideally, vegetables should be cooked and then served immediately. However, there often are occasions when you might find it helpful to prepare the vegetables in advance. One example is when you want to lightly cook a vegetable but serve it chilled, as part of a crudité platter or salad, or to prepare vegetables for the freezer.

Boiled or steamed vegetables generally are refreshed in cold water immediately after they are properly cooked, thoroughly drained, and then held, covered and refrigerated, until you are ready to serve them. Starchy vegetables that can readily absorb water (winter squash and turnips, for example) should be well-drained and spread out in a single layer at room temperature to allow them to briefly dry. Baked or roasted vegetables can be held, uncovered, in a warm oven or holding drawer for up to 2 hours before you serve them, although the texture may change from dry and fluffy to more moist and dense. Braised or stewed vegetables, unlike most vegetables, will withstand being kept warm in the oven for a few hours without losing any quality.

PROPER REHEATING

Vegetables can be reheated in simmering stock or water, in a microwave oven, or by sautéing.

SIMMERING STOCK OR WATER Place the vegetables in a sieve or perforated basket, and lower them into a pot of simmering stock or water just long enough to heat them through. Drain and immediately dress them as appropriate with butter, sauce, etc.

MICROWAVE This technique is generally best for small amounts. Evenly space the vegetables on a flat, round, or oval plate or other microwave-safe container. Reheat them on the highest power setting for the shortest possible time and dress with a sauce or other condiments, if using, and serve immediately.

FINISHING IN BUTTER, CREAM, OR A SAUCE Heat a small amount of butter, cream, or sauce in a sauté pan, add the vegetable, and then toss or "roll" repeatedly during the heating. You can do this by flipping the vegetables or simply turning them over and over with a pair of tongs.

SPECIAL CONCERNS

Another important aim of vegetable cookery is to produce dishes that retain the greatest nutritive value, the best color, and the freshest, most appealing flavor. Outlined next are some of the factors that affect nutrient, color, and flavor retention in cooked vegetables.

COLOR RETENTION A vegetable's color is determined by the pigments it contains. Although most vegetables contain more than one pigment, the overall color is determined by the one that is predominant. The various plant pigments react differently in the presence of heat, acids, metals, water, and fat. Strategies you can use to reduce or eliminate color loss during cooking are explained in succeeding sections outlining specific cooking techniques.

Generally speaking, the best color is retained when vegetables are cooked for as short a time as possible. Overcooked or improperly cooked vegetables take on unappealing dull or gray colors. In many cases, this indicates that the vegetable has been robbed not only of its color, but also of nutrients, texture, and flavor.

NUTRIENT RETENTION There is no way to retain all of a vegetable's nutrients during cooking. The major culprits in nutrient loss are heat, air, water, and enzymes. In trying to minimize this loss, you must balance practical concerns with nutritional ones. To minimize the loss of nutrients during cooking, observe the following preparation standards:

1. *Avoid holding vegetables in liquid before or after cooking.*

2. *Rinse, trim, peel, and cut vegetables as close as possible to cooking time.*

3. *Cook vegetables as quickly as possible, in as little liquid as possible.*

4. *Cook vegetables as close to the time you plan to serve them as possible.*

5. *When feasible, steam or microwave vegetables, or bake them whole, in their skins.*

FLAVOR RETENTION Any vegetable's flavor changes once the vegetable is cooked. In some cases the change is subtle, in others it is more pronounced. The degree of change depends on both the type of vegetable and the technique used.

The compounds in vegetables responsible for their characteristic flavors and odors are as readily affected by heat, water, and enzymes as are the nutrients. Overcooking tends to give some vegetables (especially members of the cabbage family) a strong flavor. Other vegetables may become flat or dull.

Holding a vegetable in water either prior to or after cooking robs it of most of its flavor, along with leaching out

nutrients and making it unacceptably soggy. Prolonged heat exposure also tends to worsen the flavor, resulting in either inappropriately bland or strong flavors.

Cooking Techniques

There is no single "perfect" vegetable cookery method. You must make a decision based on how the dish should taste and appear. The size and shape of the cut, if any, as well as whether moist heat or dry heat is applied, greatly incluences the cooked vegetable's texture, color, appearance, and flavor.

BOILING

It is difficult to think of any vegetable that cannot be boiled. Even though many people tend to think of boiled vegetables as bland or boring, boiling is of great importance in vegetable cookery. Whether one is thinking of tiny sweet peas to be bathed in butter, fresh sweet corn to be served on the cob, or slender spring asparagus, these vegetable dishes are appealing, fresh, and flavorful when properly boiled and served.

This technique's applications go much further than simply boiling up a pot of vegetables that will be doused with butter and served. Boiling also forms the basis for such fundamental operations as blanching and parcooking.

BLANCHING This step is important for several reasons—to make skins easy to remove, to eliminate or reduce strong odors or flavors, to "set" the color of vegetables to be served cold, or as the first step in other cooking techniques.

PARCOOKING/PARBOILING This is done to partially cook vegetables to be used in other preparations such as braises, grills, or gratins.

Prior to cooking, rinse the vegetable thoroughly and scrub, if necessary, to remove surface dirt. Trim and peel the vegetable, as appropriate, immediately prior to cooking. If vegetables are to be cooked whole, choose those of a similar size, shape, and diameter to assure even cooking. If the vegetable is to be cut prior to boiling, make sure that the cuts are uniform in size and shape to promote even cooking and good ap-

pearance. Cut the vegetable immediately prior to boiling and avoid holding it in water.

Water is the most commonly used liquid. However, other liquids may be appropriate, depending upon the desired flavor of the finished dish. Various stocks, court bouillons, and, in some cases, milk may be used. Add salt to the water, if desired. Add enough salt to make the liquid taste noticeably salty, like sea water. Bring the liquid to a rolling boil. Covering the pot will cause the liquid to boil more rapidly.

Seasonings and aromatics may be added to the cooking liquid or they may be combined with the vegetable once it is boiled. Ingredients, especially acidic ingredients such as citrus juice or zest, wine, or vinegar should be added to the cooking liquid of certain vegetables (white vegetables, beets, and red cabbage) to help maintain the best color. Other ingredients, such as herbs, spices, and additional vegetables added for flavor, are added according to the desired result. Boiled vegetables often are tossed with fresh herbs or freshly ground spices just before they are served. Butter, cream, and sauces may be combined with the vegetable while it is still hot or they may be added as it reheats just before serving (see "Sautéing," page 21).

1. Bring the liquid to a full boil.

The amount of liquid required will vary, depending upon the vegetable and the length of cooking time. In general, there should be enough water to hold the vegetables comfortably, without excessive crowding. Add any seasonings, acids, and/or aromatic ingredients that are appropriate to the liquid at this point.

2. Add the vegetables to the boiling liquid.

Add them in small enough batches so that the liquid's temperature does not drop dramatically. Returning the cover to the pot allows for the best color in red cabbage, beets, and white vegetables (cauliflower, for example); doing so retains acids that help to set color in these vegetables. It is acceptable to cover the pot while boiling orange and yellow vegetables (carrots and squash, for example). If preparing a green vegetable that will cook rapidly, such as peas or spinach, the lid may be returned to the pot to help shorten cooking time. Denser green vegetables, such as broccoli, should be boiled uncovered, at least for the first 2 to 3 minutes, to allow natural acids to escape. These acids could cause the vegetable's color to turn a dull olive- or yellow-green.

3. Cook the vegetables to the desired doneness. (See above.)

4. Drain the vegetables thoroughly in a colander or sieve.

At this point the vegetable either may be served as is; combined with butter, fresh herbs, spices or other aromatics, or sauces; refreshed to hold for later service; or used in other vegetable preparations, such as braises, gratins, grills, or purees.

STEAMING AND "PAN-STEAMING"

Steaming is an efficient and practical way to prepare vegetables, especially those that are naturally tender or thin, or that have been cut into small, uniform pieces. This is one of the gentler cooking techniques for vegetables. Because the vegetables are cooked in a vapor bath and are not in direct contact with water, fewer of the vitamins and minerals are lost.

Steaming can be used to fully cook vegetables or to blanch or parcook them. (See the explanation of parcooking under "Boiling.") The effects of steaming are similar to those of boiling, and any vegetable that can be boiled also can be steamed.

Vegetables are prepared for steaming and pan-steaming the same way that they are prepared for boiling (above).

Although the most commonly used liquid is water, a flavorful stock or court bouillon also is appropriate. The amount required depends upon how long the vegetables will take to cook—the more delicate the vegetable, the less liquid required.

It often is appropriate to add aromatics such as spices, herbs, citrus zest, or additional vegetables to the steaming liquid to produce specific flavors. Salt, pepper, and other seasonings can be combined with the vegetable once it is steamed. The steamed vegetable can be combined with butter, some oils (including olive and walnut), heavy cream, or a sauce while the vegetable is still hot, or these items may be used just prior to service as a medium for reheating vegetables.

1. In the bottom of a steamer, bring the liquid to a full boil with the lid on the pot.

Add any additional seasonings or aromatics to the liquid as it comes to a boil to help release their flavors.

2. Add the vegetables to the steamer in a single layer so that the steam can circulate freely.

This shortens cooking time and results in better flavor, color, and nutrient retention.

3. Return the lid to the steamer and steam the vegetables to the desired doneness.

The appropriate degree of doneness is determined by how the particular vegetable will be handled once it is steamed. Vegetables may be blanched, parcooked, or fully cooked.

4. Remove the vegetables from the steamer.

Serve them at once or hold and refresh them, if necessary. Once the appropriate doneness is reached, the vegetable may be served immediately. The vegetable may be handled in any of the same ways that boiled vegetables are.

MICROWAVING

Microwaving, essentially a moist-heat cooking method, works by causing a food's molecules to vibrate against each other, creating friction that generates heat. That heat causes a food's natural liquids to "steam" the item. Vegetables can be cooked in two ways in a microwave oven.

In the first method, they are placed in an appropriate container with a small amount of liquid and covered; the added liquid turns to steam and cooks the vegetable. In the second method, which is used for dense vegetables, the vegetable is left whole, with skin or peel intact, and steamed using the moisture held in by its own skin.

Microwave ovens also frequently are used just before service to reheat vegetables that were prepared by other techniques. This is an extremely useful application, because the vegetable can be reheated rapidly with little loss of color, nutrients, or texture.

Before microwaving, prepare the vegetable according to the type and desired result. For a vegetable that is to be combined with a small amount of liquid, rinse, peel, trim, and cut the vegetable into even pieces, as necessary. Arrange the pieces on a shallow platter or dish; they should be evenly spread over the surface. For a vegetable that is to be cooked whole, such as squash or beets, rinse the vegetable well and pierce the skin in two or three places to allow the steam to escape.

There should be only enough liquid to produce steam during the relatively short cooking time required by the microwave process. No additional liquid is needed for vegetables that are left whole.

Vegetables that are cooked with additional liquid often are combined with various seasonings and aromatics *before* they are microwaved. Vegetables microwaved whole are combined with aromatics and seasonings *after* they have been cooked. Finishing ingredients may include butter, certain oils, heavy cream, or a sauce.

1. Place the vegetable on a suitable dish or plate.

Add any liquid, if necessary, and cover the dish tightly. If plastic wrap is used, it should be punctured to allow steam to vent.

2. Place the dish in a microwave oven.

Cook the vegetable at the highest power setting for the appropriate amount of time. It may be necessary to stir, turn, or rearrange some vegetables to assure even cooking. There will be some carryover cooking because the heat produced within the vegetable itself is responsible for the cooking.

3. Serve the vegetable with the appropriate finishing ingredients or sauces; vegetables cooked whole are ready to be used in a secondary technique.

ROASTING/BAKING

This technique should not be confused with other techniques that cook vegetables in an oven, such as in braised dishes and gratins. To some extent, roasting or baking vegetables involves the same principles applied to roasting meats: The vegetable is generally left whole or cut into large pieces, no additional liquid is used, and the moisture already present in the vegetable carries the heat from the exterior to the interior.

Roasting or baking is best suited to vegetables which have thick skins that will protect the interior from drying or scorching. Examples include various winter squashes and eggplant.

This method is used frequently to prepare vegetables that might otherwise be difficult to peel, such as sweet bell peppers that will be used in a puree. The aim is to create a special flavor and texture. Browning produces the expected "roasted" flavor. The absence of added liquid means that the vegetable should have a dry, fluffy texture.

Rinse, peel, trim, and cut the vegetable as necessary. To assure even cooking, vegetables should be cut into pieces of uniform size and shape. If necessary, pierce the skin; thick-skin vegetables, such as acorn squash, beets, or turnips, need to have their skins pierced. This allows the steam that builds up during cooking to escape. Rub the skin with oil to prevent excessive drying and scorching.

A marinade can influence flavor and give additional protection to the vegetable as it cooks in the dry heat. Rub or coat the surface of the vegetable with seasonings or aromatics such as salt, pepper, or garlic cloves, as appropriate. Have available finishing ingredients, such as whole or compound butter, reduced heavy cream, or a sauce prepared separately, as desired or according to the particular recipe.

1. Place the prepared vegetable in a hot or moderate oven.

The oven's temperature depends upon the vegetable's size and density. The longer the roasting time—also determined by the vegetable's size, the diameter of its cut, and its density—the lower the temperature should be. Vegetables may be roasted on baking sheets or roasting pans, or, in some cases, directly on the oven rack, which allows the hot air to circulate readily.

2. Roast the vegetable to the desired doneness.

Generally, vegetables are thoroughly roasted when they can be pierced easily with the tip of a knife or fork. Vegetables should be rotated as they roast to promote even cooking because most ovens have hot spots. The placement of other items in the oven also could cause uneven cooking.

3. Serve the vegetable immediately on heated plates with the appropriate finishing ingredients; hold it, covered, in a warm place; or use it in a secondary cooking technique.

If the vegetable is to be pureed, it should be pureed while it is still hot (see the section on pureeing on page 27).

SAUTÉING

Some vegetables are sautéed or stirfried from their raw state. Examples of such vegetables include mushrooms, summer squashes, and onions. Denser vegetables, such as green beans, carrots, and Brussels sprouts, need to be fully or partially cooked by boiling, steaming, microwaving, or roasting before they are sautéed or stirfried.

Cooked vegetables can be sautéed just before you serve them to reheat. Chefs may refer to this technique as "finishing in butter." Instead of butter, you may prefer to use small amounts of stock, cream, or some sauces.

Glazing is another finishing technique. A small amount of honey, sugar, or maple syrup is added to the vegetable as it reheats. The sugars liquify, coating the vegetable evenly to give it some sheen and a sweet flavor. (There is a second way to "glaze" vegetables: The prepared vegetable may be cooked in a lightly sweetened liquid, which is allowed to reduce, coating the vegetable with a glaze.)

Rinse, peel, trim, and cut the raw vegetable, if required. Partially or wholly cook the vegetable by boiling, steaming, roasting, or microwaving it, if necessary. This is especially important for vegetable "mixtures." Each vegetable should be cooked separately in advance, and then reheated and mixed only at the time of service.

Have available whole or clarified butter. Because sautéing vegetables does not require the high temperatures necessary for sautéing meats or fish, whole butter is acceptable. If oil is used, the oil's flavor should complement that of the vegetable. For example, extra-virgin olive oil may be best suited to a stirfry of zucchini and red peppers, wheras peanut or sesame oil is best for an Asian-style stirfry. Use only enough of the cooking medium to lightly coat the vegetable and to effectively conduct heat from the pan to the vegetable.

Select seasonings and aromatics, such as salt, pepper, and/or lemon juice, to adjust or heighten the flavor. Finely mince or chop fresh herbs and add them at the last moment. Small amounts of ingredients that contain a high sugar concentration may be added to vegetables, generally near the end of the cooking time, to act as a glaze, giving additional flavor, sheen, and a golden color. Have available honey, sugar, maple syrup, or fruit juice.

1. Heat the pan, add the cooking medium, and heat it.

2. Add the vegetable.

If more than one type is being used, as in a stirfry, add the vegetables in the proper sequence, beginning with those with the longest cooking times, to assure that all components complete cooking at the same point.

3. Keep the vegetable in motion in the pan and sauté it only until it is very hot and tender to the bite.

HELPING HOOVER IN OUR
U.S. SCHOOL GARDEN

4. Add any aromatics, seasonings, or ingredients for a glaze. Heat them thoroughly.

5. Serve the vegetable immediately on heated plates.

STIRFRYING

Stirfries usually include vegetables that are cooked until very hot and tender yet still crisp. Stirfries lend themselves well to improvisation, so you can add more vegetables or substitute one for another.

1. Prepare all the ingredients

A successful stirfry depends upon a complete mise en place. Every ingredient needs to be ready to go into the wok or skillet. You should have it close to the stovetop and ready to add at the right point. Cut vegetables into thin slices or fine shreds so that they cook fully. Arrange your ingredients so it is easy to add them in the correct order, longest cooking time to shortest.

2. Heat the wok and the oil before you add the aromatic ingredients.

One of the biggest challenges when you stirfry at home is to get the pan very hot and to keep it hot for the entire cooking time. Preheat the pan over high heat for a few minutes before you add the oil, then add the oil to the hot pan in a swirl around the edge so that it coats the sides and runs down to the bottom of the wok. The first ingredient to add to the wok is the aromatic base: onions, shallots, garlic, or ginger, for instance. This ingredient infuses the oil with flavor so that it is carried throughout the entire dish.

3. Add the ingredients to the wok in sequence and keep them in motion as they cook.

To keep the wok as hot as possible, add only a handful or two of ingredients at a time. Use wide spoons or wok tools to keep the ingredients moving. As each ingredient is stirred into the wok and gets hot, push it up on the sides so the bot-tom can get very hot again before you add the next ingredient. Once all the ingredients are added, continue to stir and toss the ingredients until fully cooked.

4. Add the final seasonings, flavorings, and garnishes.

In addition to the aromatic base you added to the wok at the start of the stirfry, be sure to include seasonings. Salt and pepper certainly are important, but you also will want to add other pungent flavorful ingredients like soy or tamari sauce or herbs such as chives or cilantro. Stir these final additions into the dish just enough to blend them evenly. Serve stirfrys very hot, straight from the wok.

PANFRYING

Panfrying is similar to sautéing. The main difference is that in panfrying, the amount of oil used as a cooking medium is greater than that used for sautéing. Also, any sauce served with panfried vegetables is made separately. In some cases, the main item is breaded or coated with flour or a batter. Thick or dense vegetables, such as rutabagas or carrots, which require lengthy cooking times, may need to be parcooked first by boiling or steaming. Vegetables that are prepared as fritters or croquettes are typically cooked first, diced, bound together with a cream sauce, and coated with bread crumbs.

Prepare the vegetable according to the type and the desired result. Peel, trim, rinse, and cut the vegetable into even slices, as necessary. Wholly or partially cook the vegetable, if necessary. Bread it with a standard breading, or coat it with flour or batter. (See Applying Breadings, Batters, and Coatings, page 25, for more information about this technique.)

As is true for panfried meats or fish, the cooking fat or oil must be able to reach a high temperature without breaking down or smoking during the cooking process.

Aromatics and seasonings may be added to the vegetable before or after cooking, or they may be included in the breading or batter, if appropriate. Have available salt and pepper, minced fresh herbs, grated cheeses, ground nuts, or mixtures with spices or seeds (such as sesame or mustard). In addition, the recipe may call for finishing ingredients such as a compound butter, sauce, relish, or salsa.

1. Heat the cooking medium in a heavy-gauge skillet with straight sides.

The walls of the skillet should be tall enough to hold the cooking oil and the vegetable, with enough room for the oil to expand without overflowing the sides. Cast iron skillets, sometimes known as "chicken fryers," are a good choice.

2. Add the prepared vegetable carefully.

For the best color and rapid cooking, avoid crowding the vegetables in the pan.

3. Cook the vegetable over moderate to high heat until its exterior is lightly browned and crisp and its interior is tender to the bite and very hot. The shorter the necessary cooking time, the higher the heat may be.

4. Blot the vegetable briefly on absorbent paper toweling.

5. Season the vegetable with salt and pepper, if desired, and serve it immediately on heated plates. Serve the vegetable with a compound butter, a sauce, or a relish or salsa, as desired or appropriate.

DEEP FRYING

Few vegetables are deep fried in their raw state. Most are either wholly or partially cooked by boiling, steaming, microwaving, or baking. Tempura batter often is used to coat vegetables that will be deep fried. Croquettes are also commonly deep fried—they are prepared by making an appareil that includes minced vegetables or a puree, which is then coated with a standard breading.

Prepare the vegetable according to the type and desired result. Peel, trim, rinse, and cut the vegetable, as necessary. Wholly or partially cook the vegetable, as necessary. Mince or puree the vegetable, as necessary.

For the best results, coat the vegetable with breading or

batter just before cooking it. Have available ingredients for a standard breading or a prepared batter.

The cooking medium must be able to reach a high temperature without smoking or breaking down. Use an oil with a neutral flavor heated to the proper temperature.

Optional components include aromatics and seasonings and/or finishing ingredients. See the section on panfrying vegetables for suggestions.

1. Heat the oil in a deep-fryer to approximately 350°F (176 ° C).

If you don't have a deep-fryer, you can use a heavy-gauge pot with sides tall enough to hold about 2 or 3 inches of oil with at least 4 inches of "head room" so that the oil won't overflow the pot. Use a deep fat or candy thermometer to check the oil's temperature. If you don't have a thermometer, you can use the following technique to determine how hot the oil is:

To test the temperature of frying oil without a thermometer, cut a 2-inch cube of bread (crusts removed) and drop it into the hot oil. The amount of time it takes a bread cube to become golden brown tells the temperature of the oil:

> 350°F 65 seconds
> 375°F 50 seconds
> 485°F 20 seconds

2. Fry the vegetable in the oil until it is evenly browned or golden in color.

Most vegetables will float to the surface when they are properly cooked if the oil has been properly maintained and is at the correct temperature.

3. Remove the vegetable from the oil and blot it briefly on absorbent paper toweling.

4. Adjust the seasoning and serve the vegetable immediately on heated plates, with a compound butter, sauce, or relish or salsa, as desired or appropriate.

APPLYING COATINGS AND BREADINGS

There are three options for coating a food before you panfry it: dredge lightly in flour, dip in a batter, or apply a breading. Batters are made according to a specific recipe; some examples include beer batter and tempura batter. Before you dip a food in the batter, you should coat it lightly with a thin, even layer of flour or cornstarch. Standard breading means that you have coated the ingredients with flour, milk and/or beaten eggs, and dry breadcrumbs. Season the food before applying any coating, and always handle food properly for safety.

Eggwash is made by blending eggs (whole, yolks, or whites) and water or milk, about ¼ cup milk for every egg. Some items are dipped into milk or buttermilk before applying breading, rather than using eggwash. Other ingredients may be used in place of or in addition to breadcrumbs to add flavor and texture to your coating: nuts, cornmeal, cornflakes, potato flakes, grated cheese, ground nuts or spices, or chopped herbs.

Set up your work area so that the food moves in one direction:

1. Dry the item well then dip it in flour. Shake off any excess.

2. Still using the same hand, transfer the item to the eggwash. Turn to coat evenly and transfer to the breadcrumbs.

3. Press the crumbs evenly over the surface and remove the item to a holding tray. Do not stack the breaded items or let them touch each other or they will become sticky and mat together. Discard any unused flour, eggwash, or breadcrumbs.

GRILLING AND BROILING

Some vegetables can be grilled or broiled from the raw state; others require preliminary cooking or marination in an oil-based bath to assure thorough cooking. Vegetables that hold up well when subjected to a grill's intense heat include eggplant, mushrooms, onions, summer squashes, and peppers. Vegetables may be raw or may be prepared partially or completely. Prepare the vegetable according to the type and desired result. Rinse, trim, peel, and cut it in appropriate, even pieces. Thread it on a skewer, if appropriate.

GRILLED VEGETABLES A marinade or oil may be used to provide both lubrication and additional flavor. The vegetable may be raw or partially or wholly cooked prior to marination. Have available an oil-based marinade or plain oil, according to the recipe or desired result. Aromatics and seasonings may be added to the vegetable prior to cooking or after cooking, just before taking them to the table. Have available salt and pepper, citrus zest, minced fresh herbs, or spices.

BROILED VEGETABLES The core or seeds of some vegetables can be removed and the cavity filled with an appropriate filling, as in the case of broiled stuffed tomatoes. A topping often is added before the vegetable is broiled. Have available duxelles, a forcemeat, or another stuffing, as desired or according to the recipe. Have available bread crumbs, butter, and cheese for a topping, as desired or according to the recipe. If a marinade has been used, it may also be served as a sauce with the cooked vegetable. Other possible sauces include salsa, soy sauce, a jus-based sauce, reduced heavy cream, butter sauces, or cream sauce.

The method for either grilling or broiling vegetables is:

1. Thoroughly heat the grill or broiler.

2. Place the prepared vegetable directly on a rack.

If there is a danger that the vegetable might stick easily to the rack, it can be grilled in a hand grill.

3. Grill or broil the vegetable until heated through and tender.

Baste it with a marinade or oil during the cooking time, if appropriate. Turn grilled vegetables as necessary during cooking to cook them evenly and avoid scorching them. (Do not turn broiled vegetables.) Broiled vegetables should have a browned top; grilled vegetables should be lightly browned on both sides, with well-browned crosshatch marks.

HEATING A GRILL Before you light a grill, whether it is gas or charcoal, clean the grates well by scrubbing with a grill brush or with a ball of aluminum foil. If you are using a gas grill with a cover, light the burners, set the heat to the temperature you want, cover the grill, and allow about 15 to 20 minutes for the grill to come up to the right temperature.

A good charcoal fire should burn evenly and last long enough to cook everything completely. While gas grills may take as little as 15 minutes to heat up, a charcoal fire typically takes at least 35 to 45 minutes before the coals are ready for cooking.

Lighter fluid and treated charcoal briquettes may be simpler to use, but they can leave a distinct flavor on foods. We strongly recommend avoiding lighter fluid. Never use gasoline or kerosene to start a fire.

To start a fire, open the vents in the grill to let the air in. Crumple a few sheets of newspaper and place them on the fuel grate.

Add hardwood chips, briquettes, or kindling to the paper to make a mound, and set the paper on fire. Let it burn, but keep an eye on it. Fires at this stage can go out easily if there is too much or too little air blowing on them. If you are using logs instead of briquettes or chunks, add them once the kindling has started to flame.

Let the fire burn without disturbing it. Add more wood or briquettes carefully when the flames start to die down until you have enough fuel to last for a cooking session.

TESTING THE TEMPERATURE OF YOUR GRILL Some grills have built-in thermometers to make it easy to monitor how hot the grill is. If you don't have such a feature on your grill, you can use a time-honored test:

Hold your hand, palm facing down, over the heat source just above the grill rack. Count how many seconds it takes before you have to take your hand away from the grill.

- 2 seconds equals high heat
- 3 seconds equals medium-high heat
- 4 seconds equals medium heat
- 5 seconds equals medium-low heat
- 6 seconds equals low heat

STEWING AND BRAISING

Vegetable stews and braises, such as ratatouille and peas bonne femme, are excellent ways to retain the vitamins and minerals lost from the vegetable into the cooking liquid, because the liquid is served as part of the dish. The distinction between a vegetable stew and a braise is the same as for meats: The vegetables in a stew customarily are cut into small pieces, whereas those in a braise are in large pieces or are left whole. Occasionally, a thickener is added to the cooking liquid to give the finished dish more substance and to improve its appearance. The thickened sauce lightly coats the vegetable, providing an attractive sheen.

Vegetable stews and braises often are composed of more than one kind of vegetable. Prepare the vegetables according to the type and the desired result. Peel, trim, rinse, and cut the vegetables, as necessary. Blanch them to remove bitter flavors or to aid in removing peels.

The stewing process often begins with searing or sweating the main item or aromatic ingredients like garlic, shallots, ginger, or spices in fat or oil to develop a richer flavor. The particular fat or oil chosen should have a good flavor appropriate to the dish. For example, olive oil is a good choice for a ratatouille, whereas butter is better for stewed mushrooms. Dishes like succotash may rely on bacon for both the cooking medium and additional flavor (see Using Bacon as a Flavoring, page 36). Vegetables that will not release a significant amount of liquid as they cook may need additional liquid, such as stock, fumets, juices, or water.

It may be desirable to add a thickener to bind the juices and other liquids. Use a mixture of cornstarch or arrowroot and cold water (known as a slurry) or a mixture of cold butter and flour (known as beurre manié), adding them a bit at a time until the liquid reaches the desired thickness. Have available seasonings and aromatics such as salt, pepper, shallots, garlic, minced fresh herbs, spices, onions, carrots, celery; salt pork, bacon, or ham; or an acid such as vinegar, citrus zest or juice, or wine. The acid should be added near the end of the cooking time to avoid toughening the vegetable.

Various finishing ingredients may be added to give a vegetable stew a rich flavor, some sheen, and a smooth texture. Have available reduced heavy cream, a cream sauce, a liaison (page 50), or whole butter. A stew or braise may be garnished as desired or appropriate. Have available such ingredients as diced roasted peppers; bread crumbs and cheese (to create a gratin); chopped, hard-cooked eggs; or toasted nuts.

1. Heat the oil or a small amount of stock.

2. Add appropriate seasonings or aromatics and the main item.

If aromatics such as garlic, shallots, or onions are used, cook these ingredients over gentle heat with the lid on to encourage them to release their juices without developing additional color, or over more intense heat with the cover off, for a more pronounced flavor and a darker color.

3. Add the liquid, if appropriate, and bring it to a simmer.

Cook the vegetable over low heat or in a moderate oven.

4. Introduce additional vegetables and aromatics in the proper sequence so that all components complete their cooking times at the same point.

5. Cook the stew or braise until the vegetables are tender; then add a thickener and/or finishing ingredients, if appropriate.

Stews are typically cooked completely on the stovetop, whereas braises are more frequently cooked in a moderate oven (325 to 375°F). It may be necessary to strain out the vegetables before adding the thickener to the liquid. If that is the case, return the vegetable to the sauce once it is properly thickened or finished.

6. Adjust the seasoning as necessary. Serve it immediately on heated plates.

Stewed and braised vegetables can be held for a longer time than other vegetables without losing significant quality. Hold them, loosely covered, in a steam table.

PUREEING

Pureed vegetables may be served as is or they may be used in other preparations, such as timbales, custards, or soufflés. They also may be used as ingredients in other dishes once they are properly pureed. For example, a watercress puree may be used to flavor a sauce; a red pepper puree may be used as an ingredient to flavor and color a fresh pasta dough. Most purees can be stored frozen for later use.

The vegetable must be cooked until tender enough to puree easily, by either pushing it through a sieve or food mill, or pureeing it with a food processor or handheld blender. You may sieve purees made with a blender or food processor for further smoothness. Some vegetables, such as spinach, cucumbers, and tomatoes, occasionally are pureed in the raw state.

Optional components include aromatics and seasonings and finishing ingredients. Have available salt and pepper, minced fresh herbs, spices, or citrus juice or zest. Finishing ingredients, like butter or heavy cream, should be added gradually to the pureed vegetable to ensure proper consistency.

1. Boil, steam, roast, or microwave the vegetable until it is extremely tender.

2. If the vegetable has been cooked in water, drain it well and remove any excess moisture by either spreading it on a sheet tray and placing the tray in a warm oven to dry, or by gently wringing the vegetable in cheesecloth.

3. Puree the vegetable by pushing it through a sieve or food mill, or use a food processor or blender. The puree's consistency is determined by its intended use. For a smoother puree, strain a second time through a fine sieve.

4. Adjust the seasoning, finish the puree, and serve it immediately on heated plates. Finishing ingredients should be added gradually until the desired consistency and flavor are reached. Note that the pureed vegetable and heavy cream or other liquids should be at the same temperature; butter should be soft but not melted.

Soups

EGETABLE SOUPS WORK for any season and any occasion. Hearty vegetable soups, full of a rich combination of vegetables, and often including grains, beans, and a bit of meat, are perfect for cooler weather. Sophisticated cream soups make an elegant first course for a dinner party. This chapter covers soup-making techniques for broth-based soups like minestrone and thickened soups like our cream of broccoli. You'll find not only basic steps for great soups, but also the information you need to improvise your own soups to capture the season's bounty and savor the flavor of your favorite vegetables in delicious soups.

Soup Basics

The best soups are made from the freshest and best available ingredients. Many vegetable soups are made from a combination of ingredients, while others feature just one. Aromatics add an extra flavor dimension to any soup, and your options include spices and herbs, and vegetable combinations, including mirepoix, sachet d'épices, or bouquet garni.

Good quality broths are the basis of most soups, but water, fumets, vegetable essences, fruit and vegetable juices, and milk also may be called for in some soups.

The following are general preparation guidelines that pertain to most soups.

- *Cook soups at a gentle simmer, just long enough to develop a good flavor and the appropriate body.*

- *Vegetables may be added in a staggered manner, according to their cooking times.*

- *Stir the soup from time to time to keep starchy ingredients, like pasta, potatoes, carrots, and flour, from sticking to the bottom of the pot.*

- *Use a skimmer or ladle to remove any scum or foam that rises to the top of the soup as it simmers for the best flavor, texture, and appearance.*

- *Taste the soup frequently as it cooks. When the flavor is fully developed and all of the ingredients are tender, it is ready to finish*

or garnish and serve right away, or you may prefer to cool and store the soup to serve later. See below for more about cooling and storing soups.

FINISHING AND GARNISHING

Soups can be "finished" by adding cream, butter, liaisons, or herb mixtures such as pesto. It is best to add the finishing ingredients as close as possible to the time you plan to serve the soup, to keep flavors fresh and bright. Remember to check the seasoning of the soup again after you add any finishing ingredients.

Clear soups should be garnished just before serving to prevent the broth from becoming cloudy and to keep the garnish fresh. Some garnishes are best added to individual servings just before they are served: croutons, grated cheese, or a drizzle of sherry are some examples. Still other garnishes are an integral part of the soup and are usually stirred into the entire pot.

COOLING AND REHEATING SOUPS

Many soups can be prepared in large batches to have on hand in the refrigerator or freezer. The recipe will indicate when you should cool the batch in order to store it. Then, as you reheat it, you add the final ingredients. To keep your soups flavorful and wholesome, be sure to remember the following instructions:

TO COOL SOUPS QUICKLY AND SAFELY, set up an ice bath using a large bowl or your sink. Fill the bowl or sink with a few inches of water and then add plenty of ice. As soon as your soup has reached the right stage, take the pot from the heat. Puree or strain the soup if you are instructed to do so (for more about how to puree soups, see page 47). Place the soup, either in the pot you used to cook it or in a metal bowl, in the ice bath. Add more water and ice so that the ice water comes to the same level as the soup in the pot. Don't add too much, however, or the pot could begin to float and the soup spill out. Stir the soup occasionally as it cools down. Once the soup cools, you can transfer it to storage containers. Be sure to label and date the soup.

REHEAT SOUPS THOROUGHLY. Bring clear soups just up to a boil quickly over medium-high or high heat and check the seasoning and consistency. A little salt and pepper, a few drops of lemon juice, sherry, or other seasonings can make all the difference.

REHEAT THICK SOUPS, SUCH AS CREAMS, PUREES, OR BISQUES, GENTLY. Before you add the soup to the pot, add a thin layer of water or broth to the pot to act as a buffer between the soup and the pot. Put the pot over low heat and stir frequently as the soup softens slightly. Then you can increase the heat slightly and bring the soup up to a simmer. As always, be sure to check the seasoning carefully once the soup is at a simmer and make any adjustments you like.

If your soup has become too thick or too thin, you can adjust its consistency. Thick soups, especially those made with starchy vegetables or dried beans, may continue to thicken during cooking and storage. As a general rule, purees, creams, and bisques should be about as thick as heavy cream and liquid enough to pour from a ladle into a bowl. The following steps may be taken to adjust consistency:

FOR A SOUP THAT HAS BECOME TOO THICK, water or an appropriately flavored broth may be added in small amounts until the proper consistency is reached. The seasoning should be rechecked before serving.

FOR A SOUP THAT IS TOO THIN, a small amount of diluted cornstarch or arrowroot may be added. The soup should be at a simmer or slow boil when the starch is added. It should be stirred continuously and should continue simmering for 2 or 3 minutes.

DEGREASING

Some soups, especially broth-based ones, may be prepared in advance, and then cooled and refrigerated. This makes it easy to remove any fat from the soup, as the refrigeration hardens the fat enough to let you simply lift it away. If you must serve the soup right away, use a serving spoon or a shallow ladle to skim away as much of the fat as you can. Remember, though, that a few droplets of fat on the surface of brothy soups can give the soup additional richness; in fact, you might want to add a drizzle of olive oil for precisely that reason.

SERVING

Hot soups should be served very hot. The thinner the soup, the more important this is. Brothy soups lose their heat rapidly, so bring them to a near-boil before you ladle them into heated soup plates or cups. Cold soups should be thoroughly chilled and served in chilled cups, bowls, or glasses.

Hearty Vegetable Soups

Minestrone is a great example of a rich, robust vegetable soup. It is built from an aromatic base (known as a *sofrito*) that includes onions, celery, and a bit of bacon. It gets body from the addition of beans and pasta. A bit of Parmesan cheese rind adds a special flavor.

THE BASIC STEPS FOR A HEARTY VEGETABLE SOUP

1. Cook the aromatic ingredients in a little fat. (See Aromatic Options on page 32)

2. Add the broth and ingredients that require the longest cooking times. Season the soup throughout cooking time.

3. Add the remaining ingredients in sequence. (See Ingredient Options below)

4. Simmer the soup, skimming as necessary, until all of the ingredients are tender.

5. Add any final flavoring adjustments and serve, or cool the soup according to the preceding instructions, transfer to a storage container, and store in the refrigerator or freezer.

6. Reheat the soup and serve in heated bowls with garnishes as desired. (See Garnishing Options on page 33)

INGREDIENT OPTIONS

You can choose a wide array of ingredients to include in your own improvised vegetable soups. If you want to add precooked ingredients, remember that they only need to simmer in the soup long enough to get hot. Use the following as a guideline to determine when to add these ingredients.

MEATS, POULTRY, AND FISH Cuts of meat that are more mature and less tender or poultry should be added to the soup early in the cooking process so that it will flavor the broth properly and finish cooking at the same time as the other ingredients. Add fish or shellfish to hearty broths close to the end of cooking time to prevent them from becoming overcooked. Add cubed or shredded cooked meats, poultry, or fish meant as a garnish during the final 10 minutes of cooking time, just long enough to heat them.

GRAINS AND PASTA Allow grains and pasta a little more time than would be necessary to cook them in boiling salted water. These ingredients also will give some body to the soup.

LEGUMES Lentils and black-eyed peas are added to the soup along with the stock so that they will cook fully. Other beans should be cooked separately and added during the final 10 or 15 minutes of cooking time, just long enough to fully heat them.

DENSE OR STARCHY VEGETABLES Turnips, carrots, potatoes, winter squash, rutabagas, beets, parsnips, and potatoes cut into small dice typically require 30 to 45 minutes to fully cook through.

GREEN VEGETABLES Peas, green beans, and leafy vegetables such as spinach or kale are added during the final 15 to 20 minutes of simmering time for the soup. Some chefs prefer to blanch these vegetables (see page 18) to help set the colors before adding them to a soup.

TOMATOES In some cases, tomatoes may be added at the beginning of cooking time, along with the aromatic ingredients, to act as a broth flavoring. A tomato garnish may be added during the final 5 or 10 minutes of simmering time.

HERBS AND SPICES Dried herbs and most spices are added to the aromatic vegetables to release flavor into the broth throughout cooking time. Fresh or dried herbs and spices also may be added in the form of a sachet or bouquet during the final 15 to 20 minutes of simmering time, or as a final addition of fresh herbs just before service, for the freshest flavor.

AROMATIC OPTIONS

The first step when you prepare hearty vegetables soups is to build a flavorful base out of a variety of aromatics. The ingredients you choose as the aromatic base will influence the entire soup. Members of the onion family, including leeks, shallots, garlic, and onions, are universally appreciated. Combinations of vegetables, like mirepoix (onions, carrots, and celery), the Cajun Trinity (onions, peppers, and celery), or Asian-influenced mixtures, are usually cooked gently in a bit of oil or fat. Mushrooms, both fresh and dried, scallions, ginger, galangal, and other intensely flavored ingredients typically are cooked in fat as the first step in soup making. Not only does the fat help to cook the aromatics, it also helps to distribute flavor throughout the soup.

The degree to which the aromatics are cooked has a strong influence on a soup's final flavor and color. Some recipes ask you to cook the aromatics until they are just limp and translucent; professionals refer to this as "sweating" the vegetables because the vegetables actually start to release some of their own moisture. If you cover the pot, it helps to cook the aromatics a little more quickly; this technique is known as "smothering." Other recipes may instruct you to cook the aromatics until they develop a golden color or even become a rich golden brown.

If your recipe calls for spices, you may be instructed to add them to the aromatics and cook. This step helps to open up the flavor of the spice. Since the flavor in most spices is carried by fat better than it is by water, we recommend you add most of the spice at the start of cooking time. Dried herbs also are added at this point, although fresh herbs are best added near the end of cooking time.

The broth is added to the pot once the aromatic base is prepared, along with the remaining ingredients. You may add everything all at once, but very often these soups contain a selection of vegetables. The sequence you follow when you add the ingredients depends upon their individual cooking times. Some vegetables are very dense, starchy, or fibrous. Those vegetables are added near the start of cooking time. Tender or quick-cooking vegetables, like peas or corn, are added in the final minutes of cooking time. Make sure you taste the soup occasionally as it simmers so you can make small adjustments to the seasonings as you go.

Hearty vegetable soups like minestrone are best when each vegetable is cooked until it is tender, but can still hold its shape. When you introduce long-cooking ingredients like dried beans or pasta, you may find it helpful to cook them separately. Doing so maintains a lighter, brothier texture in the soup. Soups are very forgiving, however. The only important caution is this: Soups left to simmer for hours and hours lose nutrients, texture, and colors. Taste the soup carefully once all of the ingredients are properly cooked. You may find that you need a bit more salt and pepper, or you may want to add ingredients like lemon or lime juice, citrus zest, chopped fresh herbs, or a dash of wine.

Taking the time to preheat your bowls keeps the soup hot on its way from the kitchen to the table. Be sure to use an underliner to protect your hands as well as the tabletop.

FINISHING AND GARNISHING OPTIONS

Many vegetable soups are made from a combination of ingredients. Some garnishing and finishing options include a dash of lime or lemon juice or a splash of vinegar, an addition of freshly chopped herbs, grated cheese, a drizzle of oil, or diced or shredded meat, fish, or poultry. Beans, pastas, and rice (cooked directly in the soup or cooked separately and added at the last minute) are also common. Croutons and rusks are used to garnish a variety of different soups.

CROUTONS AND RUSKS

1 cup bread, with or without crusts removed, cubed

CROUTONS AND rusks keep well for several days in an airtight container, so make a large batch if you have enough bread on hand. To make croutons, remove the crust from the bread, if desired. Cut the bread into cubes. You can cut the croutons into any size you like, from tiny cubes for garnishing soups in cups to large cubes for garnishing soups served in soup plates or to add to salads.

MAKES 1 CUP CROUTONS OR RUSKS

1. Preheat the oven to 350°F. Toss the bread with enough melted butter or oil to lightly coat the cubes and season them with salt and pepper. Spread the bread cubes in a single layer on a baking sheet and bake until golden. Stir the croutons once or twice during baking so they brown evenly.

2. Rusks are actually large croutons. To make rusks, cut a baguette or other bread into slices about ½ inch thick. Brush the bread with some melted butter or olive oil and arrange on a baking sheet. Bake at 350°F until the bread is dry, crisp, and lightly browned. Turn the rusks once as they bake.

Garlic-Flavored Croutons

Mince 1 garlic clove for every cup of croutons you are preparing. Sprinkle the garlic with ¼ teaspoon of kosher salt and mash to a paste with the side of a large knife. Add the garlic paste to the butter or oil before tossing with the bread cubes or brushing onto rusks. Bake as directed above.

Cheese Croutons

After the bread cubes have been tossed with the butter as above, toss with ½ cup very finely grated Parmesan, Romano, or other grating cheese (a rotary cheese grater or a microplane grater will give you the finest texture and help the cheese adhere to the bread). Bake as directed above.

Goat Cheese or Cheddar Rusks

After the rusks are baked and crisp, top them with grated cheeses such as Cheddar or Asiago, or spread them with a soft cheese like goat cheese or brie. Return the rusks to the pan and broil or bake just long enough to heat the cheese.

Herb-Flavored Croutons

Add chopped fresh or dried herbs (such as oregano or rosemary) to the butter or oil. Toss with the bread cubes and bake as directed above.

FLAVOR is built into soups when you add aromatic ingredients to the soup at the best time. Aromatics to add at the start of cooking time include vegetables or herbs. A richly flavored broth, on its own or bolstered with ingredients like wine or citrus juice, adds another layer.

SWEAT OR SMOTHER THE AROMATICS

Both of these terms indicate a type of sautéing. Sweating is a descriptive term; as the aromatics cook, they begin to release their natural moisture. Smothered aromatics are cooked in a covered pot.

1. Heat a little oil or butter in a heavy gauge soup pot over medium heat.

2. Add the vegetables all at once, or you can choose to stagger the sequence: onions first, followed by carrots, then celery, then the more tender ingredients like mushrooms or tomatoes. Stir well to coat the vegetables with the fat, then cover the pot if you want to smother them or simply keep stirring to sweat them. Cook until the onions change color, going from relatively opaque to nearly translucent and limp.

CHOOSE A FLAVORFUL BASE LIQUID

Many soup recipes call for a base liquid that adds even more flavor to the soup. Homemade broths (see our recipes on pages 82 and 83) are a great choice, but you may want to bolster the soup even more while it simmers.

1. If you are using broth, choose a flavor that works with the main ingredients in your soup. Chicken stock has a relatively "neutral" flavor. Vegetable broth can be mild in flavor, too, but if there is a strong flavor in your vegetable broth, think about how well it will work with your soup.

2. Use flavor-building strategies like the one borrowed from Italian cooks which is shown here. For this soup, we've added a piece of Parmesan cheese rind to infuse the soup with a rich, savory flavor.

MINESTRONE

2 tbsp olive oil

4 pancetta slices, chopped

1½ cups chopped green cabbage

1 cup chopped onions

1 cup sliced carrots

1 cup chopped celery

2 garlic cloves, minced

8 cups Chicken Broth (page 83)

1 cup peeled, diced potatoes

One 3-inch piece Parmesan cheese rind

¾ cup broken vermicelli or angel hair pasta, 2-inch pieces

½ cup chopped plum tomatoes, peeled and seeded

½ cup cooked chickpeas, rinsed and drained

½ cup cooked kidney beans, rinsed and drained

Salt and pepper as needed

Freshly grated Parmesan cheese, as needed

THERE IS no one right way to make minestrone. Recipes vary from cook to cook according to individual preferences and whatever is on hand, so feel free to improvise with other vegetables, beans, or pasta shapes to suit your taste.

MAKES 8 SERVINGS

1. Heat the oil in a soup pot over medium heat. Add the pancetta and cook, stirring frequently, until the fat has rendered from the pancetta and it begins to color and crisp, about 3 minutes.

2. Add the cabbage, onions, carrots, celery, and garlic. Sauté, stirring frequently, until the onions are softened and translucent, about 8 minutes.

3. Add the broth, potatoes, and Parmesan cheese rind. Bring to a simmer and cook until the vegetables are tender, about 30 minutes. Do not overcook them.

4. When the vegetables in the soup are tender, add the vermicelli, tomatoes, chickpeas, and kidney beans and continue to simmer until the pasta is fully cooked and all of the ingredients are very hot, about 20 minutes. Remove and discard the Parmesan rind. Season the soup with salt and pepper.

5. Serve in heated bowls, sprinkled with the cheese.

USING BACON AS A FLAVORING

A bit of bacon, salt pork, or the end of a piece of cured ham such as Prosciutto or Smithfield adds depth and flavor to soups. Bacon is especially good at flavoring soups since you can gently cook out some of the fat, a procedure know as rendering, and use that fat to cook the aromatic base of your soup.

The kind of bacon you choose depends upon the flavor profile of your soup. Smoked bacons have a distinctive taste. Cured but unsmoked bacon, like pancetta, has a more subdued flavor. Pancetta is a type of Italian bacon that usually can be found in delis and butcher shops. If it is unavailable in your area, you can omit it or substitute regular bacon.

If you are choosing a bacon to render and use both as a cooking fat and for flavor, choose fatty slices, if you have an option. Put the bacon into a soup pot with a tablespoon or two of water, and then put the pot over low heat. Starting in a cold pot gives the bacon fat time to melt before the bacon gets too crisp. Stir the bacon as it cooks. The liquid will turn a cloudy color at first. Once the bacon seems to have given up most of its fat, turn the heat up a bit and keep cooking long enough for the bits to turn brown and crisp. The fat will turn clear as any moisture in the pan cooks away.

CLASSIC VEGETABLE SOUP

3 tbsp olive oil

⅔ cup diced carrots

1¼ cups diced onions

½ cup diced celery

⅓ cup diced turnip

¾ cup diced leek, white and light green portions

½ cup diced cabbage

8 cups Vegetable Broth (page 82)

Sachet: 5 black peppercorns, 5 parsley stems, 1 bay leaf, 1 thyme sprig or ½ tsp dried thyme enclosed in a large tea ball or tied in a cheesecloth pouch

½ cup chopped plum tomatoes (peeled and seeded)

½ cup peeled, diced potatoes

½ cup fresh or frozen lima beans

½ cup fresh or frozen corn kernels

¼ cup chopped flat-leaf parsley

Salt and pepper as needed

T HIS SOUP bursts with the flavor of fresh vegetables. Serve it with Cheddar Rusks (see page 34) if you like, and feel free to experiment with different combinations of vegetables.

MAKES 8 SERVINGS

1. Heat the oil in a soup pot over medium heat. Add the carrots, onions, celery, turnip, leek, and cabbage. Sauté, stirring frequently, until the onions are softened and translucent, about 15 minutes.

2. Add the broth and sachet. Bring to a simmer and cook for 10 minutes.

3. Add the tomatoes, potatoes, lima beans, corn, and parsley. Continue to simmer until the potatoes are tender, 10 to 15 minutes.

4. Remove and discard the sachet. Season to taste with the salt and pepper. Serve in heated bowls.

CHORIZO AND VEGETABLE SOUP

YOU CAN find different varieties of chorizo in the market: fresh, dried, bulk, or loose, like hamburger meat. We used a link of fresh, Mexican-style chorizo in this soup, which is made from ground pork, chiles, paprika, and other seasonings. For a more substantial soup, add cooked black or kidney beans during the final 10 minutes of simmering time.

SERVES 4 TO 6

1. Heat a soup pot over medium-high heat. Add the chorizo and sauté until browned, 5 to 6 minutes. Transfer the chorizo to absorbent towels and discard the fat from the pot.

2. Heat the oil in the same pot over medium heat. Add the onions, celery, garlic, and cumin seeds. Sauté, stirring frequently, until the onions are softened and translucent, about 5 minutes. Add the chorizo, broth, tomatoes, potatoes, peppers, tomato paste, bay leaf, half of the parsley, the oregano, and salt as needed. Simmer until the potatoes are tender, about 20 minutes.

3. Discard the bay leaf. Stir in the corn and black pepper. Simmer until thoroughly heated. Garnish each serving with the cilantro and remaining parsley.

2½ ounces diced chorizo sausage

2 tsp olive oil

¼ cup diced onions

2 tbsp diced celery

1 tsp minced garlic

¾ tsp cumin seeds

2½ cups Chicken Broth (page 83)

2 cups chopped plum tomatoes (peeled and seeded)

1 cup peeled, diced potatoes

1 small red pepper, diced

1 small green pepper, diced

1 tbsp tomato paste

½ bay leaf

1 tbsp chopped parsley

¼ tsp chopped oregano

Salt and pepper as needed

1 cup corn kernels

1 tbsp chopped cilantro

CALLALOO

CALLALOO IS the name of a soup as well as the main ingredient, the greens of the taro root. If you cannot find it in your area, fresh spinach makes a fine substitute. Whatever greens you use, be sure to wash them thoroughly to remove any grit.

MAKES 8 SERVINGS

1. Cook the bacon in a soup pot over medium heat until the fat has rendered from the bacon and it begins to color and crisp, about 3 minutes. Add the onions and garlic. Sauté, stirring frequently, until the onions are softened and translucent, about 5 minutes.

2. Add the broth, okra, callaloo or spinach, chile, and thyme along with a pinch of salt and pepper. Bring to a simmer and cook for 30 minutes.

3. Just before serving, remove the chile and add the crabmeat, scallions, coconut milk, and lime juice. Season to taste with salt and pepper. Serve in heated bowls.

2 oz slab bacon, rind removed, cut into small dice

¾ cup minced onions

1 tsp minced garlic

8 cups Chicken Broth (page 83)

4 cups fresh okra, sliced ¼ inch thick

1½ cups coarsely chopped callaloo or spinach

1 Scotch bonnet chile, pricked with a fork and left whole

4 tsp coarsely chopped thyme leaves, or 2 tsp dried

Salt and pepper as needed

10 oz crabmeat, picked over for shells

3 scallions, sliced

¾ cup coconut milk

Juice of 2 limes, or more to taste

TOMATO AND SWEET PEPPER SOUP
WITH POPPY SEED CREAM

¼ cup olive oil

1¼ cups minced onions

1 tsp minced garlic

3 cups chopped tomatoes (peeled and seeded)

2 cups red pepper julienne

1 cup thinly sliced celery

6 cups Chicken Broth (page 83)

½ cup heavy cream

1 tbsp lightly crushed poppy seeds

Salt and pepper as needed

TO PEEL fresh tomatoes: Bring a pot of water to a rolling boil. Score an X in the bottom of the tomatoes with a paring knife, and drop them into the boiling water for 15 to 30 seconds. Remove the tomatoes with a slotted spoon and place briefly in a bowl of ice water to cool. Peel away the skin with a paring knife, cut the tomato in half, and remove the seeds.

WHEN PEPPERS and tomatoes begin to ripen in the late summer and fall, this soup is a delicious way to showcase their wonderful flavors. Use a combination of red, green, and yellow peppers and tomatoes when summer farm stands offer them, or enjoy it any time of year by substituting 3 cups of chopped, drained, canned tomatoes for the fresh ones.

MAKES 8 SERVINGS

1. Heat the oil in a soup pot over medium heat. Add the onions and garlic and stir to coat evenly with the oil. Reduce the heat to low and cook, covered, until the onions are softened and translucent, about 5 minutes.

2. Add the tomatoes, red pepper, and celery to the pot, replace the cover, and continue to cook until the vegetables are tender and heated through, 6 to 8 minutes. Add the broth. Bring to a simmer and cook for 20 minutes. Skim as needed.

3. Meanwhile, whip the cream until it forms soft peaks. Fold in the poppy seeds.

4. Season the soup to taste with the salt and pepper. Serve in heated bowls, topped with the poppy seed whipped cream.

TOMATO AND ESCAROLE SOUP

T O GIVE this soup extra richness, we used canned "fire-roasted tomatoes." If you can find them in your market, give them a try. Or, try roasting your own fresh tomatoes to deepen their flavor.

SERVES 4 TO 6

1. Heat the oil in a soup pot over medium-high heat. Add the onions, shallots, and garlic and stir to coat with the oil. Sauté, stirring frequently, until the onions are softened and translucent, about 5 minutes.

2. Add the escarole and cook, stirring frequently, until it wilts, about 5 minutes. Add the broth, chopped tomatoes, and tomato sauce. Bring the soup to a boil, skimming the surface to remove any foam, and then reduce the heat to low and simmer until the escarole is very tender and all of the ingredients are very hot, about 10 minutes. Season to taste with salt and pepper. Serve in heated bowls or cups.

OVEN-ROASTING TOMATOES

Choose ripe, flavorful tomatoes for oven roasting. Plum tomatoes are a great choice since they have more flesh and less "water" than other varieties, but you will get excellent results from virtually any variety, including cherry or grape tomatoes.

First, wash the tomatoes well. Cut the core out of larger tomatoes before slicing them or cutting them into wedges. Smaller varieties, like cherry tomatoes, need only to be cut in half.

Arrange the tomatoes on an oiled baking sheet. Turn the tomatoes so they are lightly coated with the oil, then put them into a 350°F oven until they darken in color and have a sweet, rich aroma. Larger tomato slices or wedges may take up to 30 minutes, thin slices or small tomatoes will take 15 to 20 minutes.

If you want to add even more flavor, season the tomatoes before you put them into the oven with salt, pepper, minced garlic, or chopped herbs.

3 tbsp extra-virgin olive oil

1¼ cups large-dice onions

1 tbsp minced shallots

1 tsp minced garlic

6 cups coarsely chopped escarole, stemmed and washed

2 cups Chicken Broth (page 83)

1½ cups chopped tomatoes (peeled and seeded)

½ cup tomato sauce

Salt and pepper as needed

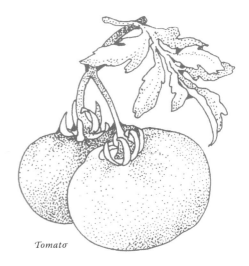

Tomato

H'LELEM (TUNISIAN VEGETABLE AND BEAN SOUP)

½ cup dried lima or butter beans

½ cup dried chickpeas

2 tbsp olive oil

¾ cup minced onions

½ cup diced celery

1 tsp minced garlic

4 cups Chicken Broth (page 83)

⅓ cup tomato paste

4 large Swiss chard leaves (stems removed and cut into 1-inch pieces, leaves shredded)

⅓ cup angel hair pasta, broken into bite-size pieces

2 tbsp Harissa (page 277)

Salt and pepper as needed

½ cup chopped parsley

P ACKED WITH beans and greens, this slightly spicy vegetable soup is both tasty and good for you. Harissa is a Tunisian hot sauce or paste usually made with hot chiles, garlic, cumin, coriander, caraway, and olive oil. It's available in cans, jars, or tubes from Middle Eastern markets and specialty stores. Or make your own (see page 277).

MAKES 8 SERVINGS

1. Separately soak the dried lima or butter beans and chickpeas overnight in three times their volume of water. Drain and cook them separately in two times their volume of fresh water until they are tender, about 45 minutes. Drain and reserve the cooking water from both the lima beans and chickpeas. Combine the lima beans and chickpeas; set aside. Combine the cooking waters and set aside.

2. Heat the olive oil in a soup pot over medium heat. Add the onions, celery, and garlic. Sauté, stirring frequently, until the onions are softened and translucent, about 5 minutes. Add the broth, reserved bean cooking liquid, and tomato paste. Mix together until well blended and bring to a simmer for 10 minutes.

3. Add the cooked beans and chickpeas, Swiss chard, and pasta. Simmer until the pasta and chard stems are tender, about 10 minutes.

4. Add the harissa and stir until blended. Season to taste with salt and pepper. Serve in heated bowls, garnished with chopped parsley.

ZUCCHINI SOUP

WHEN ZUCCHINI become large, their seeds can become a little bitter. If you have a giant-size squash, halve it from blossom to stem end, scoop out the seeds with a tablespoon, and dice the remaining flesh. Smaller zucchini can be used, seeds and all.

MAKES 8 SERVINGS

1. Cook the bacon in a soup pot over medium heat until the fat has rendered from the bacon and it begins to color and crisp, about 3 minutes. Add the onions and garlic. Sauté, stirring frequently, until the onions are a light golden brown, 8 to 10 minutes. Add the zucchini, cover the pot, and cook until the zucchini starts to become translucent, about 5 minutes.

2. Add the broth, tomatoes, tomato puree, and vinegar. Bring the soup to a simmer, and cook until all the vegetables are very tender and the soup has developed a good flavor, 15 to 20 minutes.

3. Add the basil to the soup and season to taste with the salt and pepper. Serve in heated bowls, garnished with cheddar rusks.

4 bacon strips, minced

2½ cups chopped onions

2 tsp minced garlic

7 to 8 cups diced zucchini

6 cups Chicken Broth (page 83)

1 cup chopped plum tomatoes (peeled and seeded)

½ cup tomato puree

¼ cup red wine vinegar or cider vinegar

2 tbsp minced basil

Salt and pepper as needed

8 Cheddar Rusks (page 34)

THE BACON provides a great deal of flavor to this soup; but if you prefer a vegetarian version, replace the bacon with a tablespoon or two of olive oil, replace the Chicken Broth with Vegetable Broth, and add a spoonful of minced sun-dried tomatoes along with the basil in step 3.

CORN CHOWDER WITH CHILES AND MONTEREY JACK

6 ears of corn, shucked

1 cup heavy cream

2 slices bacon, minced

1¼ cups minced onions

1 cup minced red pepper

½ cup minced celery

½ tsp minced garlic

6 cups Chicken Broth (page 83)

3 cups peeled, diced potatoes

3 cups chopped plum tomatoes (peeled and seeded, juices reserved)

One 4-oz can green chiles, drained and chopped

1 cup grated Monterey Jack cheese

Salt and pepper as needed

Tabasco sauce, to taste

1 cup toasted corn tortilla strips, optional

THIS CHOWDER is best made with fresh corn on the cob; but if corn is out of season and you are desperate for corn chowder, substitute 3 cups of frozen corn kernels, thawed. To avoid this situation altogether, however, make an extra batch or two at the height of corn season and freeze to enjoy later in the dead of winter, when fresh corn is but a distant memory.

MAKES 8 SERVINGS

1. Cut the corn kernels from the cobs with a sharp knife, capturing as much juice as possible. Reserve ¾ cup of the corn kernels and puree the rest with the heavy cream in a food processor or blender. Set aside.

2. Cook the bacon in a soup pot over medium heat until the fat has rendered from the bacon and it begins to color and crisp, about 3 minutes. Add the onions, pepper, celery, and garlic. Reduce the heat to low and cook, covered, until the vegetables are softened and translucent, about 5 minutes.

3. Add the broth, potatoes, and tomatoes, including their juices. Bring to a simmer and cook, covered, until the potatoes are tender, about 20 minutes. Skim any fat from the surface of the soup and discard.

4. Add the pureed corn-and-cream mixture, reserved corn kernels, chiles, and cheese. Heat the soup over low heat, but do not allow it to come to a full boil. Season to taste with salt, pepper, and Tabasco. Serve in heated bowls, garnished with tortilla strips, if using.

Smoked Corn and Chile Chowder

NOTE: DO not try this smoking process unless you have a well-ventilated kitchen. Turn the exhaust fan on high and monitor the process constantly.

Substitute 2 fresh poblano chiles for the canned green chiles. Core and remove the seeds from the poblanos and the red pepper. Cut into large flat pieces, approximately 4 inches square. Smoke the corn and chiles according to the directions at right. After the vegetables have cooled, cut the corn kernels from the cob as directed above, and dice the smoked chile before using.

PUREEING SOUPS

You can puree soups by a variety of means: using a handheld blender directly in the soup pot, in a countertop blender, with a sieve or a food mill, or in a food processor. Follow these guidelines to avoid scalds and burns.

FOR ALL SOUPS

The first step in pureeing a soup, regardless of what piece of equipment you intend to use, is to pull the soup pot off the heat and allow the soup to cool for at least 10 minutes. Besides possible scalds or burns from the hot soup, boiling hot liquids can splash up unexpectedly when agitated by a food processor or blender.

USING A HANDHELD BLENDER

Be sure that the soup pot is not too full. You should have at least 4 inches of space between the top of the soup and the top of the pot. If the soup fills the pot more than that, transfer some of the soup to a bowl or a pot. Put the head of the blender under the surface of the soup before you turn it on. Continue to run the blender until the soup is smooth. You can strain the soup through a fine sieve after pureeing it this way, if necessary, to remove any fibers from the vegetables.

USING A COUNTERTOP BLENDER OR A FOOD PROCESSOR

Strain the soup through a sieve to separate the solids and liquids; reserve the liquid separately. Add enough of the solids to the blender jar or bowl of the food processor to fill it by about half. Remove the "funnel" from the lid of the blender or feed tube of a food processor, to allow steam from the hot soup to escape; otherwise, pressure will build up and the soup might burst up when you remove the lid. It also permits you to add some of the reserved liquid so the soup purees more easily. Turn the motor on at a low setting. Gradually ladle some of the liquid into the soup so the blades can turn more easily. You can increase the blender speed once the soup has become a coarse puree. After the soup is smooth, transfer it to a clean pot. Continue to puree the soup, working in batches. After all of the soup is pureed and combined in the clean pot, stir it well and, if necessary, add more of the reserved liquid or additional broth to thin the soup.

TO SMOKE VEGETABLES

1. Place fine wood chips in a disposable aluminum roasting pan fitted with a wire rack (if your rack does not have feet, use balls of aluminum foil to raise the rack a few inches above the wood chips). Use only wood chips that are specifically meant for smoking food. Have ready a fitted cover or aluminum foil large enough to cover the pan. Heat the roasting pan over high heat until the wood chips begin to smolder and smoke.

2. Place the prepared vegetables on the wire rack over the smoking chips. If the chips are smoldering and creating sufficient smoke, remove the pan from the heat. Otherwise, reduce the heat to low. The idea is to keep the chips smoldering but not to catch them on fire. Cover tightly with the lid or aluminum foil and allow the vegetables to smoke for about 15 to 20 minutes. Remove the foil and allow the vegetables to cool.

VIETNAMESE WATER SPINACH AND BEEF SOUP

WATER SPINACH leaves are tender and have a sweet, mild flavor and slightly slippery texture when cooked. The edible stems provide a crisp contrast to the leaves. If you cannot find water spinach, ordinary spinach makes a fine substitute.

MAKES 6 TO 8 SERVINGS

1. Bring a medium pot of salted water to a boil. Add the water spinach or spinach leaves and cook just until wilted, 1 to 2 minutes. Remove the spinach with a slotted spoon and drain well. When cool enough to handle, squeeze the excess moisture from the spinach and chop it. Set aside.

2. Soak the bean threads in hot water to cover until tender, about 5 minutes. Drain the noodles in a colander, rinse under cool running water, separate the strands, and drain again. Chop into 2-inch pieces and set aside.

3. Heat the oil in a large wok or soup pot over medium-high heat. Add the shallots, garlic, and red pepper. Stirfry for 30 seconds. Add the beef and stirfry for 1 minute. Add the broth, soy sauce, fish sauce, lemon juice, and sugar. Bring the soup to a simmer. Add the spinach, and season to taste with the salt and black pepper.

4. Distribute the bean threads evenly between heated bowls. Ladle the soup over the bean threads and garnish with the cilantro.

1 bunch fresh water spinach (tough stem parts trimmed) or 2 cups packed spinach leaves

1 oz dried mung bean threads ("cellophane noodles")

1 tbsp vegetable oil

1 tbsp sliced shallots

½ tsp minced garlic

Pinch crushed red pepper

¼ lb beef flank steak, cut into thin strips

1 quart Chicken Broth (page 83)

1 tbsp soy sauce

1 tbsp Vietnamese fish sauce (nuoc mam)

1 tbsp lemon juice

½ tsp sugar

Salt and pepper as needed

2 tbsp chopped cilantro

WATER SPINACH is both cultivated and harvested wild throughout Asia. It grows in swamp areas and also is known as swamp cabbage. Even though it is not botanically related to ordinary (or Malabar) spinach, it can be prepared and used in much the same ways. Look for water spinach at Asian groceries. It wilts quickly, so buy only the freshest looking bunch and plan to store it no longer than two days wrapped in a plastic bag in the bottom of your refrigerator.

THE BASIC STEPS FOR A CREAM SOUP

1. Select and prepare the vegetables for cooking (see *Main Ingredient Options*).

2. Sweat the aromatic ingredients, including onions, shallots, celery, or leeks, along with the main ingredient.

3. Add flour to make a roux. (See *Thickening Options*)

4. Add the liquid and bring the soup to a very gentle simmer.

5. Skim and stir the soup frequently and season throughout cooking time.

6. Puree until smooth, finish, and serve at the best temperature. (See *Finishing and Service Options*)

MAIN INGREDIENT OPTIONS

You can use almost any fresh vegetable to make a cream soup using the method outlined above. The amount to choose depends upon the density of the vegetable. Vegetables that are similar in texture to broccoli (asparagus, cauliflower, artichokes, or peas, for example) can be interchanged easily. Replace the broccoli with an equal weight of any of those vegetables.

High moisture vegetables, like tomatoes or mushrooms, call for slightly more in order to get a rich flavor and a creamy consistency. Use 1½ times the weight of the broccoli.

THICKENING OPTIONS

The recipe for Cream of Broccoli Soup (page 52) is thickened with a classic roux using a technique known to chefs trained in classic European technique as singer. Flour is the thickener, but there are other options. One option is to use more of the basic ingredient and let the texture of the vegetable thicken the soup.

Another option calls for replacing the flour with a potato. Use a medium-size starchy potato, like an Idaho or russet, to thicken 2 quarts of soup (the amount made in this recipe). Peel the potato and cut it into thin slices or small dice. Add it along with the broccoli. It will fall apart as it cooks, thickening the soup.

Still another option is to add a little cornstarch or arrowroot to the soup after you have pureed it. Make a slurry by combining about ¼ cup of cornstarch or 2 tablespoons of arrowroot with enough cold water or broth to make it pourable. Add the slurry

to the simmering soup a little at a time as you stir it. It only takes a minute or two to thicken the soup, so keep adding small amounts until the soup is the thickness you like.

FINISHING AND SERVING OPTIONS

Cream soups can be served hot or cold. To make a cold version of your favorite cream vegetable soup, chill the soup just after you have pureed it. Once the soup is well-chilled, stir in the cold cream and then taste the soup to be sure it is properly seasoned. Cold foods often need heavier seasoning, since cold temperatures dampen flavors slightly.

Finish a cream soup by stirring in heavy cream that has been blended with an egg yolk (see *Finishing Soups with a Liaison*), but be sure you don't boil the soup once the liaison goes in. Instead of adding heavy cream, try substituting a dollop of lightly whipped unsweetened cream to finish the soup. Add a slice or rosette of plain or flavored butter to the soup just before you serve it and allow it to melt over the surface for extra richness.

Substitute crème fraîche, sour cream, or even plain yogurt for the heavy cream for a different flavor, or omit the cream altogether, for a soup that is "creamy" in texture, but not loaded with cream.

FINISHING SOUPS WITH A LIAISON

A mixture of egg yolk and cream called a liaison may be used at the end of cooking to add body and sheen to a dish. Mixing cream with egg yolks makes the yolks less likely to curdle when hot liquid is added. Adding the hot liquid carefully, as described below, "tempers" the liaison by heating it up gradually for a second line of defense against curdling.

In a large bowl, whisk the cream and egg yolk together until evenly blended. To temper the liaison, gradually add some of the hot soup you want to finish, a ladleful at a time, to the egg mixture while whisking constantly to temper the eggs and prevent curdling.

Slowly pour the tempered mixture into the pot of hot liquid while stirring constantly. Gently warm the mixture, stirring frequently, until it thickens slightly. Do not allow it to go above 185°F, or the egg yolks can still curdle. Serve as soon as possible to ensure the safety and quality of the finished dish.

CREAM SOUPS are often perceived as too rich for everyday. A great cream soup doesn't always depend upon using a lot of cream. A smooth, creamy texture is the goal. A dollop of whipped cream, crème fraîche, or yogurt adds flavor without adding too many calories or dulling the taste of your fresh vegetables.

THICKENING THE SOUP

Adding a bit of flour to the vegetables after they have sautéed until tender is a technique that chef's refer to as the *singe* method. Stir the flour into the vegetable mixture to distribute it evenly. As the flour cooks, the mixture will start to look pasty. Keep cooking and stirring for about 2 minutes to heat the flour so it will thicken the broth right away once you add it to the pot. If you don't want to use flour, you can skip this step and either add a cup of diced potatoes along with the broth or you can add a slurry to the soup after you puree it. Both techniques are described on page 50.

CONTROLLING TEXTURE AS YOU PUREE

Once the vegetables are tender enough to mash when you press on them with a fork, the soup is ready to puree. Let the soup cool for a few minutes, and then strain the soup through a sieve, catching the broth in a bowl or a measuring pitcher. Put enough of the solids into the jar of a blender to fill it halfway. Add just enough of the reserved broth to cover the solids, then cover the jar and puree. Bring the soup back to a simmer to check for seasoning and a good texture. (For more about how to puree soups safely, see page 47.)

CREAM OF BROCCOLI SOUP

2 lb broccoli

¼ cup vegetable or olive oil

1¼ cups chopped onions

½ cup chopped celery

1¼ cups chopped leeks, white and light
green parts

¼ cup all-purpose flour

6 cups Chicken Broth (page 83)

½ cup heavy cream, heated

Fresh lemon juice, to taste

Salt and pepper as needed

T HIS VELVETY soup is the essence of broccoli. It's relatively simple to make, yet tastes very elegant and refined. Try serving this soup as a first course for company.

MAKES 8 SERVINGS

1. Separate the broccoli into stems and florets. Trim away the tough outer parts of the stems. Set aside 1 cup of the nicest-looking small florets. Coarsely chop the remaining broccoli florets and the stems.

2. Heat the oil in a soup pot over medium heat. Add the onions, celery, leeks, and chopped broccoli. Sauté, stirring frequently, until the onions are softened and translucent, about 5 minutes. Add the flour and stir well to combine. Cook, stirring frequently, for 4 minutes. Gradually add the broth to the pot, whisking to work out any lumps of flour. Bring the soup to a simmer and cook for 45 minutes. Stir frequently and skim as needed.

3. Remove the pot from the heat and let the soup cool for at least 10 minutes before pureeing with a handheld blender. Strain the soup through a sieve and reserve the liquid if you are using a countertop blender or food processor. Add the solids to the blender jar or food processor bowl; do not overfill. Add a little of the liquid, replace the cover (without the vent from the lid or feed tube) and puree until smooth. Add more liquid if necessary to help puree the solids. Transfer the pureed soup to a clean pot. Continue to puree until all of the solids are pureed. Blend the soup and adjust the consistency by adding some of the remaining reserved liquid. (The soup is ready to finish now or it can be cooled and stored up to 2 days in the refrigerator or up to 1 month in the freezer.)

4. Meanwhile, steam or boil the reserved broccoli florets until just tender.

5. Return the soup to a simmer over low heat and add the heated cream. Season to taste with the lemon juice, salt, and pepper. Serve in heated bowls, garnished with the florets.

CREAM OF MUSHROOM SOUP

7 tbsp unsalted butter

8 cups chopped mushrooms

1 cup minced celery

1¼ cups thinly sliced leeks, white part only

½ cup all-purpose flour

8 cups Chicken Broth (page 83)

1 thyme sprig

1 cup sliced mushrooms

½ cup heavy cream, heated

Lemon juice to taste

Salt and pepper as needed

For a special presentation, ladle the soup into oven-proof bowls. Top the bowls with puff pastry cut to fit the bowls, seal the edges with some beaten egg, and bake until golden brown according to package directions.

MAKES 8 SERVINGS

1. Melt 6 tablespoons of the butter in a soup pot over low heat. Add the chopped mushrooms, celery, and leeks. Sauté, stirring frequently, until the leeks are softened and translucent, about 5 minutes.

2. Add the flour and cook, stirring constantly, for 3 to 4 minutes. Gradually whisk in the broth. Add the thyme sprig, bring to a simmer, and cook for 30 minutes.

3. Remove the pot from the heat, remove and discard the thyme sprig, and let the soup cool for at least 10 minutes before pureeing with a handheld blender. Strain the soup through a sieve and reserve the liquid if you are using a counter-top blender or food processor. Add the solids to the blender jar or food processor bowl; do not overfill. Add a little of the liquid, replace the cover (without the vent from the lid or feed tube), and puree until smooth. Add more liquid, if necessary, to help puree the solids. Transfer the pureed soup to a clean pot. Continue to puree until all of the solids are pureed. Blend the soup and adjust the consistency by adding some of the remaining reserved liquid. (The soup is ready to finish now or it can be cooled and stored up to 2 days in the refrigerator or up to 1 month in the freezer.)

4. Meanwhile, melt the remaining butter in a skillet. Add the sliced mushrooms and sauté until lightly browned and cooked through, about 5 minutes. Remove from the heat.

5. Return the soup to a simmer over low heat. Add the heated heavy cream and season to taste with the lemon juice, salt, and pepper. Serve in heated bowls, garnished with the cooked mushrooms.

CREAM OF TOMATO SOUP
WITH RICE AND BASIL

GOOD QUALITY canned plum tomatoes are great for this soup, but you can also use fresh, oven-roasted tomatoes for a different flavor profile. To learn about oven-roasting tomatoes, see page 43.

MAKES 8 SERVINGS

1. Drain the tomatoes and reserve the juice separately. Seed the tomatoes, if necessary, and chop them coarsely.

2. Heat the oil in a soup pot over medium heat. Add the onions and garlic. Sauté, stirring frequently, until the onions are softened and translucent, about 5 minutes. Add the broth, chopped tomatoes, and chopped basil. Season with a small pinch of salt and pepper. Bring to a simmer, lowering the heat if necessary. Simmer until all of the ingredients are tender, about 20 minutes.

3. Remove the pot from the heat and let the soup cool for at least 10 minutes before pureeing with a handheld blender. Strain the soup through a sieve and reserve the liquid if you are using a countertop blender or food processor. Add the solids to the blender jar or food processor bowl; do not overfill. Add a little of the liquid, replace the cover (without the vent from the lid or feed tube), and puree until smooth. Add more liquid if necessary to help puree the solids. Transfer the pureed soup to a clean pot. Continue to puree until all of the solids are pureed. Blend the soup and adjust the consistency by adding some of the remaining reserved liquid. (The soup is ready to finish now or it can be cooled and stored up to 2 days in the refrigerator or up to 1 month in the freezer.)

4. Return the soup to a simmer over medium heat. Stir in some of the reserved tomato juice (or additional broth) to adjust the consistency if necessary. Add the heated cream. Season to taste with more salt and pepper, if desired. Stir in the rice and immediately serve in heated bowls garnished with the basil chiffonade.

3½ cups canned plum tomatoes

2 tbsp olive oil

1½ cups chopped onions

1 tbsp minced garlic

4 cups Vegetable Broth (page 82), plus more as needed

¼ cup chopped basil

Salt and pepper as needed

½ cup heavy cream, heated

2 cups cooked rice

1 tbsp basil chiffonade

ROASTED RED PEPPER, LEEK, AND POTATO CREAM SOUP

THIS SILKY-SMOOTH cream soup derives its thickness and most of its texture from potatoes rather than roux. The sweetness of the leeks and red peppers make a wonderful combination. If you wish, substitute 1 cup of drained, bottled roasted red peppers for the freshly roasted peppers.

MAKES 8 SERVINGS

1. Preheat the broiler. Place the red peppers under the broiler and turn as they roast so that they blacken evenly on all sides. Put the peppers in a small bowl and cover. Let the peppers steam for 10 minutes, then remove them from the bowl and pull off the skin. Use the back of a knife to scrape away any bits of skin that don't come away easily. Remove the seeds, ribs, and stems from the peppers. Chop the flesh coarsely.

2. Melt the butter in a soup pot over medium heat. Add the roasted peppers and leeks. Stir them in the butter to coat well. Reduce the heat to low and cook, covered, until the leeks are softened and translucent, about 5 minutes.

3. Add the potatoes, broth, and thyme. Bring to a simmer and cook, partially covered, until the potatoes are soft enough to mash, 25 to 30 minutes. During cooking, skim away and discard any foam that rises to the surface. Keep the liquid level constant by adding additional broth as necessary.

4. Remove the pot from the heat, remove and discard the thyme, and let the soup cool for at least 10 minutes before pureeing with a handheld blender. Strain the soup through a sieve and reserve the liquid if you are using a countertop blender or food processor. Add the solids to the blender jar or food processor bowl; do not overfill. Add a little of the liquid, replace the cover (without the vent from the lid or feed tube), and puree until smooth. Add more liquid if necessary to help puree the solids. Transfer the pureed soup to a clean pot. Continue to puree until all of the solids are pureed. Blend the soup and adjust the consistency by adding some of the remaining reserved liquid. (The soup is ready to finish now or it can be cooled and stored up to 2 days in the refrigerator or up to 1 month in the freezer.)

5. Bring the soup back to a simmer over medium heat and add the heated cream. Season to taste with salt and pepper. Serve in heated bowls, garnished with the scallions or chives.

2 red peppers

4 tbsp unsalted butter

3 cups diced leeks (white and light green parts)

8 cups peeled, diced potatoes

6 cups Chicken Broth (page 83)

1 sprig thyme, or ½ teaspoon dried enclosed in a large tea ball or tied in a cheesecloth pouch

1 cup heavy cream or half-and-half, heated

Salt and pepper as needed

½ cup finely sliced scallion greens or chives

WATERCRESS SOUP

4 cups watercress, rinsed

2 tbsp unsalted butter

1¼ cups chopped leeks, white and light-
green parts

1 cup chopped onions

4 cups Chicken Broth (page 83)

3 cups thinly sliced yellow or white potatoes

1 cup sour cream

Salt and pepper as needed

THIS THICK, rich soup is tangy with the flavors of watercress and sour cream. Watercress grows wild in streams and brooks, but it also can be found in most supermarkets, sold in bunches or bags. Look for fresh, firm leaves with no sign of yellowing; store in the refrigerator, stems down, in a container of water covered loosely with a plastic bag (this storage method works well for other leafy herbs like parsley and cilantro, too).

MAKES 8 SERVINGS

1. Bring a large pot of water to a boil. Reserve 8 of the nicest looking watercress sprigs for a garnish. Remove the stems from the remaining watercress and add the leaves to the boiling water. Boil until just wilted. Drain and squeeze out any excess moisture. Puree the watercress and set aside.

2. Heat the butter in a soup pot over medium heat. Add the leeks and onions. Sauté, stirring frequently, until the onions are softened and translucent, about 5 minutes. Add the broth and bring it to a simmer. Add the potatoes and simmer until tender, about 25 minutes.

3. Remove the pot from the heat and let the soup cool for at least 10 minutes before pureeing with a handheld blender. Strain the soup through a sieve and reserve the liquid if you are using a countertop blender or food processor. Add the solids to the blender jar or food processor bowl; do not overfill. Add a little of the liquid, replace the cover (without the vent from the lid or feed tube), and puree until smooth. Add more liquid if necessary to help puree the solids. Transfer the pureed soup to a clean pot. Continue to puree until all of the solids are pureed. Blend the soup and adjust the consistency by adding some of the remaining reserved liquid. (The soup is ready to finish now or it can be cooled and stored up to 2 days in the refrigerator or up to 1 month in the freezer.)

4. Return the soup to a simmer over medium heat. Add the watercress puree. Return the soup to a simmer. Stir in the sour cream and heat through, but do not allow the soup to reach a full boil again. Season to taste with the salt and pepper. Serve in heated bowls, garnished with the watercress sprigs.

POTAGE SOLFERINO

A SMALL DICE of parboiled vegetables brings fresh color and texture to this humble puree. For a crispy garnish, use a slotted spoon to remove the crisp bacon bits in step 1, drain them on paper towels, and sprinkle them over the soup just before you serve it.

MAKES 4 TO 6 SERVINGS

1. Melt the butter in a soup pot over medium heat. Add the bacon and cook, stirring frequently, until the fat has rendered from the bacon and it begins to color and crisp, about 3 minutes.

2. Add the sliced carrots, celery, leeks, onions, turnips, and cabbage; stir to coat evenly with fat. Reduce the heat to low and cook, covered, until the onions are softened and translucent, about 10 minutes. Add the broth, potatoes, and sachet. Bring to a simmer and cook until the vegetables are tender, 25 to 30 minutes.

3. Meanwhile, boil or steam the diced carrots and green beans separately until just tender. Set aside to cool.

4. Remove the pot from the heat, remove and discard the sachet, and let the soup cool for at least 10 minutes before pureeing with a handheld blender. Strain the soup through a sieve and reserve the liquid if you are using a countertop blender or food processor. Add the solids to the blender jar or food processor bowl; do not overfill. Add a little of the liquid, replace the cover (without the vent from the lid or feed tube), and puree until smooth. Add more liquid if necessary to help puree the solids. Transfer the pureed soup to a clean pot. Continue to puree until all of the solids are pureed. Blend the soup and adjust the consistency by adding some of the remaining reserved liquid. (The soup is ready to finish now or it can be cooled and stored up to 2 days in the refrigerator or up to 1 month in the freezer.)

5. Return the soup to a simmer over medium heat. Add the diced carrots, green beans, tomato, and parsley. Season to taste with salt and pepper. Simmer until heated through, about 5 minutes. Serve in heated bowls.

2 tbsp butter

4 slices bacon, diced

⅓ cup sliced carrots

½ cup diced celery

1¼ cups sliced leeks, white and green parts

1¼ cups medium-dice onions

1½ cups diced yellow turnips

2 cups shredded cabbage

4 cups Vegetable Broth (page 82)

2 cups peeled, diced potatoes

Sachet: 1 bay leaf, 1 tsp chopped oregano or ½ tsp dried, 4 to 5 black peppercorns, 1 garlic clove, 1 tsp chopped marjoram or ½ tsp dried leaves enclosed in a large tea ball or tied in a cheesecloth pouch

¼ cup small-dice carrots

¼ cup sliced green beans

1 small tomato, peeled, seeded, and chopped

1 tbsp chopped parsley

Salt and pepper as needed

THAI FRESH PEA SOUP

6 cups Vegetable Broth, plus as needed

1 cup chopped onions

4 garlic cloves, finely minced

2 tsp green curry paste

8 cups shelled peas (thawed if frozen)

Salt and pepper as needed

1 tsp lightly toasted mustard seeds

¼ cup chopped mint

THIS SOUP adds a subtle twist to the delicate taste of peas. It is a great recipe if you have a bumper crop of fresh peas (although frozen peas work equally well), or if you are looking for an easy starter course for an evening of Thai cuisine.

SERVES 6 TO 8

1. Add about ½ cup of the broth to a soup pot and bring to a simmer over medium heat. Add the onions, garlic, and curry paste. Sauté, stirring frequently, until the onions are softened and translucent, about 5 minutes. Add the remaining broth to the pot and bring to a boil. Add the peas, cover the soup, and simmer over low heat for 10 minutes.

2. Remove the pot from the heat and let the soup cool for at least 10 minutes before pureeing with a handheld blender. Strain the soup through a sieve and reserve the liquid if you are using a countertop blender or food processor. Add the solids to the blender jar or food processor bowl; do not overfill. Add a little of the liquid, replace the cover (without the vent from the lid or feed tube), and puree until smooth. Add more liquid if necessary to help puree the solids. Transfer the pureed soup to a clean pot. Continue to puree until all of the solids are pureed. Blend the soup and adjust the consistency by adding some of the remaining reserved liquid. (The soup is ready to finish now or it can be cooled and stored up to 2 days in the refrigerator or up to 1 month in the freezer.)

3. Return the soup to a simmer over low heat. Season to taste with salt and pepper and reheat the soup, if necessary. Serve the soup in heated bowls, garnished with the toasted mustard seeds and chopped mint.

CURRIED SQUASH AND APPLE SOUP

5 cups Vegetable Broth

2½ cups leeks, white part only

¼ cup chopped celery

1 tbsp chopped garlic

2 tsp curry powder

¼ tsp ground cinnamon

⅛ tsp grated nutmeg

2½ cups diced pumpkin or Hubbard squash (peeled and seeded)

2 cups chopped apples (peeled and cored)

Salt and pepper as needed

LIME GREMOLATA

½ tsp minced garlic

2 tsp grated lime zest

½ tsp minced thyme

Tʜɪs ꜱᴏᴜᴘ tastes best after it has had a chance to mellow in the refrigerator overnight. The resting period gives the curry a chance to come to the fore. The lime gremolata, however, is best assembled immediately before you want to serve the soup.

MAKES 6 TO 8 SERVINGS

1. Add about ½ cup of the broth to a soup pot and bring to a simmer over medium heat. Add the leeks, celery, and garlic. Sauté, stirring frequently, until the leeks are softened and translucent, about 5 minutes. Add the curry powder, cinnamon, and nutmeg. Stir until blended.

2. Add the pumpkin or Hubbard squash and the remaining broth. Bring to a simmer and cook until all the squash is tender enough to mash easily, 15 to 20 minutes. Add the apples and continue to simmer until they are hot and tender, about 5 minutes.

3. Remove the pot from the heat and let the soup cool for at least 10 minutes before pureeing with a handheld blender. Strain the soup through a sieve and reserve the liquid if you are using a countertop blender or food processor. Add the solids to the blender jar or food processor bowl; do not overfill. Add a little of the liquid, replace the cover (without the vent from the lid or feed tube), and puree until smooth. Add more liquid if necessary to help puree the solids. Transfer the pureed soup to a clean pot. Continue to puree until all of the solids are pureed. Blend the soup and adjust the consistency by adding some of the remaining reserved liquid. Cool the soup quickly and refrigerate for at least 3 and up to 24 hours before serving.

4. Combine the ingredients for the gremolata just before serving the soup. Season the soup with salt and pepper, and serve in chilled bowls or cups, garnished with the gremolata.

POTATO KALE SOUP

THIS IS a robust, satisfying soup made with kale, garlic, and smoky meats in a silky pureed potato soup base. Linguiça is a Portuguese garlic sausage that can be found in many supermarkets and Latin markets.

MAKES 8 SERVINGS

1. Heat the oil in a soup pot over medium heat. Add the leek, onions, and celery. Sauté, stirring frequently, until the onions are softened and translucent, about 5 minutes. Add the broth, potatoes, and ham hock. Bring to simmer and cook until all are very tender, about 40 minutes. Remove the ham hock from the soup base. When cool enough to handle, remove the meat from the ham hock, dice, and set aside.

2. Remove the pot from the heat and let the soup cool for at least 10 minutes before pureeing with a handheld blender. Strain the soup through a sieve and reserve the liquid if you are using a countertop blender or food processor. Add the solids to the blender jar or food processor bowl; do not overfill. Add a little of the liquid, replace the cover (without the vent from the lid or feed tube), and puree until smooth. Add more liquid if necessary to help puree the solids. Transfer the pureed soup to a clean pot. Continue to puree until all of the solids are pureed. Blend the soup and adjust the consistency by adding some of the remaining reserved liquid. (The soup is ready to finish now or it can be cooled and stored up to 2 days in the refrigerator or up to 1 month in the freezer.)

3. Meanwhile, bring a large pot of salted water to a rolling boil. Use a paring knife to cut the tough stems away from the kale leaves. Blanch the kale in the boiling water until it wilts, about 3 minutes. Drain the kale, run it under cold water to stop the cooking, and drain again. Slice the kale into thin shreds.

5. Return the soup to a simmer over low heat. Add the ham hock meat, sliced kale, sausage, and bay leaf. Season to taste with salt and pepper and simmer 15 to 20 minutes longer. Remove and discard the bay leaf. Serve in heated bowls.

2 tbsp olive oil

¾ cup chopped leek, white and light-green parts

¾ cup chopped onions

¼ cup chopped celery

5 cups Chicken Broth (page 83)

4 russet potatoes, peeled, cut in sixths

1 smoked ham hock

1½ cups kale

2 ounces linguiça sausage, diced (about ½ link)

½ bay leaf

Salt and pepper as needed

ROASTED EGGPLANT AND GARLIC SOUP

1 garlic head, unpeeled

2 cups peeled, cubed eggplant

1¼ cups chopped yellow onions

½ cup chopped celery

⅓ cup chopped carrots

3 tbsp olive oil

4 cups Chicken Broth (page 83)

1 cup peeled, diced potatoes

1 sprig thyme (or ¼ tsp dried thyme)

2 tbsp tahini

Salt and pepper as needed

Lemon juice as needed

TAHINI IS a paste made from sesame seeds. It can be found in most large supermarkets (often next to the peanut butter), as well as in shops that specialize in Middle Eastern and Asian foods.

TO MAKE this a substantial main course soup, add drained, cooked chickpeas; diced roasted peppers; cooked broccoli; and/or cooked cauliflower florets. Serve with warmed whole wheat pita bread. Garnish the soup with a drizzle of extra-virgin olive oil, chopped parsley, and toasted pine nuts to add a final dash of flavor and texture.

R OASTING THE garlic and eggplant in advance adds wonderful flavor and aroma to this hearty soup. Be sure to allow the vegetables enough time to roast so they take on a deep, rich hue.

MAKES 8 SERVINGS

1. Preheat the oven to 350°F.

2. Combine the garlic, eggplant, onions, celery, and carrots in a baking dish large enough to hold the vegetables in a single layer. Drizzle the olive oil over the vegetables. Cover the pan with aluminum foil and roast for 20 minutes. Remove the foil, increase the heat to 400°F, and roast until the eggplant and garlic are very soft, about 15 minutes. When cool enough to handle, slice the garlic head in half through the middle and squeeze the garlic from its skin.

3. Combine the roasted vegetables and garlic with the broth, potatoes, and thyme in a soup pot and simmer until the potatoes are tender enough to mash easily, about 25 minutes. Remove and discard the thyme sprig. Add the tahini to the soup and whisk to combine well. Continue to simmer the soup for another 2 to 3 minutes.

4. Remove the pot from the heat and let the soup cool for at least 10 minutes before pureeing with a handheld blender. Strain the soup through a sieve and reserve the liquid if you are using a countertop blender or food processor. Add the solids to the blender jar or food processor bowl; do not overfill. Add a little of the liquid, replace the cover (without the vent from the lid or feed tube), and puree until smooth. Add more liquid if necessary to help puree the solids. Transfer the pureed soup to a clean pot. Continue to puree until all of the solids are pureed. Blend the soup and adjust the consistency by adding some of the remaining reserved liquid. (The soup is ready to finish now or it can be cooled and stored up to 2 days in the refrigerator or up to 1 month in the freezer.)

5. Return the soup to medium heat and simmer for 5 minutes, or until reduced to the desired consistency. Season to taste with salt, pepper, and lemon juice. Serve in heated bowls.

BUTTERNUT AND ACORN SQUASH SOUP

THIS SOUP has a rich, creamy texture that belies its actual calorie count. Feel free to use only one type of squash or to replace the squash with pumpkin. For a richer soup, whip a little heavy cream to form soft peaks, fold in an equal amount of sour cream, and add grated ginger root to taste. Place a dollop of this ginger-scented cream on top of each portion.

MAKES 8 SERVINGS

1 tbsp unsalted butter

1¼ cups diced onions

⅓ cup diced carrot

½ cup diced celery

1 tbsp minced ginger root

½ tsp minced garlic

3 to 4 cups Chicken Broth (page 83)

2 cups cubed butternut squash

1 cup cubed acorn squash

½ cup peeled, sliced potatoes

Salt and pepper as needed

1 tsp grated orange zest

1. Heat the butter in a soup pot over medium heat. Add the onions, carrot, celery, ginger, and garlic. Sauté, stirring frequently, until the onions are softened and translucent, about 5 minutes.

2. Add the broth, squashes, and potatoes. Bring the broth to a simmer and cook until the squashes are tender enough to mash easily with a fork, about 20 minutes.

3. Strain the soup through a sieve, reserving the liquid. Puree the solids and return to the soup pot. Add enough of the reserved liquid to achieve a soup consistency. Blend well. Return the soup to a simmer.

4. Season the soup to taste with salt, pepper, and orange zest. Serve the soup in heated bowls.

Squash Varieties

CORN AND SQUASH SOUP WITH ROASTED RED PEPPER PUREE

THIS SIMPLE soup, based on a freshly made garlic and basil broth, is a wonderful way to take advantage of fresh summer produce. If you crave a taste of summer in the middle of winter, you can also make this soup with frozen corn.

MAKES 4 TO 6 SERVINGS

1. Combine the water, basil, and garlic in a large saucepan. Bring to a simmer and cook, partially covered, for 30 minutes, skimming the surface if necessary. Strain the broth and reserve.

2. Heat the butter in a soup pot over medium heat. Add the onions and sauté, stirring frequently, until the onions are softened and translucent, about 5 minutes. Add the squash and sauté, stirring frequently, until limp, another 5 minutes. Add the corn and broth and bring the soup to a simmer. Season to taste with salt and pepper.

3. Puree the soup and strain it through a fine sieve.

4. Return the soup to a simmer. Adjust the seasoning with more salt or pepper, if necessary. Ladle it into heated soup bowls and swirl some red pepper puree through each portion.

6 cups water

3 basil sprigs

1 garlic head, halved horizontally

2 tbsp butter

1 cup diced onions

2 cups diced yellow squash

3 cups fresh or frozen corn kernels

Salt and pepper as needed

¼ cup Roasted Red Pepper Puree (page 262)

NEW ENGLAND CORN CHOWDER

2 tbsp canola oil

2 bacon slices, finely minced

½ cup minced celery

1 cup minced onions

1 bay leaf

2 tsp thyme

4 cups Chicken Broth (page 83)

1 cup peeled, diced potatoes

2 cups fresh or frozen corn kernels

2½ cups half-and-half

Salt and pepper as needed

TO GARNISH SOUP

2 tbsp whole butter

2 tbsp chopped parsley

THIS CORN chowder has a cream-enriched broth and plenty of sweet kernels of corn and tender potatoes. You can make a double batch when corn is in season. Freeze it before you add the half-and-half, and finish the soup with cream just before you are ready to serve it.

SERVES 6 TO 8

1. Heat the oil in a soup pot over medium heat. Add the bacon and cook, stirring frequently, until the fat has rendered from the bacon and it begins to color and crisp, about 3 minutes.

2. Add the celery and onions. Sauté, stirring frequently, until the onions are softened and translucent, about 5 minutes.

3. Add the bay leaf, thyme, and broth, and bring to a boil. Reduce the heat to a simmer and add the potatoes and corn. Cook the soup until both the potatoes and corn are tender, about 20 minutes.

4. Enrich the soup with the half-and-half, and adjust the seasoning with salt and pepper.

5. Ladle the soup into heated soup plates or bowls, and garnish each portion with a ½ teaspoon of whole butter, a pinch of coarsely ground black pepper, and a sprinkling of parsley.

FENNEL AND POTATO CHOWDER

FENNEL, WHICH is sometimes labeled as "anise" in supermarkets, is a vegetable with a broad, bulbous base that can be eaten raw or cooked. It has a delicate and very mild sweet licorice flavor. If you happen to find fennel with the feathery, dill-like tops still attached, chop some to use as a garnish. This is not a thickened chowder, so if you prefer a thicker consistency, try pureeing half of the soup and mixing it with the unpureed half.

MAKES 8 SERVINGS

1. Melt the butter in a soup pot over medium heat. Add the leeks, onions, shallots, and fennel. Stir to coat evenly with butter. Sauté, stirring frequently, until the onions are softened and translucent, about 5 minutes.

2. Add the broth and potatoes. Bring to a simmer and cook until the potatoes are tender, 20 to 25 minutes. Stir occasionally and skim the surface as necessary.

3. Add the cream or half-and-half, blend well, and return to a simmer. Adjust the seasoning to taste with salt and pepper. Serve in heated bowls, garnished with the chives or scallions.

¼ cup unsalted butter

2½ cups diced leeks, white and light-green parts

1¼ cups minced onions

2 tbsp minced shallots

1½ cups diced fennel

6 cups Vegetable Broth (page 82)

4 cups peeled, diced potatoes

1 cup heavy cream or half-and-half, heated

Salt and pepper as needed

6 tbsp minced chives or sliced scallions

MANHATTAN CORN CHOWDER

2 tbsp olive oil

2 slices bacon, minced

1¼ cups minced onions

1¾ cup minced celery

½ cup minced red pepper

½ cup minced green pepper

3 garlic cloves, sliced thin

2 tbsp minced thyme leaves

2 bay leaves

2 tsp dried oregano

2 cups fresh or frozen corn kernels

2 cups small-dice Yukon gold potatoes

10 cups Chicken Broth (page 83)

1½ cups chopped tomatoes (peeled and
　　seeded, juices reserved)

Salt and pepper as needed

TO GARNISH CHOWDER

¼ cup extra-virgin olive oil

2 tbsp chopped flat-leaf parsley

⅓ cup grated Parmesan cheese

THIS COLORFUL soup shares the same flavor profile as Manhattan clam chowder. A final garnish of extra-virgin olive oil adds additional flavor to the soup.

SERVES 6 TO 8

1. Heat the oil in a soup pot over medium heat. Add the bacon and cook, stirring frequently, until the fat has rendered from the bacon and it begins to color and crisp, about 3 minutes. Add the onions, celery, peppers, and garlic. Sauté, stirring frequently, until the peppers and onions are softened and translucent, about 8 minutes.

2. Add the thyme, bay leaves, oregano, corn, potatoes, and broth and bring to a boil. Reduce to a simmer and cook until the potatoes and the corn are tender, about 20 minutes. Add the tomatoes and their juices and season the soup with salt and pepper.

3. Serve the soup in heated bowls or soup plates. Garnish each portion with a drizzle of good olive oil, a sprinkle of chopped parsley, and a sprinkle of Parmesan cheese, if desired.

COLD TOMATO AND ZUCCHINI SOUP

T HIS FRESH-TASTING soup, much like gazpacho, is a great way to make use of a summer bounty of fresh vegetables and herbs. If time permits, make it a day ahead of serving to let the flavors blend. Don't store it more than 2 to 3 days, though, because tomatoes can sour quickly.

MAKES 8 SERVINGS

1. Combine all the ingredients except the broth, Tabasco, salt, pepper, and croutons in a blender or food processor, in batches if necessary. Process the soup in short pulses to a coarse puree.

2. Pour the soup into a bowl. If it is too thick, thin it slightly with broth or water. Season to taste with the Tabasco, salt, and pepper. Refrigerate for at least 30 minutes before serving. Serve in chilled bowls, garnished with croutons.

4 cups chopped tomatoes (peeled and seeded, juices reserved)

2 cups tomato juice

1¼ cups minced onions

1 cup red pepper (seeded, ribs removed, and coarsely chopped)

¾ cup cucumber (peeled, seeded, and coarsely chopped)

1½ cups coarsely chopped zucchini

¼ cup chopped cilantro

¼ cup chopped basil

¼ cup chopped parsley

2 tbsp drained, prepared horseradish

1 tbsp red wine vinegar

3 garlic cloves, chopped

Vegetable Broth (page 82) or water, as needed

Tabasco sauce, to taste

Salt and pepper as needed

½ cup Croutons (page 34)

CHILLED BORSCHT

2 medium beets

2 tbsp olive oil

2½ cups finely diced onions

1 cup celery julienne

⅔ cup parsnips julienne

⅓ cup carrots julienne

1¼ cups leeks julienne, white and light-green parts

½ savoy cabbage, shredded

8 cups Chicken Broth (page 83) or Vegetable Broth (page 82)

Sachet: 1 tsp dried marjoram, 4 to 5 parsley stems, 2 cloves peeled garlic, and 1 bay leaf enclosed in a large tea ball or tied in a cheesecloth pouch

Red wine vinegar, to taste

Salt and pepper as needed

½ cup sour cream

¼ cup minced dill

THIS COLD version of Russia's classic beet soup is a gorgeous magenta color. To keep your fingers from turning the same color, wear gloves as you work with the beets.

MAKES 8 SERVINGS

1. Simmer the beets, in enough boiling water to cover, until partially cooked, 10 to 15 minutes. When cool enough to handle, peel and reserve (use gloves to keep your hands from becoming stained).

2. Heat the olive oil in a soup pot over medium heat until it shimmers. Add the onions, celery, parsnips, carrots, leeks, and cabbage. Reduce the heat to low and cook, covered, until the vegetables are softened and translucent, about 15 minutes. Add the broth and sachet. Bring to a simmer and cook for 10 minutes.

3. Grate the parboiled beets (wear gloves) directly into the soup and simmer until all the vegetables are tender, about 10 minutes. Remove and discard the sachet. Chill the soup. Season to taste with the vinegar, salt, and pepper. Serve in chilled bowls, garnished with the sour cream and dill.

KH'YAAF B'LUBBAN (CHILLED CUCUMBER AND YOGURT SOUP)

FANS OF Indian food will find this Lebanese soup familiar, because it is quite similar in flavor to the Indian condiment kheera raita, which also is made with yogurt, cucumber, and mint. As with kheera raita, the cooling quality of this soup makes it a wonderful complement or second course to spicy-hot foods.

MAKES 6 TO 8 SERVINGS

1. Mix the garlic with the mint in a small bowl.

2. Beat the yogurt and milk together with a wire whisk or handheld blender on medium speed until smooth. Fold in the mint and garlic with a rubber spatula.

3. Combine the cucumbers with the yogurt mixture and lightly season with salt and pepper. Cover and chill for several hours or overnight.

4. After chilling, recheck seasoning and adjust as needed. Serve the kh'yaaf b'lubban in chilled bowls.

2 garlic cloves, minced

3 tbsp chopped mint

4 cups plain yogurt

1 cup whole milk

4 medium cucumbers, peeled, seeded, and finely diced

Salt and pepper as needed

Common Cucumber

GAZPACHO

3 cups ripe tomatoes (peeled, seeded, and finely diced; reserve juices)

2 cups cucumbers (peeled, seeded, and finely diced)

1¼ cups minced onions

1 cup fine-dice red peppers

1 tsp minced garlic cloves

2 tbsp tomato paste

2 tbsp extra-virgin olive oil

2 tbsp minced herbs such as tarragon, thyme, or parsley

3 cups canned tomato juice

¼ cup red wine vinegar, or to taste

Juice of ½ lemon, or to taste

Salt and pepper as needed

¼ tsp ground cayenne pepper, or to taste

1 cup Croutons (page 34)

½ cup thinly sliced chives or scallion greens

IF THE soup is too thin for your taste, add about 1 cup of freshly made white bread crumbs before chilling. If it's too thick, the consistency can be thinned by adding more tomato juice or water.

PART OF the tomato juice can be replaced with fish broth or clam juice, an apt substitution if the soup will be served before a seafood main course.

T HIS TANGY marriage of fresh tomato, cucumber, pepper, and onion is a summer favorite. The flavor of gazpacho improves if allowed to chill overnight, but thereafter this soup has a short shelf life because the tomatoes sour quickly. It is best prepared no more than a day or two before it will be eaten.

MAKES 8 SERVINGS

1. Reserve 2 tablespoons each of the tomatoes, cucumbers, onions, and peppers for the garnish.

2. Puree the remaining tomatoes, cucumbers, onions, and peppers in a food processor or blender, along with the garlic, tomato paste, olive oil, and herbs, until fairly smooth but with some texture remaining.

3. Transfer to a mixing bowl and stir in the tomato juice along with the red wine vinegar, lemon juice, salt, black pepper, and cayenne pepper to taste. Cover and chill thoroughly, at least 3 hours but preferably overnight.

4. After chilling, recheck the seasoning and adjust as needed. Serve in chilled bowls, garnished with the reserved vegetables, croutons, and chives.

WHITE GAZPACHO WITH GREEN GRAPES

THIS UNUSUAL white gazpacho derives from the Andalusian tradition of thickening a refreshing cold vegetable soup with bread and almonds. Some recipes for white gazpacho substitute melon for some or all of the cucumber, for a sweeter version.

MAKES 6 SERVINGS

1. Bring the vegetable broth to a boil. Dissolve the cornstarch in the water and whisk into the boiling broth. Remove from the heat and cool. Add the vinegar and then slowly whisk in the oil. Reserve at room temperature.

2. Soak the bread cubes in just enough cold water to barely cover them until they are evenly moistened, about 10 minutes, then squeeze the water out of the bread. Transfer half of the soaked bread to a food processor and puree along with half of the thickened broth mixture, 4 teaspoons of the almonds, and ½ teaspoon of the garlic. Puree until smooth. Add 1½ cups of the cucumbers and pulse until the soup is a relatively smooth puree. Transfer the soup to a container. Repeat to puree the rest of the soup. Season to taste with salt and pepper. Cover the soup and refrigerate until very cold.

3. Pour the chilled soup into chilled bowls, garnish with the grapes and parsley.

¾ cup Vegetable Broth

1½ tsp cornstarch

½ tsp water

3 tbsp sherry vinegar

1 tbsp extra-virgin olive oil

3 cups crustless cubed firm white bread (½ of a French loaf)

¼ cup chopped blanched almonds

1 tsp minced garlic

3 cups diced cucumbers (peeled and seeded)

Salt and pepper as needed

1½ cups halved green seedless grapes

¼ cup chopped flat-leaf parsley

TO MAKE cucumber cups for a special serving option: Select firm cucumbers that are at least 2 inches in diameter. Cut them into 4-inch sections, leaving the peel intact. Use a melon baller or a grapefruit spoon to scoop out the seeds and some of the flesh, leaving enough flesh at the bottom of the section to keep the soup in the cup. Instead of adding halved grapes directly to the soup, present them whole, strung on toothpicks or short skewers.

COLD CARROT BISQUE

2 tsp butter

⅓ cup minced onions

3 tbsp minced shallots

2 tsp minced ginger root, or to taste

1 garlic clove, minced

5½ cups thinly sliced carrots

5 cups Vegetable Broth (page 82)

2 tbsp white wine

½ tsp ground cardamom

2 cups orange juice

½ cup heavy cream, cold

1½ to 2 cups fresh carrot juice

Salt and pepper as needed

I F YOU don't own a juicer, look for fresh carrot juice at your local health or natural foods store. Try garnishing this soup with a dollop of whipped cream and a sprinkling of sliced chives.

MAKES 8 SERVINGS

1. Melt the butter in a soup pot. Add the onions, shallots, ginger, and garlic. Sauté, stirring frequently, until the onions are softened and translucent, about 5 minutes.

2. Add the carrots, broth, wine, cardamom, and orange juice. Bring to a simmer and cook until the carrots are tender, about 30 minutes.

3. Puree the soup in a food processor or blender until smooth. Cover and chill thoroughly.

4. Just before serving, stir in the cream. Thin the soup with carrot juice to a barely thick consistency. Adjust the seasoning to taste with salt and pepper and serve in chilled bowls, garnished as desired.

CHILLED CARAWAY SQUASH BISQUE

¼ cup unsalted butter

1¼ cups minced onions

½ cup minced celery

⅓ cup minced carrots

1 cup minced leeks, white part only

6 cups Vegetable Broth (page 82) or water

4 cups diced yellow squash

1 cup peeled, sliced potatoes

Sachet: 1 tsp caraway seeds, 1 garlic clove,
    1 sprig thyme or ½ tsp dried thyme en-
    closed in a large tea ball or tied up in a
    cheesecloth pouch

¾ cup heavy cream

Salt and pepper as needed

1 tsp lightly toasted caraway seeds

AROMATIC CARAWAY seeds complement the subtle flavor of yellow squash in this delicate and unusual soup. Small squash are the best choice for this soup because they have small seeds. If you only can find large squash, remove the seeds if they are big. Regardless of the size, select squash that are firm, bright, and free of spots or blemishes.

MAKES 8 SERVINGS

1. Melt the butter in a soup pot over medium heat. Add the onions, celery, carrots, and leeks. Stir to coat evenly with the butter. Reduce the heat to low and cook, covered, until the onions are softened and translucent, about 5 minutes.

2. Add the broth, squash, potatoes, and sachet. Bring to a simmer and cook, stirring occasionally, until the potatoes are tender, about 25 minutes.

3. Remove and discard the sachet. Strain the soup through a sieve, reserving the liquid. Puree the solids and return to the soup pot. Add enough of the reserved liquid to achieve a soup consistency. Blend well and return to a simmer for 2 minutes. Transfer to a bowl and chill thoroughly.

4. Add the heavy cream and blend well. Season to taste with salt and pepper. Serve in chilled bowls garnished with toasted caraway seeds.

CHILLED CREAM OF AVOCADO SOUP

THIS SOUP manages to preserve the elusive flavor of the avocado. Use only very ripe avocados for this soup. If you buy avocados that aren't ripe yet, you can speed the ripening process by placing them in a paper bag with an apple and folding the top of the bag closed. The apple will give off ethylene gas, which accelerates ripening.

MAKES 4 TO 6 SERVINGS

1. Cut each avocado in half from top to bottom, following the contour of the pit in the center. Remove the pit and scoop out the avocado flesh.

2. Puree the flesh in a food processor or blender with 4 cups of the broth or water, the chili powder, coriander, and lime juice until very smooth. If the soup is too thick, add more broth or water to correct the consistency. Transfer to a bowl, cover, and chill thoroughly.

3. Just before serving, blend in the yogurt or cream. Adjust the seasoning to taste with salt and pepper. Serve in chilled bowls, garnished with the tomato and tortilla strips, if using.

2 large ripe avocados

4 to 5 cups Vegetable Broth (page 82) or water

½ tsp chili powder

¼ tsp ground coriander

Juice of 1 lime

1 cup plain yogurt or heavy cream

Salt and pepper as needed

2 ripe plum tomatoes (peeled, seeded, and diced), optional

2 corn tortillas, cut into strips and fried, optional

YOU CAN garnish this soup with the tomato and tortilla strips called for in the recipe, or for a more elegant (albeit expensive) touch, try garnishing with lump crabmeat, cooked fresh corn kernels, and a touch of finely diced red pepper tossed in a dash of lemon or lime juice.

CHILLED INFUSION OF FRESH
VEGETABLES WITH FAVA BEANS

YOU CAN adjust the suggested vegetable garnish in this soup to suit your taste, using more or less of any particular vegetable. Or you can use different vegetables entirely. It's up to you.

MAKES 8 SERVINGS

1. Make the vegetable infusion: Combine the leeks, celeriac, shallots, parsley, chives, garlic, thyme, bay leaf, and salt and pepper with 6 cups of the water in a soup pot. Cover and simmer gently for 1 hour. Add a little water to bring it back to its original level, return briefly to a boil, remove from the heat, and cool. Strain through a fine mesh sieve or cheesecloth. Chill thoroughly.

2. Meanwhile, make a tomato broth: Combine the tomatoes with 1½ cups of the remaining water. Simmer gently for 30 minutes, and then strain through a fine sieve or cheesecloth. Chill thoroughly.

3. Bring about 1 inch of water to a boil in a saucepan. Add the carrots, cover, and pan-steam until tender. Using a slotted spoon, transfer the carrots to a colander and rinse under cold water to stop the cooking. Drain well and transfer to a bowl. Repeat this process with the peas, fava beans, and asparagus tips, cooking each vegetable separately until tender. Add the diced tomato to the cooked vegetables and toss to combine. Chill thoroughly.

4. Mix the tomato broth and the vegetable infusion. Taste and adjust the seasoning as needed. Serve in chilled bowls, garnished with the vegetables and chervil leaves, if using.

3½ cups sliced leeks, white and light-green parts

1 cup sliced celeriac

½ cup minced shallots

1¼ cups minced parsley

2 tbsp sliced chives

1 tsp minced garlic

1 thyme sprig

½ bay leaf

Salt and pepper as needed

8 cups water, or as needed

3 cups quartered ripe tomatoes

¼ cup sliced baby carrots

¼ cup small green peas, fresh or frozen

¼ cup shelled and peeled fava beans

¼ cup asparagus tips

¼ cup peeled, seeded, and diced tomato

8 chervil or flat-leaf parsley leaves, optional

FAVA BEANS, also known as broad beans, resemble large lima beans. Some supermarkets carry frozen fava beans, and in the spring you may be fortunate enough to find fresh favas. Fava beans have a tough outer skin that must be removed before cooking: Blanch the beans for about 30 seconds in boiling water, then cool slightly and slip the beans from the skins. If the skins do not come off easily, blanch the beans again for another 30 seconds. If you cannot find fava beans, simply substitute fresh or frozen lima beans.

VEGETABLE BROTH

2 tbsp olive oil

1 tbsp minced garlic

2 tsp minced shallots

10 cups water

3 cups sliced leeks, white, light-green, and
    dark-green parts

1¼ cups thinly sliced onions

1 cup thinly sliced broccoli stems

1 cup thinly sliced fennel (with some tops)

½ cup dry white wine or vermouth (optional)

½ cup thinly sliced celery

⅓ cup thinly sliced carrot

⅓ cup thinly sliced parsnip

1 tbsp salt, or to taste

4 to 5 whole black peppercorns

1 bay leaf

1 sprig fresh thyme or ¼ teaspoon dried leaves

THIS BROTH can be prepared in large batches and frozen for later use. Be sure to label and date the containers. Freeze the broth in ice cube trays, and store the frozen cubes in large freezer bags so you can thaw exactly the amount needed at any given time.

WHEN PREPARING vegetables for other dishes, save any wholesome trim or peels that you want to put into the broth. Then every few days, put on a pot of broth. You will get a nutrient boost, as well as avoid the use of canned broths that might be higher in sodium.

THE VEGETABLES listed with the ingredients below should be thought of merely as suggestions. Feel free to add other vegetables, as long as they will not give the finished broth a strong odor or color (for instance, beets and beet greens might not be appropriate). Starchy vegetables may make the broth foam over as it simmers. Beyond that, let your own taste be your guide.

MAKES ABOUT 8 CUPS

1. Heat the olive oil in a soup pot over medium heat. Add the garlic and shallots and sauté, stirring frequently, until they are translucent, 3 to 4 minutes.

2. Add the remaining ingredients and bring the broth slowly up to a simmer. Reduce the heat to low and continue to simmer until the broth has a good flavor, 45 to 50 minutes.

3. Strain the broth through a sieve and then allow it to cool completely before storing in the refrigerator.

Great or Broad-leaved Thyme

CHICKEN BROTH

CHICKEN BROTH is a crucial ingredient in soup making and the flavor of homemade broth is hard to beat. You can double or even quadruple this recipe and freeze the extra so you always have some on hand. If you freeze the broth in ice cube trays, and then transfer the frozen cubes to freezer bags, it's easy to thaw exactly the amount you need. If you're short on time and must use canned broth, choose the all-natural or fat-free, reduced-sodium varieties.

MAKES ABOUT 8 CUPS

1. Place the chicken and water in a large pot (the water should cover the chicken by at least 2 inches; add more if necessary). Bring the water slowly to a boil over medium heat. As the water comes to a boil, skim away any foam that rises to the surface and discard. Adjust the heat once a boil is reached so that a slow, lazy simmer is established. Cover the pot partially and simmer for 2 hours, skimming as often as necessary.

2. Add all of the remaining ingredients. Continue to simmer, skimming the surface as necessary, until the broth is fully flavored, about 1 hour. (If using hen or chicken parts, remove them and cool slightly. Dice or shred the meat and use to garnish the broth or save for another use.) Discard the skin and bones. Strain the broth through a colander or sieve into a large metal container. Discard the solids.

3. If you are using the broth right away, skim off any fat on the surface. If you are not using the broth right away, cool it quickly by transferring it to a metal container (if it's not in one already) and place the container in a sink filled with ice cold water. Stir the broth as it cools, and then transfer it to storage containers. Store in the refrigerator for up to 5 days, or in the freezer for up to 3 months. Label and date the containers clearly before putting them into the freezer.

4 lb stewing hen or chicken parts or meaty bones, such as backs and necks

3 quarts cold water

1¼ cups thinly sliced onions

½ cup thinly sliced celery

⅓ cup thinly sliced carrot

5 to 6 whole black peppercorns

3 to 4 parsley stems

1 bay leaf

1 sprig fresh thyme

2 tsp salt, or to taste

SOME STORES sell packages of necks and backs that can be used to prepare broth. This broth also can be made with the carcasses of roasted birds. Save the bones after all of the meat has been pulled or carved away (freeze them if you will not be making the broth within a day or two). You will need the carcasses of about 3 birds.

IF THE broth is allowed to chill overnight in the refrigerator, the fat will rise to the surface and harden, making it easy to lift away the fat. This broth will then be completely fat free, and will only have the salt that you choose to add yourself.

IF, AFTER straining the broth, you find the flavor to be weaker than you would like, put the broth back on the stove and boil it down until the flavor has concentrated to your liking.

Appetizers

EGETABLE APPETIZERS ARE a perfect way to start a meal. They run the gamut from simple dips and spreads like guacamole, made from silken smooth avocados, to complex dishes that are sophisticated enough to feature at the most elegant dinner, like our portobellos stuffed with a Tuscan-style bean salad and drizzled with celery juice. One of the most popular vegetable appetizers, and one that really requires no recipe, is crudités.

Crudités

Crudités is nothing more elaborate than fresh, raw vegetables served with a cold sauce for dipping. The name itself means "raw" in French. Nearly every cuisine has some corollary to the French crudités. Sometimes it's as simple as the "relish" platters popular in the 1950s that featured stalks of celery and radishes with the simplest of all sauces: salt. Sometimes it's an extensive selection of fresh and pickled vegetables, such as you might enjoy from an antipasto selection, or some tapas.

Crudités platters can be strictly vegetables or you might want to include pickles, olives, cured or smoked meats, and cheeses to turn your crudités into a more substantial appetizer, or even, if paired with good breads and some flavorful oils, to make into a simple supper.

SELECTING VEGETABLES FOR CRUDITÉS

The first criterion for selecting vegetables for a crudités platter is flavor and freshness. The best way to be sure your vegetables are the most flavorful is to choose them based on the season. Sniff or, if possible, taste vegetables.

The way vegetables look is important for a successful crudités platter. Look for vivid colors, good textures, and unblemished specimens. It's a good idea to be generous so you can create a bountiful array. Consider not only the flavor of the vegetables, but also the color.

PREPARING VEGETABLES FOR A CRUDITÉS PLATTER

Some vegetables are perfect to eat raw: cucumbers, tomatoes, peppers, zucchini, carrots, celery, and fennel are some examples. Rinse, peel, and cut or slice them so they are easy to pick up and eat.

Other vegetables, including green beans, sugar snap or snow peas, broccoli, cauliflower, and some baby vegetables, including zucchini, pattypan, or yellow squash, also are delicious raw, but you may prefer to quickly blanch them, and possibly even marinate them, before adding them to your platter. Blanching (page 18) makes some vegetables brighter and more vivid. It also helps remove any bitterness from vegetables like cauliflower and broccoli. Blanched vegetables should be thoroughly drained and chilled so they are crisp, not waterlogged. If you are planning to pickle or marinate the vegetables, remember that the flavor is absorbed better when the vegetables are still warm. However, acids can change the colors in green vegetables, so it's best to chill them before you add any dressings or marinades.

ARRANGING VEGETABLES ON A CRUDITÉS PLATTER.

It really doesn't matter how you arrange the vegetables themselves. You can arrange them neatly for a sophisticate look or simply toss them together for a rustic presentation. There are a few guidelines to follow, however:

- *Dry the vegetables well so that the dips can cling.*

- *Chill the vegetables and the platter, as well as the bowls you plan to use for dips.*

- *Use strong or contrasting colors for a dramatic look.*

GUACAMOLE

4 avocados, halved, pitted, and peeled

3 tbsp lime juice

2 plum tomatoes, diced (optional)

1 jalapeño (optional), seeded and minced

½ cup sliced scallions

½ cup chopped cilantro

1 tsp Tabasco sauce, or to taste

Salt and pepper as needed

GUACAMOLE IS a Mexican condiment made from mashed avocados, lemon or lime juice, and chile peppers. Variations can include tomatoes, cilantro, garlic, and scallion. It is important to remember that avocado begins to oxidize as soon as its flesh is exposed to air; cover your guacamole with a layer of plastic wrap fitted directly onto the surface of the mixture.

SERVES 8

1. Mash the avocados with a fork. Add the remaining ingredients and adjust the seasoning with lime juice, salt, and spices.

2. The guacamole is ready to serve now or it can be held in a covered container for up to 8 hours.

ARTICHOKE DIP

1½ cups cooked artichoke hearts, drained and chopped

1 cup mayonnaise

1 cup grated Parmesan cheese

½ cup diced green chiles

3 tbsp sliced scallions, cut thin on the diagonal, optional

2 tbsp small-dice tomatoes, peeled and seeded, optional

THIS DIP can be served hot or at room temperature. Just be careful not to leave it at room temperature for more than an hour or so because it does contain mayonnaise.

MAKES ABOUT 3 CUPS

1. Preheat oven to 350°F.

2. Combine the artichoke hearts, mayonnaise, cheese, and green chiles. Mix well and pour into a 2-quart casserole dish. Bake for 20 to 25 minutes or until lightly browned.

3. Garnish with chopped green onions and chopped tomato, if desired.

SPINACH DIP

YOU CAN bake this dip in small ramekins if you prefer, but we like it baked in a small, round pumpernickel, rye, or sourdough loaf.

MAKES ABOUT 3 CUPS

1. Preheat oven to 350°F.
2. Stir the spinach, artichoke, sour cream, chiles, Parmesan, and garlic together in an oven-proof bowl. Fold in the Monterey Jack cheese. Season to taste with salt and pepper. Bake until the mixture is very hot and bubbly, about 10 to 15 minutes.
3. To prepare the bread, cut a circle from the top of the loaf, keeping it intact to use as a lid. Pull out the bread from the center of the loaf to make room for the dip. Pour the dip into the bread bowl, replace the "lid" and serve.

2 cups chopped spinach, cooked or thawed if frozen and squeezed dry and drained

1 cup finely chopped artichoke hearts or bottoms

1 cup sour cream

½ cup minced green chiles

⅓ cup grated Parmesan cheese

2 tsp minced garlic

1 cup coarsely grated Monterey Jack cheese

Salt and pepper as needed

1 small round bread loaf (rye, pumpernickel, or sourdough), optional

ONION DIP

IF YOU'VE never had a made-from-fresh onion dip, this recipe will convince you that it's well worth the 5 minutes of preparation time!

MAKES ABOUT 3 CUPS

1. Heat a sauté pan over medium heat. Add the oil and heat until it shimmers. Add the onions and season them with a pinch of salt. Sauté, stirring frequently, until the onions are a deep, rich brown, about 20 minutes. Remove from heat and set aside to cool.
2. Mix the remaining ingredients in a bowl, and then add the cooled onions. Refrigerate for an hour. Stir and season with additional salt and pepper, if needed, before serving.

2 tbsp olive oil

1½ cups diced onions

Salt and pepper as needed

1½ cups sour cream

¾ cup mayonnaise

¼ tsp garlic powder

WORKING WITH ARTICHOKES

Before you serve artichokes or just their hearts, trim away the thorns and scoop out the choke.

TRIMMING WHOLE ARTICHOKES

Once artichokes are cut and exposed to air they start to turn brown. An acid such as lemon juice slows this discoloration. Whenever you are cutting artichokes, cut a lemon in half to rub on cut surfaces or fill a bowl with water and add a squeeze of lemon juice and salt to hold the artichokes after trimming.

Cut the stem flush with the base of the artichoke or leave it intact, but peel the stem and trim off the rough bottom. For artichokes served whole, use a chef's knife to cut off the top inch of the artichoke, and then use kitchen scissors to remove any remaining barbed leaf tips and create a neat appearance. For artichoke hearts, pull away the outer leaves, leaving only the tender inner leaves at the center. To remove the choke before cooking, spread open the leaves of the artichoke. Use a grapefruit spoon, tablespoon, or melon baller to scoop out and discard the pale, purple-tinged leaves.

TRIMMING ARTICHOKE BOTTOMS

To prepare artichoke bottoms, cut away the outer leaves with a paring knife. Trim and peel the stem or cut it flush with the artichoke base. Make a cut crosswise through the artichoke at its widest point. Scoop out the choke at the center with a grapefruit spoon or teaspoon. The bottom should look like a bowl. Hold the trimmed artichoke bottoms in lemon water to prevent browning.

COOKING ARTICHOKES

Artichokes are typically cooked by boiling them. Fill a pot with enough water to completely submerge the artichokes and add salt and lemon juice to season the water. The taste of salt and lemon juice should be noticeable. (You can substitute other citrus fruits such as limes or grapefruits, or replace the lemon juice with a white vinegar.) When the water is simmering, add the artichokes and cover them with a clean plate small enough to fit down into the pot, so that it can keep the artichokes under the surface as they cook.

An alternative is to use thawed frozen artichokes, if you can find them in your market. Canned artichokes (both hearts and bottoms) are widely available as both brine-packed or marinated. Brine-packed versions can be used in most recipes with good results, as long as you carefully rinse the artichokes to remove the brine. Reserve marinated artichokes to feature in salads or antipasto platters, rather than use them in cooked dishes.

SERVING ARTICHOKES

There are a number of ways to serve artichokes. Whole artichokes, cooked and chilled, are often served with a vinaigrette; if they are served warm, you might want to pair them with Hollandaise Sauce (page 284). Cut artichokes into slices or wedges and use them as an ingredient in a cold salad or ceviche, or use them as ingredients in pasta and rice dishes, added to stews or braises, as a topping for pizzas or crostini, or served on their own as a side dish.

ARTICHOKES, more properly, the variety known as globe artichokes, have been prized since Roman times as a food, and today there are over 50 varieties of this edible thistle grown throughout the world. Artichokes are actually the flower bud of the plant, protected by sharp barbs at the tip of each leaf.

PREPARING ARTICHOKES FOR COOKING

The way you plan to serve artichokes determines what steps need to be followed to prepare them. Fill a bowl with a mixture of water and lemon juice to hold artichokes after they are cut. Whole artichokes for stuffing or serving with a dip need to be trimmed of sharp barbs; kitchen scissors are the best tool for this task. Spread open the leaves and scoop out the purple tipped leaves and hairy filaments with a spoon. For artichoke hearts, cut away most of the tough outer leaves, leaving behind the base and tender inner leaves. To make an artichoke bottom, cut the leaves completely away from the base of the artichoke.

COOKING ARTICHOKES

Cook artichokes in boiling water you've seasoned with lemon juice, wine or vinegar, and salt. These ingredients are acidic so they flavor the artichokes as well as help them become tender. The artichokes may bob up above the surface of the water. To keep them submerged, top them with a clean plate or the lid of a pot that is slightly smaller in diameter than the pot you are using. Test the artichoke by piercing the stem or base with a knife tip; it should slide in easily. Once artichokes are tender, you can add them to salads, appetizers, stews, or braises.

ARTICHOKE CEVICHE IN BELGIAN ENDIVE

4 artichokes

1 lemon, sliced

Salt and pepper as needed

1 cup diced plum tomato

½ cup red onion julienne

1 scallion, split and sliced thinly on
    the diagonal

2 tbsp chopped cilantro, or as needed

2 tsp minced garlic

½ tsp minced jalapeño, or to taste

2 tbsp extra-virgin olive oil

1 tbsp lime juice, or as needed

12 Belgian endive spears

A CEVICHE IS a marinated dish that you may be more familiar with when made with fish or seafood. Here the lime juice is important both for its flavor and for its ability to keep the artichokes from turning brown when they are exposed to the air.

SERVES 4

1. Trim the stems, leaves, and choke from the artichokes. Place the hearts in a small pot with enough water to generously cover. Add the lemon slices and salt to taste. Bring the water to a simmer over high heat. Reduce the heat to medium and simmer until the artichoke hearts are very tender, about 12 to 15 minutes. Cool the hearts and slice thinly or quarter.

2. Toss together the artichokes, tomato, red onion, scallion, cilantro, garlic, and jalapeño. Drizzle the olive oil and lime juice over the ceviche and season generously with salt and pepper. Toss until the ingredients are evenly coated. Cover the bowl and marinate the ceviche in the refrigerator for at least 2, and up to 12, hours.

3. Taste the ceviche just before serving and season with additional cilantro, lime juice, coarsely ground black pepper, and salt to taste. Spoon the ceviche into the endive spears and serve on a chilled platter or plates.

SPINACH AND SAUSAGE
STUFFED MUSHROOMS

12 large white mushrooms

½ lb Italian (sweet or hot) sausage

1 cup chopped chopped fresh spinach leaves

½ cup minced flat-leaf parsley

½ cup grated Parmesan cheese

½ cup minced scallions

1 large egg, lightly beaten

Salt and pepper as needed

¼ cup butter

¼ cup plain breadcrumbs

W E USED white mushrooms in this recipe, but you can substitute other mushrooms in this dish. You can stuff the mushrooms up to 2 days before baking them.

SERVES 6

1. Preheat the oven to 400°F.

2. Cut the stems away from the mushroom caps and trim to remove any dirt or bruised portions. Chop the stems and reserve. Scrape the gills from the mushroom caps and reserve separately.

3. Remove the sausage from its casing and crumble. Heat a large skillet over medium-high heat. Add the sausage and cook, stirring with a wooden spoon to break up any large clumps, until the sausage is no longer pink, about 5 minutes. Use a slotted spoon to lift the sausage from the skillet. Drain the sausage in a sieve to allow any grease to drain away. Transfer to a mixing bowl when cool.

4. Return the skillet to medium-high heat. Add the chopped mushroom stems and sauté until they are tender and any moisture they release has cooked away, 2 to 3 minutes. Add the spinach and sauté until the spinach is tender, about 4 minutes. Add the spinach mixture to the sausage and stir to combine. When the mixture has cooled to room temperature, stir in the parsley, 1/4 cup of Parmesan, the scallions, and egg. Stir until blended. Season to taste with salt and pepper.

5. Return the skillet to medium heat. Add the butter and heat until the butter is melted but not foaming. Add the mushroom caps to the butter and roll or toss the caps in the butter until they are evenly coated. Continue to cook, partially covered, until the caps are heated through, 2 to 3 minutes. Remove them from the pan using a slotted spoon and transfer to a baking dish. Fill the mushroom caps with the sausage stuffing mixture. Combine the remaining 1/4 cup Parmesan with the breadcrumbs and sprinkle evenly over the tops of the mushrooms. Bake until the tops of the mushrooms are golden and crisp, 10 to 12 minutes. Serve at once.

AVOCADO WITH MARINATED FIDDLEHEAD FERNS

FIDDLEHEAD FERNS are available from April to early July. They should be a soft jade-green in color, firm, and no more than about 1 inch across. If fresh fiddleheads are not available, frozen can be used.

SERVES 8

1. To make the dressing, combine the vinegar, shallots, garlic, thyme, marjoram, basil, salt, and pepper in a large bowl. Gradually whisk in the oil until thoroughly blended. Reserve half the dressing. Toss the portobellos in the remaining dressing and marinate in the refrigerator for at least 2, and up to 12, hours.

2. Preheat a grill to medium heat and oil the rack lightly. Remove the portobellos from the marinade and grill them for 4 to 8 minutes on each side, or until well marked and tender. Let cool slightly before cutting into ¼-inch slices.

3. Heat the remaining 2 tablespoons of oil in a small sauté pan over high heat. Add the blanched fiddleheads and sauté until heated through, about 1 minute. Season to taste with salt and pepper. Add the croutons and toss to combine.

4. Toss the spring greens with the reserved dressing and divide among chilled salad plates. Divide the mushroom slices among the salads and garnish with fiddleheads and croutons.

5 tbsp red wine vinegar

2 shallots, minced

1 tsp minced garlic

1 tsp chopped thyme

1 tsp chopped marjoram

1 tsp chopped basil

Salt and pepper as needed

⅔ cup olive oil

Four 4- to 5-inch-diameter portobello mushrooms, stemmed

2 tbsp olive oil

½ lb fiddlehead ferns, blanched (page 18)

Salt and pepper as needed

1 cup Croutons (page 34)

10 cups mixed spring greens, rinsed and dried

SPRING GREENS can include combinations of red and green oak leaf lettuces, mâche, mizuna, or Bibb lettuce.

STUFFED CHERRY TOMATOES WITH MINTED BARLEY CUCUMBER SALAD

THE BARLEY salad can be prepared up to 2 days in advance. You may want to double the ingredients for the filling to have on hand as an accompaniment to grilled or broiled salmon. The tomatoes can be stuffed up to 6 hours before they are served.

SERVES 8

1. Soak the barley in enough cold water to cover for 30 minutes and drain well.
2. Bring the barley and enough water to cover to a boil. Reduce the heat and simmer until tender, about 40 minutes. Strain through a sieve, transfer to a bowl of ice water, and let cool for 1 minute. Set the sieve over a bowl and let the barley drain.
3. Combine the barley, tomato, cucumber, parsley, mint, and scallions in a large mixing bowl. Stir in the olive oil, lemon juice, salt, and pepper.
4. Cut the core from the cherry tomatoes and make two cuts into the tomato to open it out like a flower. Stuff with some of the salad. Serve on a chilled platter or individual plates.

½ cup pearl barley

¼ cup diced tomato

¼ cup diced cucumber

⅓ cup chopped flat-leaf parsley

2 tbsp chopped mint

1 tbsp finely sliced scallions, white portion only

2 tsp extra-virgin olive oil

1 tsp lemon juice

Salt and pepper as needed

16 cherry tomatoes

TOMATO SAMPLER WITH PAN-FRIED CALAMARI

¾ lb fresh calamari, cleaned and rinsed

½ cup all-purpose flour, or as needed for dredging

2 tsp Old Bay seasoning mix

Salt and pepper as needed

½ cup milk

1 cup olive or canola oil, or as needed for pan frying

¾ cup arugula leaves

3 cups torn frisée

1 cup Balsamic Vinaigrette (page 131)

1 yellow beefsteak tomato, sliced thick

1 red beefsteak tomato, sliced thick

½ cup red cherry tomatoes, halved

½ cup yellow cherry tomatoes, halved

*S*OME FARM stands offer baskets of an assortment of tomato varieties with colors that range from a brilliant yellow to a deep dusky maroon that is almost black. We especially enjoy the contrast of hot, crunchy, pan-fried calamari against the juicy tomatoes.

MAKES 4 SERVINGS

1. Cut the squid's body into thin rings approximately ⅛ inch thick. Rinse the rings and tentacles thoroughly in cold water, then blot dry on absorbent toweling.

2. Combine the flour, Old Bay seasoning, salt, and pepper in a large plate or pan. Pour milk into a shallow bowl.

3. Add the oil to a skillet (there should be about ¼ inch covering the bottom) and preheat the oil over medium-high heat.

4. Dip the squid rings and tentacles into the milk first and then in the seasoned flour, turning to coat evenly. Immediately lower the coated calamari into the hot oil. Cook, turning occasionally, until the squid is golden brown on all sides, about 6 to 8 minutes. Remove the calamari from the oil and drain briefly on absorbent toweling.

5. Toss together the arugula and frisée with the vinaigrette and mound the dressed greens on a serving platter or individual plates. Add the tomatoes to the vinaigrette remaining in the bowl and very gently toss to coat. Top the greens with the tomatoes and calamari. Serve at once.

BAKED TOMATOES WITH GOAT CHEESE

¾ cup crumbled fresh goat cheese

3¼ cup diced roasted red peppers

2 tbsp currants, plumped

2 tbsp chopped basil

2 tbsp chopped flat-leaf parsley

Freshly ground pepper to taste

6 plum tomatoes

TOMATOES ARE known to promote health because they contain lycopene, a type of carotene, as well as vitamin C and potassium. To give tomatoes even more impact, serve them nestled on a bed of mâche or other baby greens. Their juices and the filling ingredients will dress the greens, so there is no need for a vinaigrette.

SERVES 6

1. Preheat oven to 350°F. Make six small rings from aluminum foil to hold the tomatoes and set in a small baking dish.

2. To make the filling, crumble the goat cheese in a large bowl. Add the red peppers, currants, basil, parsley, and pepper.

3. Cut a thin slice from the bottom of each tomato so it can stand upright. Remove the core and scoop out some of the flesh with a melon baller. Set the tomatoes in the aluminum foil rings. Divide the filling between the tomatoes. Bake until the tomatoes are hot and the cheese has just started to brown, about 15 minutes. Serve hot.

BAKED VIDALIA ONIONS

To prepare onions to bake whole, trim away a thin slice from the root ends, but leave enough root intact to hold the onions together as they cook. Other herbs to try with these onions include chives, flat-leaf parsley, marjoram, or sage. Prepare the onion pouches up to 12 hours before grilling, but serve them directly from the grill for the best flavor.

SERVES 8

8 small Vidalia onions

2 tsp chopped rosemary

2 tsp chopped thyme

Salt and pepper as needed

¼ cup balsamic vinegar

1. Preheat a grill. Cut 16 squares of aluminum foil, each piece approximately 12 inches square.

2. Peel the onions and trim the root ends, leaving the cores intact. Make 3 or 4 cuts across the top of each onion, cutting only two-thirds of the way down. Set each onion in the center of a double layer of aluminum foil squares, root end down.

3. Divide the rosemary, thyme, salt, and pepper evenly between the onions. Pull the aluminum foil up over each onion to create a pouch, leaving the top of the onion exposed. Pour 1½ teaspoons of the vinegar into each pouch.

4. On a gas grill, place the onions on the top shelf over medium-high heat. On a charcoal grill, place the onions on the side farthest away from the direct heat of the charcoal. Cook the onions, turning them occasionally, until they are very tender, about 1 hour. Remove the aluminum foil. Serve drizzled with any juices that accumulated in the aluminum foil pouch.

IF YOUR grill is too full, try baking these onions in an oven preheated to 375°F. Place them in a baking dish large enough to hold them without touching and bake until the onions are very tender, 35 to 40 minutes.

MAKING CROSTINI OR CANAPÉS

Crostini and canapés are bite-size, open-faced sandwiches. Simple and quick to make, they offer the busy cook a wide range of flavors, textures, and colors.

All canapés have a base of bread, a spread, a main item, and a garnish. Crostini, meaning "little toasts" in Italian, are not held to the same rigid guidelines of a canapé. Crostini refers both to a toasted piece of Italian or French bread, and the hors d'oeuvre that is created when a savory item is placed on top of the toast.

Crostini and canapés should be easy to pick up, and small enough to eat in one or two bites. For the most appealing crostini and canapés, choose your ingredients with attention to color, shape, and texture. In the following recipes, the terms crostini and canapé can be used interchangeably.

PREPARE THE CROSTINI OR CANAPÉ BASE

Select the bread for your crostini or canapé base and cut it into shapes, if necessary. Cocktail rye or pumpernickel bread is easy to use for canapés, but you can use other breads as well. Trim away the crust, and cut the cocktail bread in half on the diagonal to make triangles. For an elegant affair, use small, round cutters to create a more uniform and finished-looking base. When making crostini, you can choose to toast, grill, or broil the bread slices for more flavor and texture.

ADD A FLAVORFUL SPREAD TO THE BASE

A spread acts as a moisture barrier between the main item and the bread, as well as to hold the topping in place. It also adds mouthfeel and flavor. Spread a thin layer of softened butter, cream cheese, mustard, a bean spread, or mayonnaise from edge to edge. Add flavoring ingredients to the spread if you like: minced garlic, shallots, or scallions; purees of roasted peppers or chilies, Parmesan cheese, or olives can be blended into the spread.

GARNISH THE CROSTINI OR CANAPÉ WITH THE TOPPING

Sliced toppings should be very thin and cut or trimmed so they won't hang over the edge of the base. Another option is to dice or mince the main item and fold it into the spread to make a flavorful salad topping for the base. When you plan to make larger numbers of crostini or canapés for a party or reception, you can add the spread and topping to an entire slice of bread, then use cutters to trim or cut them into shape. Garnishes like a bit of fresh fruit, vegetables, or herbs can add additional color, texture, and flavor.

GARLIC AND PARSLEY BUTTER

VERSATILE AND delicious, this is a compound butter used in classical French cuisine. The butter holds well, so make enough to enjoy with crostini, on toasted bread as an accompaniment to pasta dishes, or as a final seasoning and sauce for simply steamed or boiled vegetables.

MAKES 2 CUPS

1½ bunches flat-leaf parsley, stems removed

4 garlic cloves, roughly chopped

1 tsp salt, or to taste

1 lb butter, diced into small cubes, cold

1. Place the parsley, garlic, and salt in a food processor fitted with a metal chopping blade and pulse until evenly minced and well blended.

2. Add the cubed butter to the parsley-garlic mixture. Process, scraping down the sides as needed, until the butter is softened and the mixture is well blended. The butter should be light green in color.

3. The butter may be placed into a ramekin or shaped into a log and rolled in plastic wrap. Refrigerate until ready for use. The butter be can be held for at least a week in the refrigerator, or frozen for several weeks.

Garden Parsley

AVOCADO AND BLACK BEAN CROSTINI

CROSTINI IS a general term that refers to "little toasts," which are usually topped with one or more garnish items. This southwestern version combines the creaminess of black beans with the heat from the guacamole for a dynamite hors d'oeuvre or snack idea.

SERVES 8

1. Preheat the oven to 400°F.
2. Toast the baguette slices in the oven for 5–7 minutes, or until the outside edges are golden brown. Spread each baguette slice with approximately ½ teaspoon of the garlic butter. Reserve the toasts until needed.
3. Combine the onions, tomatoes, black beans, cilantro, and vinegar. Season to taste with salt and pepper.
4. Peel and core one of the avocados and dice into ¼-inch pieces. Combine the avocado with 1 tablespoon of the lime juice, garlic, chili powder, and cumin. Season to taste with salt and pepper.
5. Peel and core the remaining avocado. Slice each half across the meridian into 8 slices. Sprinkle the avocado with the remaining lime juice to prevent oxidation.
6. Spread 1 heaping teaspoon of the avocado mixture on each crostini. Top with 1 tablespoon of the black bean mixture. Garnish with an avocado slice and a cilantro leaf.

24 baguette slices, ¼-inch thick

¼ cup Garlic and Parsley Butter

½ cup small-dice Vidalia onions

½ cup small-dice plum tomatoes

¾ cup cooked or canned black beans, drained and rinsed

2 tbsp cilantro, chopped

1 tsp white wine vinegar

Salt and pepper as needed

2 avocados

2 tbsp lime juice

1 garlic clove, minced

¼ tsp chili powder

⅛ tsp ground cumin

24 cilantro or parsley leaves, washed

RED PEPPER MOUSSE IN ENDIVE

1 tsp olive oil

½ cup minced onions

1 tsp minced garlic

3 red peppers, seeded and finely chopped

1 cup Vegetable or Chicken Broth
   (pages 82–83)

1 tbsp tomato paste

Pinch saffron threads, crushed

Salt and pepper as needed

1 tbsp powdered gelatin

¼ cup dry white wine, cold

¼ cup heavy cream, whipped to
   medium peaks

30 endive spears (2 or 3 heads)

¼ cup finely sliced red pepper for garnish

WORKING WITH gelatin requires a little attention, but the reward for your effort is a delicate mousse that melts in your mouth as soon as you take a bite. Pipe or spoon the mousse into the endive spears before the gelatin has completely set up. Once the spears are filled, however, the appetizer can be held in the refrigerator, loosely covered with plastic wrap, for up to 24 hours.

SERVES 12

1. Heat a medium nonstick skillet over medium heat. Swirl in the oil, then add the onions and garlic. Sauté until the onions are translucent, about 3 minutes. Add the red peppers, broth, tomato paste, saffron, salt, and pepper. Simmer until all ingredients are tender and liquid is reduced by half, 20 to 30 minutes. Remove from the heat and cool slightly. Transfer to a blender or food processor and purée.

2. Sprinkle the gelatin over the wine in a small bowl and let stand until softened, about 5 minutes. Heat the gelatin mixture in a microwave at high power until the gelatin dissolves and clears, 30 to 40 seconds. Stir the melted gelatin into the red pepper purée. Chill the mixture in the refrigerator until it mounds when dropped from a spoon, about 20 minutes.

3. Fold the whipped cream into the red pepper purée. Pipe the mousse into endive spears and garnish with a sliver of red pepper.

PORTOBELLO WITH TUSCAN BEAN SALAD AND CELERY JUICE

TUSCAN DISHES are vibrant with the strong flavors of their wonderful foods. Savor the interplay of sharp, subtle, earthy ingredients in this hearty dish.

SERVES 4

1. Bring the celery juice or broth to a boil in a small saucepan. Dissolve the cornstarch in the water and whisk into the boiling broth. Transfer to a large bowl and cool. Add the vinegar and then slowly whisk in the oil. Add the beans, carrot, celery, peppers, scallions, salt, and pepper, tossing gently to coat. Cover and let stand at room temperature for 1 hour (refrigerate the salad if holding longer than 1 hour).

2. Preheat the oven to 350°F. Place the mushrooms in a baking pan and spray with olive oil nonstick spray. Cover with aluminum foil and bake until tender, 15 to 20 minutes. Transfer to a platter and cool.

3. Divide the bean salad between the mushroom caps. Sprinkle with the chives and cilantro just before serving.

¼ cup celery juice or Vegetable or Chicken Broth (pages 82–83)

½ tsp cornstarch

1 tsp water

2 tbsp champagne vinegar

2 tbsp extra-virgin olive oil

½ cup cooked cannelloni beans, drained and rinsed

¼ cup minced carrot

¼ cup minced celery

¼ cup minced red pepper

¼ cup minced yellow pepper

2 tbsp minced scallions

Salt and pepper as needed

8 small (2-inch diameter) portobello mushrooms, cleaned

Olive oil nonstick spray

1 tbsp minced chives

2 tsp chopped cilantro

PORTOBELLO MUSHROOMS have a wonderful, meaty texture that pairs well with substantial fillings. Before roasting them, cut away the stems and gently scrape out the gills. You can save the stems to add to a pot of broth later on.

CELERY JUICE is available in most large markets or health food stores; but if you have difficulty finding it, make your own by puréeing chopped, fresh celery with a little water. Strain the purée and use the juice any time you want to add a hint of celery to a soup or rice dish.

CHILLED ASPARAGUS WITH MUSTARD HERB VINAIGRETTE

2 lb asparagus

MUSTARD HERB VINAIGRETTE

2 tbsp white wine or cider vinegar

2 tsp Dijon mustard

1 tsp chopped flat leaf parsley

½ tsp chopped tarragon leaves

Salt and pepper as needed

Dash of onion powder

Dash of garlic powder

¼ cup extra-virgin olive oil

I F YOU have a choice at the market, opt for larger asparagus. It has a richer, more satisfying flavor than very slender asparagus.

MAKES 8 SERVINGS

1. Bring a large pot of salted water to a rolling boil.

2. Trim the asparagus to remove the white, fibrous ends. Cut the asparagus into 2-inch pieces on the diagonal.

3. Add the asparagus to the boiling water and cook until the spears are bright green and just tender, 4-5 minutes. (If necessary, cook the asparagus in batches.) Drain the asparagus in a colander and rinse with cold water until the asparagus is chilled. The asparagus is ready to dress and serve now, or it can be held in a covered container in the refrigerator for up to 6 hours.

4. To make the vinaigrette, whisk together the vinegar, mustard, parsley, tarragon, salt, pepper, onion powder, and garlic powder until blended. Add the oil to the vinegar mixture in a thin stream, whisking constantly. Season with additional salt and pepper, if needed.

5. Toss the chilled asparagus with the vinaigrette or pass it separately on the side. Serve immediately on a chilled platter or plates.

STUFFED GRAPE LEAVES

½ cup olive oil

1 cup minced onions

½ cup minced fennel

2 tbsp minced garlic

1 cup short-grain rice

1½ cups fine-dice tomatoes

Salt and pepper as needed

¼ cup minced scallions, white portion only

¼ cup minced parsley

¼ cup chopped dill

¼ cup chopped mint

18 to 20 brine-packed grape leaves, rinsed
and drained

2 cups thinly sliced potatoes

4 cups Vegetable Broth (page 82) or water,
as needed

¼ cup lemon juice

Lemon wedges for garnish

Plain yogurt for garnish

P LAN TO make this recipe the day before you want to serve it so that the stuffed grape leaves can rest overnight; this allows them to firm up and their flavor to develop more fully. You can keep cooked stuffed grape leaves in the refrigerator to add to salads or enjoy on their own. Adding a layer of potatoes to the baking dish keeps the grape leaves from sticking as you cook them.

SERVES 8 TO 10

1. Heat 2 tablespoons of the oil in a sauté pan over medium-high heat. Add the onions, fennel, and garlic and sauté, stirring frequently, until they are fragrant and just starting to become translucent, about 4 minutes.

2. Add the rice and stir to coat completely with the oil. Continue to sauté, stirring constantly, until the rice develops a toasty flavor, about 2 minutes. Add the tomatoes and season with salt and pepper. Continue to cook until the tomatoes are very hot, another 3 minutes. Remove the pan from the heat and stir in the scallions, parsley, dill, and mint. Season with additional salt and pepper, if needed.

3. Cool the rice mixture to room temperature (or it can be kept in the refrigerator in a covered container for up to 12 hours, if you want to prepare the rice ahead of time and assemble the grape leaves later.)

4. Bring a pot of water to a boil. Add the grape leaves and cook until they are softened, about 5 minutes. Drain well.

5. Arrange the sliced potatoes in a rectangular baking dish and add enough of the broth to barely cover them (this will prevent the potatoes from discoloring as you fill and roll the grape leaves).

6. Spread each grape leaf flat on a work surface. The veins should be facing up and the smooth side of the leaf facing down. Place 1 tablespoon of the rice mixture in the center of the leaf. Fold in the sides and then roll up the leaf like a cigar so that the rice is completely encased in the leaf. Place the filled grape leaves in the baking dish, with the seam facing down so the grape leaves won't unroll. The grape leaves can be close to each other, but should not be touching.

7. Season the grape leaves with lemon juice and a little salt and pepper. Add the remaining olive oil, the lemon juice, and enough additional broth or water to barely cover the grape leaves. Cover the grape leaves with a clean, heat-proof plate (this will keep them submerged as they cook). Place over medium heat and bring the broth or water to a simmer. Reduce the heat to low and cook until the rice filling is very tender, 30 to 45 minutes.

8. Remove the grape leaves from the pan, cool to room temperature, and then chill for at least 8 hours in a covered container in the refrigerator. You may wish to add some of the broth to the storage container to keep the grape leaves moistened. Serve the stuffed grape leaves chilled or at room temperature with lemon wedges and yogurt.

Grape Vine

VIETNAMESE FRIED SPRING ROLLS

SPRING ROLL wrappers usually can be found in the produce section. We opted to panfry these spring rolls, rather than deep fry them. Be sure the oil is heated properly. (If you don't have a deep fat thermometer, use the bread cube test described on page 24.)

MAKES 20 PIECES

1. Heat the oil in a wok over high heat, add the gingerroot and the white portion of the scallions. Stirfry until aromatic, about 30 seconds. Add the pork and stirfry until cooked through, about 5 minutes. Add the black fungus and stirfry until hot, about 30 seconds. Add the cabbage, bean sprouts, mushrooms, and scallion greens. Stirfry until all vegetables are very hot and tender crisp, 2 to 3 minutes.

2. Add the soy sauce, rice wine, sesame oil, sugar, salt, and pepper. Stirfry until the ingredients are evenly coated, and then push the solid ingredients up onto the sides of the wok, allowing the liquid to settle in the bottom. When the liquid is boiling rapidly, stir in the slurry. Return the liquid to a simmer, and then pull the ingredients from the sides of the wok into the sauce. Stirfry until all of the ingredients are coated with the sauce. Transfer the mixture to a bowl and cool to room temperature. The filling is ready to use now, or it can be stored in a covered container in the refrigerator for up to 2 days.

3. Sprinkle a baking sheet liberally with cornstarch. Place 2 tablespoons of filling on each spring roll sheet and brush the edges of the sheet with egg wash. Fold the narrow ends in on both sides (fold about 1 inch of the wrapper) and then roll the wrapper around the filling. The filling should be completely enclosed in the wrapper. Seal the seam on the bottom of the roll by pressing it gently. Place the finished rolls on the lined baking sheet. The spring rolls are ready to panfry now, or they can be covered and held in the refrigerator for up to 8 hours.

4. Add enough corn or peanut oil to come to a depth of 1 inch in a deep pot or Dutch oven and heat the oil over medium-high heat to 350°F. Add a few spring rolls to the hot oil, a few at a time. Panfry on the first side until the wrapper is blistered and deep golden brown, about 4 minutes. Turn and fry on the second side until golden and crisp, another 3 to 4 minutes. Drain briefly on absorbent toweling. Serve at once on a heated platter or plates and pass the mustard on the side.

---

2 tbsp peanut oil

2 tsp minced gingerroot

¼ cup thinly sliced scallions, white portion only

1 lb ground pork

½ oz dry black fungus, rehydrated and drained (see page 15)

2 cups shredded napa cabbage

1½ cups bean sprouts

1 cup thinly sliced shiitake mushrooms

½ cup thinly sliced scallions, green portion only

2 tbsp dark soy sauce

1 tbsp rice wine

1 tbsp sesame oil

1 tbsp sugar

2 tsp salt

1 tsp ground white pepper

Slurry of 2 tbsp cornstarch mixed with 1 tbsp cold water

Cornstarch to line baking sheets

1 package spring roll sheets

Egg wash of 2 eggs beaten with 1 tbsp water

Corn or peanut oil as needed for frying

½ cup Chinese-style mustard, or as needed

MIXED GRILL OF GARDEN VEGETABLES WITH CHARMOULA

CHARMOULA

¼ cup olive oil

2 tbsp fresh lemon juice

3 tbsp chopped parsley

2 tbsp chopped cilantro

1 tsp minced garlic

¾ tsp paprika

½ tsp ground cumin

Pinch of cayenne pepper

Salt and pepper as needed

3 artichokes, cooked (page 90)

1 zucchini, halved lengthwise

2 new potatoes

1 fennel bulbs, trimmed

12 baby carrots

12 asparagus stalks, trimmed

½ cup olive oil

3 tbsp minced garlic

Salt and pepper as needed

2 onions, sliced ½ inch thick

18 mushroom caps, trimmed

2 red or yellow peppers, cored and
   cut into thirds

CHARMOULA IS a fresh, pungent sauce made with fresh lemon juice, parsley, cilantro, paprika, cumin, and cayenne pepper—perfect for brightening and enhancing the rich, smoky taste of grill vegetables.

SERVES 6

1. Combine the ingredients for the charmoula and set aside. (The charmoula is best when freshly prepared, but it can be made up to 8 hours in advance and held in a covered container in the refrigerator.)

2. Halve the artichokes and remove the chokes. Set aside. Score the zucchini with the tines of a fork. Set aside.

3. Cook the potatoes in salted boiling water until tender, about 15 minutes. Drain and let cool to the touch. Cut the potatoes in half. Set aside.

4. Blanch the fennel, carrots, and asparagus separately for 2 minutes, or until tender-crisp. Drain and let cool to the touch. Cut the fennel into quarters and core them. Set aside.

5. Combine the olive oil, garlic, salt, and pepper in a large bowl. Add all the vegetables, turn to coat, and let sit for 30 minutes.

6. Light a fire in a charcoal or gas grill. Grill the vegetables, adding them to the grill in the order given in the ingredients list. Grill the vegetables until they begin to take on color and are cooked through.

7. Arrange the grilled vegetables on a platter, drizzle them with the charmoula, and serve either hot or at room temperature.

Grilled Vegetables with a Parsley Salad

Dress 2 cups of curly parsley sprigs with a dressing made from 4 tablespoons extra-virgin olive oil, ½ teaspoon minced garlic, 1 tablespoon fresh lemon juice, and 1 tablespoon grated Parmesan. Sprinkle the salad over the grilled vegetables instead of preparing the charmoula.

Greek Grilled Vegetables

Top the grilled vegetables with ½ cup crumbled feta cheese and 3 tablespoons minced dill before seasoning with lemon juice, salt, and cracked pepper to taste. Serve either hot or at room temperature.

HOW TO CUT VEGETABLES FOR TEMPURA

One of the delights of tempura is the interesting shapes that the food takes on during frying. You can take some liberties in how you prepare the vegetables, but be sure that they're cut so that they will be tender inside just when the batter is crisp and golden. Here are some suggested cutting techniques. Remember to dry all ingredients thoroughly before dunking them in the tempura batter.

ZUCCHINI AND YELLOW SQUASH: Cut on a sharp diagonal to make elongated ovals, ½ inch thick, or cut in lengthwise wedges, 3 to 4 inches long.

BELL PEPPERS: Core and seed, remove the ribs, and cut lengthwise into strips ½ inch wide.

SHIITAKE MUSHROOMS: Remove stems and fry the caps whole or cut out a decorative star on top.

GREEN BEANS: Trim ends and fry whole.

SWEET ONIONS: Before peeling, cut into rings 1 inch thick; then pull off outer layer of skin.

EGGPLANT: Cut in half lengthwise, cut half moons ¼ inch thick; sprinkle lightly with salt and let sit for 20 minutes to purge excess bitter juices; rinse and pat dry.

ASPARAGUS: Trim off the woody base with a diagonal cut.

SWEET POTATOES AND MOST ROOT VEGETABLES: Cut into slices, ¼ inch thick.

CARROTS AND PARSNIPS: Cut on a sharp angle to make elongated ovals, ¼ inch thick.

LOTUS ROOT: Cut in cross-sections to reveal the beautiful seed pod pattern, ¼ inch thick.

VEGETABLE TEMPURA

DIPPING SAUCE

2 scallions, minced

¼ cup soy sauce, plus as needed

¼ cup water

2 tbsp rice vinegar

2 tbsp honey

1 tbsp minced gingerroot

2 garlic cloves, minced

1 tsp dry mustard

1 tsp hot chili sauce, plus as needed

BATTER

2 cups all-purpose flour

4 tsp baking powder

2 cups cold water

¼ cup dark sesame oil

1 cup red pepper strips

1 cup yellow pepper strips

1 cup broccoli florets

1 cup quartered mushrooms

1 small zucchini, cut on the diagonal,
⅛ inch thick

1 small yellow squash, cut on the diagonal,
⅛ inch thick

Salt and pepper as needed

Vegetable oil for deep frying

T HE POPULARITY of these crisp, batter-dipped vegetables as an appetizer has spread beyond Japanese restaurants.

SERVES 4 TO 6 AS AN APPETIZER

1. For the dipping sauce: Combine the scallions, soy sauce, water, vinegar, honey, ginger, garlic, mustard, and hot sauce in a bowl. Cover and refrigerate to let the flavors blend for at least 1 hour or up to 12 hours. Taste and adjust the seasoning with soy sauce and hot sauce before serving.

2. For the batter: Whisk together the flour and baking powder. Add the cold water and sesame oil all at once and whisk until about the thickness of pancake batter and very smooth. Refrigerate until ready to prepare the tempura.

3. Blot the vegetables dry, season with salt and pepper, and dip them in the batter to coat evenly.

4. Pour the oil into a tall pot to a depth of 3 inches. Heat over medium heat until the oil registers 350°F on a deep-frying thermometer. Work in batches to avoid crowding. Slip the batter-coated vegetables into the hot oil. Deep fry until the batter is golden brown and puffy, 3 to 4 minutes. Turn the vegetables, if necessary, to brown and cook evenly. Remove from the pot with tongs and drain briefly on absorbent towels. Serve the vegetables at once with the dipping sauce.

CHEDDAR CORN FRITTERS

Wcorn and then scrape the cobs with a table knife to release all the milk.
HEN FRESH corn on the cob is available, cut the kernels from the ears of
Catch this milk in a bowl and add it to the batter.

SERVES 6 TO 8

1. Stir together the flour, sugar, chili powder, if using, salt, and pepper in a mixing bowl. Set aside.

2. Combine the corn and corn milk, if available, pepper, if using, eggs, water, and the cheese in a bowl. Add to the flour mixture all at once. Stir just until the batter is evenly moistened. Stir in the melted butter.

3. Pour the oil into a large skillet to a depth of ¼ inch. Heat over medium heat until it registers 350°F on a deep-frying thermometer. Using a serving spoon and working in batches to avoid crowding, drop spoonfuls of batter into the hot oil to make 16 fritters in all. Pan fry on the first side until golden brown and crisp, about 2 minutes. Turn once and fry until golden brown on the second side, 2 minutes more. Drain the fritters on absorbent towels and season with salt. If needed, you can keep the first batches of fritters warm in an oven at 200°F while you finish frying the rest. Serve at once.

¾ cup all-purpose flour

2 tsp sugar

1 to 2 tsp chili powder, optional

Salt and pepper as needed

3 ears corn, plus corn milk if available, or
   2 cups corn kernels

3 tbsp diced red or green pepper, optional

2 large eggs, lightly beaten

½ cup water

½ cup grated Cheddar

2 tbsp melted butter

Vegetable oil for pan frying

SPANAKOPITA

2 lb spinach

¼ cup olive oil

1 cup minced onions

2 tbsp minced garlic

Salt and pepper as needed

3 large eggs, beaten

Two 3-oz packages cream cheese,
 room temperature

1¼ cups crumbled feta cheese

¼ cup chopped dill

¼ cup chopped parsley

½ tsp ground coriander

¼ tsp grated nutmeg

One 1-lb box phyllo sheets, thawed

1½ cups melted butter

IF YOU have frozen the spanakopita, they can be baked without thawing them first. Increase the baking time to 20 to 25 minutes.

YOU CAN skip the first step of this recipe if you choose to substitute two 10-ounce boxes of frozen spinach for fresh. Place the frozen spinach in a colander; let it thaw completely and squeeze out the moisture. As an alternative to individual spanakopita, try the Spinach Pie variation on page 124, which can be prepared in a baking pan.

MAKES 40 PIECES

1. Rinse and drain the spinach until all traces of sand and dirt are gone. Bring a large pot of salted water to a rolling boil. Add the spinach (this can be done in two or more batches, if necessary). Stir the spinach until all of the leaves are submerged and wilted. Simmer, uncovered, until the spinach is just tender, about 3 minutes. Drain the spinach, rinse well with cold water to stop the cooking, and press or squeeze out as much additional moisture as possible. Chop the spinach and set aside.

2. To make the spinach filling: Heat the oil in a sauté pan over medium-high heat until it shimmers. Add the onions and garlic and sauté, stirring frequently, until the onions are tender and translucent, 4 to 5 minutes. Add the spinach and sauté until very hot, another 3 minutes. Season well with salt and pepper. Transfer to a bowl or plate and cool completely. Blend the eggs into the cream cheese until smooth, and then stir into the spinach mixture. Fold in the feta, dill, parsley, coriander, and nutmeg. The filling is ready to use now, or it may be stored in a covered container in the refrigerator for up to 24 hours.

3. To assemble the spanakopita: Set up the phyllo as described on page 124. Make a stack of three phyllo sheets, brushing each layer with melted butter. Cut the sheets into five strips with a sharp knife or pastry cutter. Mound about 1 tablespoon of the filling mixture at the base of each strip. Fold the dough up into triangles. Brush the top of each triangle with a little additional butter and transfer to a baking sheet. They can be placed fairly close together, but they should not be touching. The spanakopita is ready to bake now or they can be packed into a container and frozen for up to 1 month.

4. Preheat the oven to 375°F. Bake the spanakopita until the phyllo is crisp and golden brown and the filling is completely cooked and very hot, 16 to 18 minutes. Serve hot or at room temperature.

Spinach

Spinach Pie

Some cookbooks refer to this as the "pan" version of spanakopita. Instead of making individual triangles, half of the phyllo sheets are layered into a lasagna pan or rectangular baking dish that measures approximately 10 inches by 15 inches, brushing the layers with butter. The edges of the phyllo should hang over the edges of the pan by about 1 inch. Add the spinach filling and spread it into an even layer. Fold the phyllo back onto the filling. Add the remaining sheets of phyllo as the top layer, again brushing with butter. Tuck the edges of the top layer of phyllo down into the pan so that the filling is completely enclosed. Brush the top of the pie with a little more melted butter and then refrigerate the pie until the butter is firm. Score the top layer of phyllo into 3-inch squares. Bake the pie at 350°F until the phyllo is light golden brown and the filling is cooked and very hot, 45 to 50 minutes. Let the pie rest for 10 minutes before cutting it into pieces and serving.

WORKING WITH PREPARED PHYLLO DOUGH

Phyllo dough is nothing more than a simple flour-and-water dough stretched into thin sheets. Working with prepared phyllo is much easier than stretching it yourself. It is available in the freezer section of well-stocked supermarkets and from Greek and Middle Eastern groceries.

GETTING READY TO WORK

Thaw frozen phyllo dough either in the refrigerator overnight or at room temperature for 2 hours. Once thawed, the individual sheets should pull apart easily and be very flexible. However, contact with the air soon dries out phyllo unless it is covered. Set your work area up so that your phyllo stays moist and flexible as you work with it. Place a large baking sheet or a piece of plastic wrap down, remove the phyllo from the box, and unroll the number of sheets needed. Set the sheets flat on the baking sheet or plastic wrap. Cover the sheets completely with a large piece of plastic wrap, and then lay a piece of lightly dampened paper towel or a barely moistened kitchen towel over the plastic to keep the air around the phyllo moist.

LAYERING PHYLLO

Transfer one sheet of the phyllo at a time to your flat work area and immediately re-cover the remaining sheets. Brush or spray the entire sheet with butter or oil. For a very flaky texture and extra flavor in the finished dish, you can scatter bread crumbs over the sheet. Keep working this way, one sheet at a time, until you have the correct number of layers for your recipe. If necessary, cut the phyllo stack into strips to fold into triangles for appetizer-size spanakopita.

SCORING PHYLLO

Large items that you will need to cut into portions should be scored before they go into the oven. Otherwise, the fragile, crisp pastry would shatter as you try to slice it. It is easiest to cut the dough when it is firm, so we suggest that you chill it first. The butter will firm up in about 20 minutes. Then use a pizza cutter or the tip of your sharpest paring knife to cut almost through the layers. It is best to leave a layer or two uncut so that the filling doesn't ooze out as the pie bakes, but if it should, the pie will still taste great.

7217   All the delicacies of the season, Rome.

Salads

ALADS ARE ONE of the most delightful ways to enjoy vegetables. Most of the salads in this chapter feature fresh, uncooked vegetables, but some are based on cooked vegetables—roasted, grilled, steamed, and boiled—that have been combined with a dressing to marinate as they chill.

Whether you are making a green salad or a mixed vegetable salad, leafy greens are an important component in many salads. They may be an ingredient in a salad, or they can be a bed for a composed salad or a selection of salads served as a sampler. The information below is useful not only for selecting and preparing greens to use in salads, but also for preparing greens for cooking.

Selecting and Preparing Salad Greens

Salad greens include lettuce of all types, as well as other leafy vegetables, such as Belgian endive and watercress. The selection of greens and their complementary dressings lend themselves to many forms and appearances. In its most basic form, a green salad is one or two lettuces tossed with a dressing and garnished with vegetables, croutons, or cheeses. More complex or composed salads usually are served as main-course meals or appetizers rather than an accompaniment.

Today, you can feature a wider variety and better quality of greens than ever before in your salad bowl. Salad greens can be grouped according to their flavors and/or textures:

MILD GREENS: Bibb, Boston, green or red leaf, iceberg, mâche, oak, romaine, various baby varieties of cooking greens

SPICY GREENS: Amaranth, arugula, mizuna, tat-soi, watercress

BITTER GREENS AND CHICORIES: Belgian endive (or witloof), curly endive (known as chicory or frisée), radicchio

HERBS AND FLOWERS: Basil, chives, chervil, mint, parsley, chrysanthemums, nasturtiums, pansies

Lettuce blends are readily available in virtually every market. You can select from precut lettuces such as romaine, iceberg, or baby spinach; or try more exotic blends, sometimes referred to by their French name, *mesclun*. These precut and cleaned greens can be purchased in your local market. A great boon to the time-challenged cook, precut and packaged salad greens still need a thorough rinse and a few turns in your salad spinner. If you have a bit more time, you can prepare your own blend from individual greens, using the preceding list as a flavor guide and your own sense of color to guide you. Using more than one color, flavor, or texture is a great way to make your own custom blend.

Once the greens are selected and prepared, you can add to the artistry of your salad through garnishing. Depending on what's in season (or in your refrigerator), choose from such items as slices or wedges of tomatoes, cucumbers, carrots, radishes, mushrooms, olives, and peppers. For a more substantial salad, add eggs, cheese, raw or blanched vegetables, potatoes, and cooked meats. These additions give your salads yet another level of interest in terms of flavor, texture, and nourishment.

CLEAN THE GREENS

Nothing is worse than a gritty salad or one that forces your friends and family to use a knife to cut the lettuce. All greens, including prepackaged salad mixes and "triple-washed" bagged spinach, must be washed and dried prior to serving and should be kept properly chilled until ready to eat.

Salad greens are highly perishable and require proper handling. More tender greens, such as Boston lettuce or mâche, last only a day or two; romaine and iceberg are heartier and last much longer. If you purchase your fresh produce at a weekly farmer's market, be sure to enjoy tender greens right away and save the longer-lasting ones for later in the week.

The salad spinner is a relatively inexpensive, key piece of timesaving equipment for salad washing. Through centrifugal force, the salad spinner cleans the greens while spinning away water. This ensures the greens will have better flavor and the dressing will cling to them more evenly.

Wash the greens thoroughly in plenty of cool water to remove all traces of dirt and sand:

1. Separate the greens into leaves, and trim coarse rims or stem ends or ribs.

2. Fill a large bowl or a clean sink with cold water, and then add the lettuce. Swish it gently through the water and lift it away.

3. Check the bottom of the bowl or sink; if you feel any grit or sand, drain the water and repeat until all traces of grit are gone.

4. Dry the greens completely. Greens that are properly dried have more flavor and, when stored, last longer. Fill the basket of a salad spinner and spin until the leaves are dry.

5. Store cleaned and dried greens in the refrigerator until ready to dress and serve. Keep them in plastic containers or zipper-lock bags with a piece of paper towel to absorb any excess moisture, or in your salad spinner. Use the greens within a day or two.

CUT OR TEAR THE GREENS INTO BITE-SIZE PIECES

Use clean fingers to tear lettuce into pieces or use a knife to cut greens into pieces or to shred them. If you are using a knife, make it a habit to sharpen the blade before you begin. A sharp edge will cut cleanly through the leafy greens and you won't bruise or crush the lettuce. Use a high-carbon, stainless steel blade so you don't discolor the leaves.

Garnish and dress your salads just before you serve them. Add just enough dressing for the greens; don't drown the salad. Plan on about 2 or 3 tablespoons for each serving. Use less if the dressing is thin, like a vinaigrette. You may need to use a bit more if the dressing is heavier. Use clean hands, tongs, or a salad spoon and fork and a lifting and tossing motion until each piece of lettuce is coated completely.

STEP-BY-STEP VINAIGRETTES

Many of our salads feature freshly made, flavorful vinaigrettes. Most vinaigrette recipes can be doubled, tripled, or even quadrupled without any problem. Making a large batch of vinaigrette gives you a head start on a variety of vegetable dishes. Vinaigrettes are used as a marinade or a dip, as well as to dress salads. Conversely, there's no need to make large batches; simply combine the ingredients for a small amount of dressing right in the salad bowl, leaving one less thing to wash.

DETERMINE THE BALANCE OF ACID AND OIL

A good vinaigrette balances the sharpness of the vinegar or juice by combining it with oil. One of the simplest of all recipes, a basic vinaigrette is a combination that you can express as a ratio: three parts oil to one part acid.

This works well as a starting point, but you may find with experience that you prefer a combination that changes the ratio slightly. If your oil is so strongly flavored that it could overpower the vinegar, you may wish to replace some of the intensely flavored oil with a more subtly flavored one. Very sharp or strong vinegars can be adjusted by either adding a bit of water to dilute them or sugar to soften their acidity.

ADD ANY ADDITIONAL INGREDIENTS

When preparing a vinaigrette, add the salt, pepper, herbs, mustard, or other ingredients to the vinegar before adding the oil so they will be blended evenly throughout the sauce. Herbs give vinaigrettes a wonderful flavor and color. However, if they are added too far in advance, the vinegar can start to discolor them and flatten their lively flavors. When preparing a large batch of vinaigrette that you want to last through several meals, you might prefer to add the herbs to the dressing just before you serve it.

GRADUALLY ADD THE OIL

Slowly pour or ladle a few droplets of oil at a time into the bowl, whisking constantly. Once the vinaigrette starts to thicken, you can add the oil more quickly. If the vinaigrette sits for a short time, it will start to separate. Whisk it vigorously before you dress your salad or serve it as a dip.

Use a handheld or countertop blender to make a vinaigrette quickly. Vinaigrettes made with a blender will be thicker, and can hold their emulsion longer than those that are simply whipped together.

CHECK THE SEASONING

To be certain your dressing is balanced, put a few leaves of lettuce in a small bowl and add a teaspoon of the vinaigrette. Toss the greens until they are lightly coated and then taste them. If you taste a vinaigrette full strength, it may seem too strong or biting; once on your greens, however, the flavor may be perfect. Adjust the seasoning or the ratio of oil to vinegar, if necessary, whisk well, and serve.

RED WINE VINAIGRETTE

WE'VE COMBINED two oils here for a well-balanced flavor in the vinaigrette. Try other oils instead of the extra-virgin olive oil. Options include walnut or peanut oil.

MAKES 2 CUPS

½ cup red wine vinegar

1 tsp Dijon-style mustard

Salt and pepper as needed

¾ cup extra-virgin olive oil

¾ cup corn or safflower oil

2 to 3 tbsp minced herbs, optional

1. Whisk together the vinegar, mustard, about ½ teaspooon salt, and a pinch of black pepper. Gradually whisk in the oils until they are all incorporated and the vinaigrette is smooth and lightly thickened (as the vinaigrette sits, it will start to separate). Season with additional salt and pepper, if needed.

2. Just before serving, whisk the vinaigrette to recombine the oils and vinegar. Check the seasoning again and add the herbs, if using.

BALSAMIC VINAIGRETTE

THERE ARE different grades of balsamic vinegar. Save the rich, syrupy, authentic balsamic to savor in small droplets as a dressing for perfect strawberries or a slice of melon, and use a less expensive variety for this salad dressing. Balsamic vinegar has a bold flavor and a dark color, so we've blended it with a bit of red wine vinegar.

MAKES 2 CUPS

¼ cup balsamic vinegar

¼ cup red wine vinegar

1 tsp Dijon-style mustard

Salt and pepper as needed

1½ cups extra-virgin olive oil

2 to 3 tbsp minced herbs, optional

1. Whisk together the vinegars, mustard, about ½ teaspoon salt, and a pinch of black pepper. Gradually whisk in the oil until it is all incorporated and the vinaigrette is smooth and lightly thickened (as the vinaigrette sits, it will start to separate). Season with additional salt and pepper, if needed.

2. Just before serving, whisk the vinaigrette to recombine the oil and vinegars. Check the seasoning again and add the herbs, if using.

GRAPEFRUIT VINAIGRETTE

⅓ cup grapefruit juice

¼ cup white wine vinegar

Salt and pepper as needed

1½ cups peanut or light sesame oil

2 tsp minced grapefruit zest, optional

Y OU NEED pure, unsweetened grapefruit juice for this salad dressing. If you are using a purchased grapefruit juice, check the label to be sure it isn't a sweetened fruit "cocktail" instead of pure juice.

MAKES 2 CUPS

1. Whisk together the grapefruit juice, vinegar, ½ teaspoon salt, and a pinch of black pepper. Gradually whisk in the oil until it is all incorporated and the vinaigrette is smooth and lightly thickened (as the vinaigrette sits, it will start to separate). Season with additional salt and pepper, if needed.

2. Just before serving, whisk the vinaigrette to recombine the vinaigrette. Check the seasoning again and add the grapefruit zest, if using.

CUCUMBER, TOMATO, AND FETA SALAD

¼ cup red wine vinegar

1 tbsp coarsely chopped oregano

Salt and pepper, as needed

½ cup extra-virgin olive oil

3½ cups diced cucumbers

1½ cups diced tomatoes

¼ pound crumbled feta

1 cup thinly sliced red onions

T HIS SALAD is simple to prepare and perfect for a summer lunch when tomatoes and cucumbers are just ripe and waiting to be enjoyed. Try making this salad with different varieties of tomatoes when they appear in your local market throughout the season.

SERVES 6

1. Combine the vinegar, oregano, salt, and pepper in a salad bowl. Add the olive oil gradually while whisking constantly.

2. Add the cucumbers, tomatoes, feta, and onions to the dressing and toss until the ingredients are evenly coated. Season the salad with additional salt and pepper, if needed.

WATERMELON AND RED ONION SALAD
WITH WATERCRESS

Y OU CAN cut the red onion up to 8 hours ahead of time, and actually improve its flavor and color. Put the sliced onion in a bowl, cover with cold water, and refrigerate for at least 4, and up to 8, hours to remove the bitterness and odor.

SERVES 6

Combine the vinegar, oil, salt, and pepper in a salad bowl. Add the watermelon and watercress and toss gently to coat. Top with the onion rings and pine nuts. Serve immediately on a chilled platter or plates, or the salad can be held in a covered container in the refrigerator for up to 8 hours.

2 tbsp white wine vinegar

1 tbsp vegetable oil

Salt and pepper, as needed

3 cups cubed seedless watermelon

1 bunch watercress (trimmed, rinsed, and dried)

½ medium red onion (sliced thin and separated into rings)

1 tbsp toasted pine nuts

YOU CAN simplify your life and give a little performance tableside by layering the watermelon, watercress, and onion rings in a salad bowl, and refrigerating it, covered, earlier in the day. Prepare the dressing mixture, combine the salad, and toss in front your guests, then scatter the pine nuts over the salad before serving..

Spanish Melon

JÍCAMA AND RED PEPPER SALAD

Jícama might not look too promising when you buy it, but underneath its coarse skin lies a sweet, crunchy, refreshing vegetable.

SERVES 8

1. To make the dressing, combine the lime juice, sugar, Tabasco, salt, and pepper in a medium bowl. Add the oil in a steady stream, whisking constantly.

2. Add the jícama, red pepper, cilantro, scallions, and garlic to the dressing and toss to combine.

3. Cover the salad and marinate in the refrigerator for at least 30 minutes and up to 3 days before serving. Serve the salad chilled or at room temperature.

3 tbsp lime juice, about 2 limes

1 tbsp sugar

1 tsp Tabasco sauce

Salt and pepper as needed

⅓ cup canola oil

1 medium jícama, peeled and julienned

1 large red pepper, cut into julienne

2 tbsp chopped cilantro

2 scallions, sliced thin on the bias

2 tsp minced garlic

LEMON-INFUSED GREEK SALAD
WITH GRAPE LEAVES

2 tbsp lemon juice

2 tsp balsamic vinegar

1 tbsp chopped parsley

Salt and pepper as needed

3 tbsp canola oil

2 tbsp extra-virgin olive oil

1½ lb romaine hearts, rinsed, dried,
    and torn into pieces

1 cup Greek olives, cut in half lengthwise

2 cups sliced, peeled seedless cucumber

2 cups halved cherry tomatoes

1 yellow pepper (seeded, thinly sliced)

1 red onion, sliced ⅛-inch thick

2¼ cups crumbled feta

4 whole wheat pitas, toasted,
    cut into 16 wedges

16 Stuffed Grape Leaves (page 110)

T HE FINAL additions to this salad—toasted pita wedges and grape leaves—
add some substance and texture to this classic salad. If you have a good
source for prepared grape leaves, use them any time you want a quick and satisfying salad that is substantial enough to feature as a main course.

SERVES 8

1. Combine the lemon juice, vinegar, parsley, ½ teaspoon salt, and ⅛ teaspoon
pepper and stir until the salt is dissolved. Add the canola and olive oils in a
stream, whisking constantly, until the oil is blended into the dressing. Season
with additional salt and pepper, if needed.

2. Place the cleaned romaine into the salad bowl. Add the sliced olives, cucumbers, cherry tomatoes, pepper, and red onion to the mixing bowl. Toss the salad
ingredients together with the vinaigrette until evenly coated.

3. Top with the feta and garnish with the pita wedges and stuffed grape leaves.

BLT SALAD WITH BUTTERMILK-CHIVE DRESSING

12 bacon strips

4 whole wheat rolls, cubed

2 tbsp olive oil

3 minced garlic cloves

Salt and pepper, as needed

1 head Boston lettuce, separated into leaves, rinsed and dried

2 large tomatoes, sliced ¼ inch thick

½ cup Buttermilk-Chive Dressing (recipe follows)

DRESSING

⅓ cup buttermilk

¼ cup prepared mayonnaise

2 tbsp corn oil

2 tbsp minced chives

1 tbsp red wine vinegar

Dash Tabasco sauce

½ tsp lemon juice, freshly squeezed

⅛ tsp Old Bay seasoning

Dash Worcestershire sauce

THIS SALAD is most successful when the bacon is freshly cooked. The croutons can be prepared in advance, but try to cook the bacon just before you serve the salad.

THE DRESSING will stay fresh for up to 3 days in the refrigerator. Be sure to stir or shake well before serving to recombine the ingredients.

ONE OF the most popular offerings at lunch in any diner or cafe, this salad reinterprets the classic "bacon, lettuce, and tomato" sandwich. If you can find yellow tomatoes, try alternating slices of red and yellow tomatoes to give this dish some extra eye-appeal.

SERVES 4

1. Preheat the oven to 400°F. Lay the bacon strips on a baking sheet, and bake them for about 8 minutes, or until brown and crisp. Transfer them to a plate lined with paper towels to allow the grease to drain.

2. Toss the cubed whole wheat rolls, olive oil, garlic, and salt and pepper to taste together in a baking dish; toast the bread for 8 to 10 minutes to prepare croutons.

3. Arrange the lettuce in a salad bowl or on individual plates. Top with the sliced tomatoes, bacon strips, and croutons. Drizzle the dressing over the salad and serve immediately.

Buttermilk-Chive Dressing

THIS DRESSING is used on the BLT Salad, but it would be equally good in a potato salad or as a dip for crudités, and would make an excellent topping for a baked potato.

MAKES ¾ CUP

Combine all of the ingredients in a bowl or jar. Stir or shake to blend. Adjust the seasoning to taste by adding more salt, pepper, lemon juice, Worcestershire sauce, or chives. The dressing is ready to serve now, or it can be stored in a covered container in the refrigerator for up to 3 days.

SALADS don't have to be simply tossed greens with a slice of cucumber. Shifting the emphasis toward vegetables other than lettuce improves the nutritional value of a salad. It also adds rich textures and flavors. Lots of vegetables in your salad can even "upgrade" a side dish to an entrée or appetizer.

AVOCADOS IN SALADS

Avocados add creaminess, richness, and a wealth of nutrients to a dish. Choose avocados that are ripe, or nearly ripe. To check for ripeness, cradle the avocado in the palm of your hand, wrap your fingers gently around the avocado, and press very gently. A ripe avocado will give very slightly. Use the following guidelines to keep ripe avocados from turning brown.

Peel avocadoes just before you use them. Make a single cut, starting at the stem end and cutting completely around the avocado. Twist the two halves in opposite directions and pull the avocado apart to expose the seed (a large, round pit). Pry out the pit with your finger tips or a spoon. If the avocado is ripe, the skin will pull easily away from the flesh. Just bend the skin back slightly. Or you may use a serving spoon to scoop out the flesh. Use a very sharp knife to cut the slices and sprinkle them with lemon or lime juice to prevent browning.

CORN IN SALADS

Although corn on the cob, served hot from the pot or grill, is a classic accompaniment to a main dish, it is a perfect addition to salads. Plump, sweet kernels add a refreshing burst of flavor, as well as a flash of color. To prepare corn to serve cold, prepare it as you normally would. We chose to grill the corn in this instance for a subtle, smoky taste. Steaming, boiling, and roasting are also great options.

Pull the husk and silk away from the corn, if you haven't already. Set the broad end of the ear of corn down on a stable work surface. Use a chef's or a utility knife. Cut the kernels away from the cob by making a slice from the tip to the end. The kernels should feel like they are "popping" off the cob. Once you've cut the kernels from the cob, you can break the large pieces up if you wish.

TOMATO, AVOCADO, AND ROASTED CORN SALAD

4 ears corn on the cob with husks
    still attached

Salt, as needed

6 cups mesclun lettuce mix, rinsed and dried

1 cup Chipotle-Sherry Vinaigrette
    (recipe follows)

3 red beefsteak tomatoes, sliced ¼ inch thick

2 avocados, cut into slices

1 medium red onion, sliced thin

1 cup small-diced aged Cheddar cheese

2 tsp freshly ground black pepper

VINAIGRETTE

3 tbsp sherry vinegar

1 tbsp fresh lime juice

1 tbsp minced shallots

1 tbsp chopped cilantro

1 tsp chopped thyme

1 tbsp chopped parsley

2 canned chipotles, drained and minced

1 garlic clove, minced

1 tsp real maple syrup

¾ cup olive oil

IF YOU have the grill going, you can cook the corn on the grill instead of in the oven.

SERVES 8

1. Preheat oven to 400°F. Roast the unhusked ears of corn until tender, about 45 minutes. Check their doneness after about 45 minutes; pull the husk partially away from the biggest ear. If you can pierce a kernel easily with a fork, it is done. Remove from the oven and cool completely.

2. Shuck the corn and cut the kernels from the cobs. Place the corn kernels in a mixing bowl and toss with 1 teaspoon of the salt. Keep the corn at room temperature if you are making the salad right away, or cover and refrigerate for up to 12 hours.

3. Toss the mesclun mix with ½ cup vinaigrette. Mound the dressed mesclun on a chilled platter or individual plates. Arrange the tomatoes, avocados, and red onion over the mesclun. Sprinkle with the cheese and reserved corn. Drizzle with the remaining ½ cup dressing. Season to taste with salt and pepper. Serve immediately.

Chipotle-Sherry Vinaigrette

MAKES 1 CUP

In a medium bowl, combine all the ingredients except the olive oil. Gradually whisk in the olive oil until the dressing is lightly thickened. Taste and adjust the seasoning.

FRISÉE WITH ALMONDS, APPLES, GRAPES, AND GOAT CHEESE

¾ cup apple cider

¼ cup cider vinegar

¼ cup diced Granny Smith apple

½ cup peanut oil

1 tbsp tarragon leaves, chopped

½ tsp salt, or to taste

Pinch ground white pepper

1½ pounds frisée lettuce

2 Granny Smith apples, or other tart apple

1 cup red grapes, cut in half lengthwise

½ cup toasted slivered almonds

1 cup crumbled goat cheese

F RISÉE, A light-green variety of endive with very curly leaves, is the base for a delicious combination of early autumn produce, crunchy walnuts, and pungent blue cheese.

SERVES 8

1. To prepare the vinaigrette, whisk together apple cider, cider vinegar, apple, peanut oil, tarragon, salt, and white pepper by hand or by mixing with a hand blender.

2. To make the salad, clean and thoroughly dry the frisée. Slice the apples ⅛ inch thick. If necessary, hold the apple slices in water with a splash of lemon juice. This will prevent the apple slices from browning.

3. Just before serving, whisk the vinaigrette vigorously and season with additional salt and pepper, if needed. Toss the frisée with the vinaigrette. Arrange the frisée on chilled plates, top with apple slices, about 2 tablespoons of grapes, 1 tablespoon of almonds, and 2 tablespoons of goat cheese. Serve immediately.

MIXED GREEN SALAD WITH WARM BRIE DRESSING

BRIE IS a soft cheese with a smooth white rind. To get the best flavor, make sure it is perfectly ripe. Press the piece you are considering to make sure it is plump yet slightly resilient to the touch. If possible, ask for a sample; it should taste buttery.

SERVES 6

1. Put the Brie in the oven at 200°F to soften.

2. Meanwhile, in a small saucepan over medium heat, heat the oil and sauté the shallots until they are translucent, about 3 minutes. Mix in the mustard. Remove from the heat and stir in the vinegar. Return to the heat and whisk in the softened cheese until it is fully melted and forms a uniform dressing. Season to taste with salt and pepper.

3. Toss with the greens and serve immediately. For additional texture, garnish with croutons and/or bacon bits.

6 ounces Brie (cut into ¼-inch slices, rind removed)

1 tbsp olive oil

2 tbsp minced shallots

1 tbsp Dijon mustard

¼ cup sherry wine vinegar

Salt and pepper as needed

4 cups mixed salad greens (romaine, radicchio, endive, red oak, etc.)

¾ cup Croutons (page 34) and/or bacon bits for garnish, optional

ALTHOUGH THIS dressing is best when served just after you prepare it, it can be made ahead of time and refrigerated. To serve, heat it in a saucepan or microwave, then mix well to incorporate the ingredients.

SPINACH AND ARUGULA SALAD
WITH STRAWBERRIES

1 tbsp red wine vinegar

1 tbsp balsamic vinegar

¼ tsp salt

3 tbsp olive oil

2 cups baby spinach leaves

2 cups arugula leaves

1 cup sliced strawberries

Freshly ground pepper

YOU CAN replace these greens with 2 cups frisée (or chicory, tender yellow inner leaves only) and 2 cups mixed mild greens.

T O SERVE this as an appetizer or a savory course, add a broiled goat cheese "button." Use four 1-oz buttons, or cut a log into 1-inch pieces; press fresh white bread crumbs and 1 tablespoon toasted sliced almonds over the surface, and broil until the cheese is hot and the bread crumbs on the top turn golden brown.

SERVES 4

1. For the vinaigrette, measure the vinegars and salt into a salad bowl, then gradually add the oil while whisking until emulsified.

2. Add the greens to the vinaigrette and toss gently, using a lifting motion. When the greens are lightly coated, transfer to chilled plates, top with the strawberries, and finish with a generous grinding of pepper.

RADISH SALAD WITH PEARS

36 small radishes, cut into very thin slices

2 pears (peeled, quartered, and cut into very thin slices)

¼ cup distilled white vinegar

2 tbsp olive oil

1 tsp sugar, or to taste

Salt and freshly ground pepper, to taste

3 tbsp plain yogurt

S ERVE THIS refreshing salad with slightly spicy foods. It's a great foil for bold flavors and brings a touch of sweetness to the plate.

SERVES 6

Combine the sliced radishes and pears in a large bowl. Add the vinegar, oil, sugar, salt, and pepper. Stir gently until well combined. Cover and marinate at room temperature for 15 minutes. Blend in the yogurt. Taste and adjust the seasoning, if necessary. Cover and refrigerate for at least 1 to 2 hours before serving.

ROASTED PEPPER AND FLAT-LEAF PARSLEY SALAD

FEATURING HERBS as a salad ingredient is typical throughout the Middle East. Be sure to smell the parsley before you buy it to check for a strong, pleasing aroma.

SERVES 6 TO 8

1. To prepare the red and green peppers, char the peppers in an open gas flame, in a broiler, or over hot coals until blackened on all surfaces. Transfer the charred peppers to a plastic bag or a covered bowl and allow them to cool until they can be easily handled. Pull away the blackened skin (use a paring knife if necessary to remove any parts that are not easy to pull away). Halve the peppers and remove the stem, seeds, and ribs. Cut the cleaned pepper flesh into neat dice.

2. Combine the diced peppers, serrano, onions, and cucumbers in a bowl. Whisk together the oil, lemon juice, and zest until evenly blended. Pour over the peppers. Cover and refrigerate for at least ½ hour, up to overnight.

3. Add the olives and oregano to the salad. Taste and adjust the seasoning with salt and pepper, if necessary. Fold in the parsley. Serve this salad chilled or at room temperature, to accompany grilled fish or seafood.

3 red peppers

3 green peppers

1 serrano (seeded and minced)

2 red onions, thinly sliced

3 cucumbers (peeled, seeded, and sliced thin)

⅓ cup olive oil

2 lemons, zest and juice

20 Kalamata olives, pitted and sliced

2 tsp minced oregano

Salt and pepper as needed

1 bunch flat-leaf parsley, leaves only

Bell Pepper

CHOPPED STEAKHOUSE SALAD
WITH MAYTAG BLUE CHEESE AND
RED WINE VINAIGRETTE

CHOPPED SALAD is a classic steakhouse offering. Maytag blue cheese gives it a rich, savory appeal. If unavailable, substitute any other good quality blue cheese. The croutons, made with roasted garlic, add a special touch to the dish.

SERVES 6

Combine the lettuce, pepper, cucumber, tomato, celery, radishes, corn, and capers in a large bowl. Add the vinaigrette to the salad ingredients, and toss until the salad is thoroughly coated. Arrange on chilled plates and scatter the crumbled cheese over the salad. Top with garlic croutons.

PEELING AND SEEDING TOMATOES

Bring a pot of water to a rolling boil. Fill a bowl with ice water and have it near the stove. Core the tomatoes and score an X through the skin at the bottom of each. Submerge a few tomatoes at a time in the boiling water for 15 to 30 seconds. Using a slotted spoon, transfer the tomatoes to the ice water. Drain the tomatoes and pull the skin away. Cut, slicing tomatoes in half crosswise. Plum tomatoes should be halved from top to bottom. Squeeze or scrape out the seeds and chop the flesh.

2 heads Bibb or Boston lettuce, torn into bite-size pieces

½ red pepper (peeled, seeded, and diced)

½ cucumber (peeled, seeded, and diced)

½ tomato (peeled, seeded, and diced; see note below)

½ diced celery stalk

4 radishes, sliced thin

Kernels cut from 1 fresh corn ear, grilled or broiled

2 tbsp drained capers

¾ cup Red Wine Vinaigrette (page 131)

⅓ cup crumbled Maytag blue cheese

Garlic Croutons (page 34)

GREEN BEANS WITH FRIZZLED PROSCIUTTO AND GRUYÈRE

I F YOU can find slender little haricots verts, use them in this salad. Large green beans can be left whole or sliced on the diagonal if you wish. Try Romano beans for an even richer bean taste. Cut the Gruyère into sticks that are about the same size and length as your green beans.

SERVES 8

1. Combine the lemon juice, vinegar, shallots, ½ teaspoon salt, and ¼ teaspoon pepper. Gradually whisk in 6 tablespoons olive oil. Season with additional salt and pepper, if needed. Set aside.

2. Bring a large pot of salted water to a boil. Add the green beans and cook until bright green and just barely tender to the bite, about 3 minutes. Drain the green beans and rinse with cold water until they feel cool. Drain well.

3. Toss the greens beans and the dressing together and let them marinate at room temperature for 10 minutes.

4. Heat the remaining olive oil in a sauté pan over medium-high heat until it shimmers. Add the prosciutto to the hot oil and cook until it "frizzles," about 2 minutes. Add the prosciutto and the Gruyère. Season with additional salt and pepper if necessary. Serve at room temperature.

3 tbsp lemon juice, or to taste

1 tbsp white wine vinegar

2 tbsp minced shallots

Salt and pepper as needed

7 tbsp extra-virgin olive oil

1 lb green beans, ends trimmed

¼ lb prosciutto, thinly sliced

¼ lb Gruyère cheese cut into sticks

SPINACH SALAD WITH MARINATED SHIITAKES AND RED ONIONS

2 tbsp peanut oil

3 cups sliced shiitake mushrooms

2 tsp reduced-sodium soy sauce

1 tbsp cider vinegar

⅛ tsp salt, or to taste

⅛ tsp freshly ground black pepper,
   or to taste

Dash Tabasco sauce

2 tsp olive oil

½ cup diced red onion

6 cups fresh spinach (trimmed, washed,
   and torn)

2 cups radicchio chiffonade

¼ cup Balsamic Vinaigrette (page 131)

SAUTÉED SHIITAKE mushrooms add an earthy flavor and heartiness to this salad, making it perfect for an autumn lunch.

SERVES 8

1. Heat the peanut oil in a sauté pan until it shimmers.

2. Add the mushrooms and sauté for 2 minutes. Add the soy sauce and cook until dry. Remove from the heat and place in a bowl. Add the vinegar, salt, pepper, and Tabasco sauce. Cool completely.

3. Add the olive oil to the pan and sauté the onion over low heat, stirring frequently, until translucent, about 5 to 7 minutes. Allow to cool.

4. Toss the mushrooms, onions, spinach, and radicchio together with the vinaigrette. Adjust the seasoning with salt and pepper to taste. Serve immediately.

PREPARED SALAD MIXES AND BAGGED GREENS

If you were ever tempted to skip the washing and drying step when using prepared, bagged lettuces and greens, you were no doubt concerned over news stories of illnesses related to fresh spinach and lettuce. No matter how many times the bag proclaims your spinach or Mediterranean mix was washed, you need to wash it again and dry it well.

There is another important message from the food borne outbreaks associated with lettuce and spinach, however. After stringent investigations, the source of the contamination was found, and it appears that the contamination occurred before the produce arrived at the store or a consumer's home kitchen. Cross contamination between pasture land and fields filled with growing produce infected the crops before they ever reached the processing plant.

There is nothing the consumer can do to make greens safe if they have come in contact with pathogens like *E. coli*. Washing, even cooking, does not remove or inactivate the pathogens. This does not mean that you should not eat these delicious, healthy vegetables. It is in the interest of your local markets to know the origins of your food. It is in your interest to opt for locally grown and processed vegetables. Large-scale operations have the potential to spread a food borne disease rapidly over a wide area. Scrupulous food processors do all they can to assure that foods stay safe at each step of processing.

TOMATO SALAD WITH WARM RICOTTA CHEESE

2 lb ricotta cheese

1 tsp salt

¼ cup olive oil

1 tsp coarse-grind black pepper

3 tbsp fine-dice shallots

3 tbsp red wine vinegar

2 tbsp sherry vinegar

Salt and freshly ground pepper, to taste

1 basil sprig

½ cup pure olive oil

½ cup extra-virgin olive oil

2 lb red, yellow, and orange cherry and
    pear tomatoes

3 tsp minced basil

Try this unique and interesting way of serving ricotta cheese for a twist on a favorite summer treat. The dressing includes a blend of olive oils to achieve a light flavor, but you can use all extra-virgin olive oil if you prefer.

SERVES 6

1. To make the ricotta cheese, preheat the oven to 350°F. Mix the ricotta and salt together well. Put the mixture in a small baking dish or casserole. Drizzle with the olive oil and pepper. Bake until browned on top and bubbling around the edges, about 20 minutes. Let sit for about 10 minutes before serving.

2. Meanwhile, combine the shallots, vinegars, salt, pepper, and basil in a bowl; let sit for 20 minutes.

3. Remove and discard the basil sprig. Whisk in the olive oils. Adjust the flavor as necessary with additional vinegar, salt, and pepper.

4. Cut any large tomatoes into halves or quarters; leave small ones whole. Add the tomatoes to the vinaigrette and toss to coat them evenly. Divide the tomatoes among six salad plates. Add a spoonful of the warm ricotta to each. Scatter the minced basil over the top of the salads.

TOMATO, ARUGULA, AND MOZZARELLA SALAD

6 ripe tomatoes, sliced ½ inch thick

12 oz fresh mozzarella, sliced
    ¼ inch thick

½ cup extra-virgin olive oil

¼ cup red wine vinegar

2 bunches stemmed arugula

Kosher salt and freshly cracked pepper,
    to taste

12 basil leaves, thinly sliced, for garnish

With just a few ingredients in the dish, you have to be sure that everything is as fresh and flavorful as possible, making this a seasonal favorite to enjoy when tomatoes are at their best in your market or garden.

SERVES 8

1. Overlap alternating tomato and mozzarella slices around the edge of a platter.

2. Whisk the olive oil and vinegar together in a small bowl. Combine the arugula with half of the oil and vinegar mixture in a large bowl and toss.

3. Place the arugula in the center of the platter. Drizzle the remaining oil and vinegar mixture over the tomatoes and mozzarella. Sprinkle with the salt and pepper and garnish with basil.

VINAIGRETTES can be more than simple combinations of oil and vinegar. You can add flavor and reduce calories from fat by introducing other ingredients. Here, we've roasted vegetables before juicing them, to make an intensely flavored juice that has enough body to allow you to cut back a bit on the oil.

ROASTING THE VEGETABLES

The basic information about roasting vegetables can be found on pages 20 and 21.

1. Choose a selection of vegetables with flavors that complement each other. A combination of mild flavors (zucchini and yellow squash), sweet flavors (carrots, onions, and peppers), tart flavors (tomatoes), and a touch of bitterness (celery) results in a balanced flavor.

2. Cut the vegetables into pieces that are about the same size so they cook evenly. Spread them in an even layer. Once you put the pan into the oven, remember to stir the vegetables so they roast evenly. Let the vegetables cool before you put them in a juicer or a blender to liquefy.

DRESSING THE SALAD

To dress tender lettuces and leafy greens without crushing them, combine the greens with the dressing first. Add garnishes (we added crumbled blue cheese, grilled onions slices, and pine nuts here) after the greens are lightly and evenly coated with dressing.

1. Put all the greens into a salad bowl. Spoon the dressing over the greens. A good guideline is to use about 2 or 3 tablespoons for each cup of greens.

2. Use a pair of tongs or a salad spoon and fork to lift and toss the greens. This action lets them roll gently in the dressing and distributes the dressing evenly for the best salad.

WINTER GREENS WITH WARM VEGETABLE VINAIGRETTE

¾ cup Roasted Vegetable Vinaigrette
 (recipe follows)

1½ cups torn frisée

1½ cups torn radicchio

1½ cups torn arugula

1½ cups baby spinach leaves

12 to 18 Belgian endive spears

12 grilled red onion slices

¾ cup crumbled blue cheese

6 tbsp toasted pine nuts

VINAIGRETTE

¾ cup chopped leeks

⅔ cup chopped peppers

⅔ cup chopped onions

⅔ cup chopped celery

½ cup chopped carrots

½ cup chopped zucchini

½ cup chopped yellow squash

¼ cup small-dice tomatoes,
 peeled and seeded

5 tbsp extra-virgin olive oil

Vegetable Broth (page 82), as needed

1 tbsp Dijon mustard

2 tsp crushed black peppercorns

1 tsp minced garlic

⅛ tsp salt

3 tbsp chopped herbs (parsley, chives,
 tarragon, and/or chervil)

W E'VE PAIRED some sturdy greens with an unusual dressing that is exceptionally low in fat but loaded with flavor. The dressing also is good to combine with leftover pasta, rice, or potatoes for a quick-to-prepare salad.

SERVES 4 TO 6

1. Heat the roasted vegetable vinaigrette in a small saucepan. Keep warm.

2. Wash and dry frisée, radicchio, arugula, and spinach. Place in a bowl and toss together.

3. Arrange the endive spears on a chilled platter or plates and top with the frisée mix. Garnish with the grilled onion slices, blue cheese, and the pine nuts. Drizzle the warm dressing over the salad.

Roasted Vegetable Vinaigrette

MAKES 2 CUPS

1. To roast the vegetables, toss the vegetables in the oil and roast in the oven at 350°F until tender, 45 to 60 minutes.

2. Pass the vegetables through a juicer. The vegetables should yield 9 fluid ounces/270 milliliters of roasted vegetable juice. If they do not, add enough vegetable broth to equal 9 fluid ounces.

3. Add the remaining ingredients, except the herbs, and purée to evenly incorporate. Thin the consistency of the vinaigrette with vegetable broth, if necessary.

4. Stir the herbs into the vinaigrette. Refrigerate until needed.

SOUTHERN-STYLE GREEN BEAN SALAD

1½ cups Chicken or Vegetable Broth
(pages 82–83)

1 tbsp cornstarch diluted with 1 tbsp water

3 tbsp tarragon vinegar

2 tbsp minced onion

1 tbsp olive oil

1 tbsp minced thyme

1 tbsp minced savory or 1 tsp dried savory

¼ cup minced flat-leaf parsley

½ tsp dry mustard

½ tsp salt

Freshly ground pepper, to taste

1 pound fresh green beans, trimmed and cut
diagonally in 1½-inch pieces

1 thick slice bacon, quartered

2 heads Boston lettuce

4 scallions, sliced thin

THIS TAKE on classic southern-style green beans is served on a bed of buttery Boston lettuce. We've included savory, an herb related to the mint family. Some describe its flavor as a cross between thyme and mint. Savory has a strong taste, so if it's your first experience with it, you may want to cut back the amount we suggest here. Prepare the beans and the dressing up to 24 hours ahead of time, but reserve them separately until just before you assemble the finished salad.

SERVES 6 TO 8

1. To make the dressing, bring the broth to a simmer over medium heat and add the diluted cornstarch. Return the broth to a simmer and continue to cook for another 2 minutes. Remove the broth from the heat and pour it into a bowl. When the broth has cooled to room temperature, add the tarragon vinegar, onion, oil, thyme, savory, parsley, mustard, salt, and pepper.

2. To prepare the green beans, trim the ends from the green beans and cut them on the bias into 2-inch pieces. Cook the green beans with the bacon in boiling water until tender, 6 to 8 minutes. Using tongs, transfer the green beans to a large bowl of ice water. Cool the green beans for 1 minute, and then drain on layers of paper towels. Discard the bacon.

3. To assemble the salad, toss together the green beans, lettuce, and scallions with the dressing until the ingredients are evenly coated. Serve directly from the salad bowl or on chilled plates.

SHAVED VEGETABLE SALAD

Other seasonal vegetables may be used, such as whole haricots verts, Romano beans, cucumbers, Belgian endive, or carrots.

SERVES 6

1. To make the dressing, combine 1 tablespoon lemon juice, the garlic, vinegar, salt, and pepper in a small bowl. Let sit at room temperature for 30 minutes. Gradually whisk in 6 tablespoons olive oil until thoroughly combined. Taste and adjust the seasoning with additional salt and pepper, if needed.

2. No more than 2 hours before serving the salad, cut the vegetables into paper-thin slices with a sharp knife or a mandoline (see note at right). If you are not serving the salad immediately, toss the fennel with 2 teaspoons lemon juice, seal in a plastic bag, and refrigerate; wrap the other shaved vegetables in a clean, damp dish towel or napkin and refrigerate.

3. When you are ready to serve the salad, toss all the shaved vegetables together in a bowl with the remaining 2 tablespoons of olive oil. Put them on chilled plates or a serving platter and sprinkle the vegetables with salt and pepper. Remove the garlic from the dressing and whisk it until thoroughly blended. Drizzle the dressing over the vegetables. Garnish the salad with parsley.

1 tbsp fresh lemon juice, or as needed

1 garlic clove, crushed

1 tsp champagne vinegar

Salt and pepper as needed

½ cup extra-virgin olive oil, or as needed

3 large fennel bulbs (trimmed of stalks and halved from top to bottom)

6 celery stalks

6 radishes

1 small summer squash

1 red or yellow pepper (seeded, deribbed, and cut into ½-inch strips)

¼ cup chopped flat-leaf parsley

THE MANDOLINE, named for the stroking motion the hand makes while using it, is an indispensable tool in most professional kitchens. The French model may be purchased in specialty cookware stores. An inexpensive Japanese version is found in Asian food markets. Exercise extreme caution when using this tool, as the blade is razor sharp.

TWO-CABBAGE SLAW WITH AVOCADO AND RED ONION

2 cups finely shredded leaf spinach

1 cup finely shredded red cabbage

1 cup finely shredded savoy cabbage

½ cup red onion julienne

¾ cup Grapefruit Vinaigrette (see page 132)

1 avocado

1 grapefruit (peeled, cut into segments; see
    note on page 161)

2 tsp cracked black peppercorns

T HIS VEGETABLE salad has brilliant color and a taste to match. The grape-fruit vinaigrette gives a definite boost to the dish.

SERVES 4

1. Toss together the spinach, cabbages, red onion, and ½ cup of the vinaigrette in a salad bowl.

2. Peel the avocado, slice the flesh about ¼ inch thick, and toss gently with the remaining vinaigrette to coat.

3. Arrange the avocado on top of the cabbage mixture and top with the grape-fruit segments and cracked peppercorns.

Savoy Cabbage

TOMATO SALAD WITH POTATOES AND OLIVES

For the best flavor, combine the potatoes while still very warm with the other ingredients in this salad.

SERVES 6

1. Scrub the potatoes well, if leaving the skins intact. Cook in simmering salted water until they are tender enough to pierce easily with a skewer or the tip of a paring knife, about 25 to 40 minutes, depending on the size of the potatoes.

2. Drain the potatoes and return them to the pot. Place the pot over low heat and let the potatoes dry, shaking the pan frequently, until the steam has been driven off the potatoes. Transfer them to a shallow dish or pan and let them cool until they can be handled (they should still be quite warm, however). Cut or slice the potatoes and place in a salad bowl.

3. Add the tomatoes, onion, olives, capers, and oregano. Drizzle with a little olive oil and toss gently to combine the ingredients (be gentle so that the potatoes don't break apart). Taste the salad and adjust the seasoning with salt and pepper, if necessary.

4. Serve the salad at room temperature. (This salad may be prepared up to 24 hours in advance; store under refrigeration until ready to serve.)

12 red bliss potatoes

2 yellow slicing tomatoes (seeded and cut into medium dice)

2 red slicing tomatoes (seeded and cut into medium dice)

1 red onion, sliced thinly with the grain

½ cup pitted oil-cured olives

1 tbsp drained capers

2 tsp dry oregano

¼ cup olive oil, or to taste

Salt and pepper, as needed

ROASTED BEET AND ORANGE SALAD

TAKE ADVANTAGE of the amazing variety of beets available at local farm-stands. Choose among red, golden, or candy-stripe varieties, or try using a combination of different varieties of beets for this colorful salad. As an alternative to serving this salad on individual salad plates, alternate the dressed beets with the orange slices on a serving platter or in a large serving bowl, topped with slices of red onion, shelled walnut halves, and crumbled goat cheese.

SERVES 8

1. Preheat oven to 375°F.
2. Place the beets in a baking dish, add about ¼ inch of water, and cover tightly with aluminum foil. Roast the beets until tender, about 20 minutes. Allow to cool slightly, and slip off their skins. Cut the beets into quarters.
3. Blend together the olive oil, vinegar, lemon juice, salt, and cayenne pepper. Toss the beets in the dressing while they are still warm.
4. Divide the beets into eight portions and serve each portion with five orange segments, topped with 1 tablespoon each of the onion and walnut, and 2 tablespoons of crumbled goat cheese.

8 beets, green tops trimmed

5 tbsp olive oil

2 tbsp red wine vinegar

2 tbsp lemon juice

1 tsp salt, or to taste

Pinch cayenne pepper

40 orange segments (skin removed, see note below)

½ cup red onion julienne

½ cup shelled walnut halves

1 cup crumbled goat cheese

TO PREPARE citrus segments, cut away both ends of the fruit. Using a sharp paring knife, follow the curve of the fruit and cut away the skin, pith, and membrane, leaving the flesh completely exposed. Working to release each segment and keep it intact, slice the connective membrane on either side of the segment.

ARTICHOKE AND OLIVE SALAD

1 tsp anchovy paste

½ tsp arrowroot

⅓ cup Vegetable Broth (page 82)

3 tbsp red wine vinegar

3 tbsp extra-virgin olive oil

¼ tsp dried oregano

¼ tsp ground black pepper

1 cup artichoke hearts (cooked if fresh, thawed if frozen), quartered

½ cup peas, cooked if fresh, thawed if frozen

⅓ cup carrot julienne

¼ cup picholine olives, pitted and cut into slivers

¼ cup niçoise olives, pitted and cut into slivers

3 cups mesclun greens, washed and dried (about 6 oz)

2 tbsp grated Asiago cheese

1 tbsp chopped parsley

I F YOUR market has a selection of olives, try your favorites or explore some new varieties. If you aren't a fan of anchovies, don't be put off by them in the dressing. They add a rich, savory taste that isn't at all fishy.

SERVES 4

1. Blend the anchovy paste, arrowroot, and 1 tablespoon of the broth together in a small bowl. Bring the remaining broth to a boil in a small saucepan and add the anchovy mixture, stirring constantly until thickened. Remove from the heat, stir in the vinegar, and cool completely. Gradually whisk in the oil. Stir in the oregano and pepper.

2. Combine the artichoke hearts, peas, carrot, and olives in a bowl. Stir in the dressing, cover, and marinate for 1 hour.

3. Divide the greens and arrange as a bed on four chilled salad plates. Mound the artichoke mixture in the center or the greens and garnish with the cheese and parsley. Serve immediately.

CHINESE LONG BEAN SALAD WITH TANGERINES AND SHERRY-MUSTARD VINAIGRETTE

CHINESE LONG beans also are known as yard-long beans, but they are seldom left to grow to this length. They are part of the same plant family as the black-eyed pea. Green beans may be substituted if Chinese long beans are unavailable. Use mandarin oranges or navel oranges if tangerines aren't in season.

SERVES 4

1. Trim the beans and cut into 1½-inch lengths. Cook in boiling water until barely tender, about 3 minutes. Drain and cool.

2. Working over a large bowl to catch the juices, cut the tangerine sections out from between the membranes.

3. Add the beans, onions, and sunflower seeds to the tangerine sections and juice. Season with the salt and pepper, and set aside.

4. Place the vegetable broth in a small saucepan over medium heat. Whisk the cornstarch with 1 teaspoon water in a small bowl and add it to the broth; stir until the mixture thickens. Remove from the heat and set aside to cool.

5. Combine the olive oil, vinegar, orange juice, mustard, brown sugar, shallot, and garlic in a small bowl. Then whisk into the thickened broth. Season to taste with salt and pepper as needed.

6. Toss the bean mixture with the vinaigrette.

1 pound Chinese long beans

2 tangerines, peeled

½ cup thinly sliced Vidalia onions

¼ cup toasted sunflower seeds

¼ tsp salt

⅛ tsp ground black pepper

½ cup Vegetable Broth (page 82)

1 tsp cornstarch

2 tbsp olive oil

1 tbsp sherry vinegar

1 tbsp fresh orange juice

1 tbsp Dijon mustard

½ tbsp light-brown sugar

1 shallot, minced

1 tsp minced garlic

Salt and pepper as needed

MOROCCAN CARROT SALAD

2 lb carrots (peeled and thinly sliced)

2 garlic cloves

4 tbsp olive oil

Juice of 1 lemon

1 tbsp ground cumin

Small pinch of cayenne pepper

1 tsp minced cilantro

1 tsp minced parsley

2 onions, finely chopped

1 cup chopped dates

THIS UNUSUAL carrot salad gets its mysteriously rich flavor from melting dates with onions to a soft purée.

SERVES 8

1. In a medium saucepan, combine the carrots and garlic. Add water to cover by 1 or 2 inches. Bring to a simmer and cook until tender, about 5 minutes. Using a slotted spoon, transfer the carrots to a bowl.

2. Cook the cooking liquid over medium heat to reduce to ½ cup. Whisk in 2 tablespoons of the olive oil and the lemon juice to the reduced cooking liquid. Pour the mixture over the carrots. Add the cumin, cayenne, cilantro, and parsley. Set aside.

3. Heat the remaining olive oil in a medium saucepan over medium heat. Add the onions and sauté until translucent, about 5 minutes. Add the dates and cook until the dates are softened. Toss the onion and date mixture with the carrots. Let cool. Cover and refrigerate for 1 to 2 hours.

Entrees

AIN DISHES THAT feature vegetables are a wonderful way to add variety and flavor to your meals. Throughout this chapter are recipes for entrees that are either made primarily or exclusively from vegetables, or that feature a special vegetable paired with meat, fish, or poultry.

In addition to the recipes in this chapter, you can feature a selection of vegetables from the next chapter, Side Dishes, to make a satisfying main course. Or you might choose to serve one of the recipes in this chapter in a smaller portion, as either an appetizer or a side dish.

Vegetables to Stuff and Bake

Some vegetables make perfect containers to hold a savory filling that can be topped and baked. Preparing the vegetables requires no special skills. Eggplant, zucchini and other soft-skinned squashes, peppers, and tomatoes are all perfect for stuffing, once you've prepared them properly.

SELECT THE VEGETABLES FOR STUFFING

Since stuffed vegetables are typically baked, it is helpful to choose vegetables of a relatively uniform size. When they are nearly the same size and shape, they will bake evenly and you won't end up with some that are fully cooked, some that are overcooked, and some that are undercooked. Eggplants,

White Mushrooms

zucchinis, and similar vegetables can be made as single servings, or you can opt to use one or two large vegetables, and then cut them into portions.

PREPARE THE VEGETABLE FOR STUFFING

TO PREPARE EGGPLANT, ZUCCHINI, AND SOFT-SKINNED SQUASHES, rinse the vegetable well and cut away the stem end. Next, cut the vegetable in half lengthwise. Scoop out the seeds and some of the flesh to create a space for the stuffing. Use a serving spoon, a grapefruit spoon, or a melon baller to scoop out the vegetable. Leave an even layer of the flesh behind and try not to poke through the skin or peel. You may be able to chop the flesh you scooped out and incorporate it into the stuffing.

TO PREPARE TOMATOES, cut out the stem end (you can use a paring knife, a melon baller, or a tool called a tomato witch). For small tomatoes, you may choose to make two cuts so you can open out the tomato like a flower. Make a cut from the stem end toward the bottom of the tomato, but leave the bottom of the tomato intact. Make a second cut so that you create four equal-sized "petals." Scoop out the seeds from the interior. You can make a thin slice on the bottom of the tomato to create a flat surface to keep the tomato from tipping over after you place it in a baking dish.

TO PREPARE MUSHROOMS FOR STUFFING, pull or cut away the stem, leaving behind the cap. If you trim the stems before you cut them away, you can save the stems to add to broths, soups, stews, or to add to the mushroom stuffing. Scrape out the gills from the underside of the cap.

TO PREPARE PEPPERS, cut away the top (the stem end) just below the widest portion, and pull out the seeds and ribs. To keep peppers from falling over in the pan, cut a thin slice away from the bottom of the pepper, making sure to cut just enough to make a flat surface. If you cut away too much, you'll create an opening through which the stuffing might ooze out as the peppers bake.

EGGPLANT can be found in a number of different varieties. Western, or globe, eggplant is the most familiar in this country, large, with glossy black skin and green leaves. Italian or baby eggplant, also referred to as a small globe eggplant, is similar in shape. Japanese or Asian eggplants are long and slim, more like a zucchini, with brown leaves and tender flesh. There is even a variety of white eggplant.

PREPARING EGGPLANT

Eggplant is technically a fruit, and is related to both tomatoes and potatoes. As with potatoes, the soft, spongy, white flesh tends to darken once it is cut.

Unlike potatoes, however, holding eggplant in water or sprinkling it with lemon juice or vinegar is not recommended. Cooked eggplant does darken in color, so, although you should cut them open just before you plan to cook them, some darkening is not a concern.

BAKING EGGPLANT

You can bake eggplant whole. It will cook in its skin into a rich, smooth texture that is easy to puree. To roast whole eggplant, pierce the skin in a few places so it doesn't explode. Or, you can stuff it, as we have done here.

Eggplant contains a lot of moisture that is driven out of the vegetable as it bakes. The filling (we used lentils here, but there are many other options including meat and bread stuffings) absorbs the moisture and takes on a great flavor and texture. Leave room around the eggplant as it bakes so that it develops a dark, roasted exterior.

ROASTED EGGPLANT STUFFED WITH CURRIED LENTILS

½ cup brown lentils

2 cups Vegetable Broth (page 82) or water

2 small globe eggplants

1 tbsp olive oil, plus more for greasing pan

¼ cup minced yellow onion

2 tsp minced garlic

½ tsp grated gingerroot

½ cup minced white mushrooms

½ tsp lemon zest

½ tsp curry powder

¼ tsp ground cinnamon

¼ tsp ground turmeric

Salt and pepper as needed

SMALL GLOBE eggplants are the perfect size for this dish and sometimes can be found in the supermarket produce section or at farm stands. If you cannot find them, however, use a larger eggplant, leaving the same size wall but cooking for up to 10 minutes longer; cut it into serving portions after baking.

SERVES 4

1. Bring the lentils and broth or water to a boil in a small pot. Cover and reduce the heat to low. Simmer until the lentils are tender to the bite, 25 to 30 minutes. Remove from the heat and set the lentils aside, still in their cooking liquid.

2. Preheat the oven to 350°F. Grease an 8 × 11-inch baking pan. Halve the eggplants lengthwise and scoop out some of the flesh, leaving a ½- to ¾-inch wall. Mince the scooped flesh and set aside. Transfer the eggplant halves to the prepared baking pan, skin side down.

3. Heat a large skillet over medium heat. Add the oil and heat until it shimmers. Add the onion, garlic, and ginger. Sauté, stirring occasionally, until the onion is golden brown, 6 to 8 minutes. Add the minced eggplant, mushrooms, lemon zest, curry, cinnamon, turmeric, and salt and pepper to taste. Sauté over medium heat, stirring occasionally, until the mushrooms begin to release some moisture, about 5 minutes.

4. Drain the lentils, reserving the cooking liquid, and add the lentils to the eggplant and mushroom mixture. Add enough of the cooking liquid (about ¼ cup) to moisten the vegetables well, and then simmer until the liquid is reduced, 6 to 8 minutes.

5. Fill the hollowed eggplant halves with the lentil mixture. Cover with aluminum foil and bake until the eggplants are tender and cooked through, 35 to 40 minutes. Serve immediately.

SPICY EGGPLANT, WILD MUSHROOM, AND TOMATO CASSEROLE

YOU CAN prepare this dish in one large casserole or in individual gratin dishes. It can be assembled and kept in the refrigerator for up to 2 days prior to baking. In that case, increase the baking time by 10 or 12 minutes.

SERVES 4

1. Preheat the oven to 400°F.
2. Heat 1 tablespoon of the oil in a large skillet over medium-high heat until it shimmers. Add the sliced eggplants and zucchinis in batches (the slices should not overlap) and sauté on the first side until golden brown, 1 to 2 minutes. Turn and sauté until golden brown on the second side, and then another minute on each side. Remove the slices from the pan as they are cooked and place on absorbent paper to drain briefly. Repeat until all of the eggplants and zucchini are cooked, adding more oil to the skillet as necessary as you work.
3. Return the skillet to the heat and add enough oil to lightly coat the pan. Add the red and green peppers and scallions and sauté, stirring frequently, until the peppers are very hot and limp, about 2 minutes.
4. Grease a casserole dish and add the eggplants, tomatoes, zucchini, red and green peppers, and scallions in layers, finishing with a layer of eggplant.
5. To make the sauce, combine the cornstarch with 2 tablespoons of the chicken broth to make a slurry and set aside. Heat the sesame oil in a saucepan over medium heat. Add the garlic and ginger and sauté, stirring constantly, until aromatic, about 1 minute. Add the remaining chicken broth, the hot bean paste, rice vinegar, sugar, soy sauce, and sherry. Bring the sauce to a full boil for 1 minute. Gradually add the cornstarch slurry, adding just enough to lightly thicken the sauce (you may not need to add all the slurry, or you may wish to make a bit more slurry for a thicker sauce).
6. Pierce the eggplant layer with a kitchen fork in several places. Pour the sauce over the eggplant. Bake the casserole until the eggplant and zucchini are completely tender, 30 to 40 minutes. Serve the casserole accompanied with hot steamed rice.

2 tbsp peanut or corn oil, plus as needed

3 eggplants (peeled, sliced ½ inch thick)

3 zucchinis, sliced ½ thick

½ cup fine-dice red pepper

½ cup fine-dice green pepper

1 tbsp chopped scallions

2 tomatoes, sliced ½ inch thick

2 tbsp cornstarch, or as needed

½ cup Chicken Broth (page 83)

⅓ cup sesame oil

1 tsp minced garlic

1 tsp minced ginger

1 tbsp hot bean paste

¾ cup rice vinegar

½ cup sugar

½ cup soy sauce

½ cup sherry wine

2 cups cooked rice, hot

EGGPLANT ROLLATINI

18 eggplant slices, cut lengthwise

1½ cups ricotta cheese

2 cups grated mozzarella cheese

½ cup grated Romano

½ cup minced flat-leaf parsley

Salt and pepper as needed

4 large eggs

⅔ cup milk

2 cups flour

2 cups dry bread crumbs, or as needed

4 cups canola oil, use as needed

3 cups Basic Tomato Sauce (page 260), heated

TO PREPARE eggplant for frying: Many recipes instruct you to salt eggplant before you cook it. Some say this step is necessary because it draws out any bitterness in the eggplant. We think it is a good idea if you plan to fry the eggplant, even if it isn't large or bitter. Drawing out some of the moisture helps to collapse the vegetable a little, so that it doesn't act like a sponge, soaking up too much oil as you fry it. Peel and slice the eggplant as directed in your recipe. Place in a colander, sprinkle liberally with kosher salt, and let rest until the salt begins to draw out some of the liquid, about 20 minutes. Rinse the eggplant thoroughly, let drain, and blot dry.

I NSTEAD OF eggplant, you can make this dish with large zucchini or yellow squash. If you wish, add chopped vegetables to the filling mixture for a heartier entrée.

SERVES 6

1. Peel, salt, and rinse the eggplant if desired (see the note on preparing eggplant at left).

2. Blend the ricotta, 1 cup mozzarella cheese, the Romano, parsley, ½ teaspoon salt, ¼ teaspoon pepper, and 1 egg until smooth. Keep refrigerated until needed.

2. Blend the remaining 3 eggs with the milk in a shallow bowl to make an egg wash. Put the flour in a second shallow bowl and season with a pinch of salt and pepper. Put the bread crumbs in a third shallow bowl. Dip the eggplant slices one at a time into the flour, then the egg wash, and last, the bread crumbs, patting the crumbs evenly over all sides of the eggplant. Transfer the eggplant slices to a plate or baking sheet.

3. Pour about ½ inch of oil into a deep skillet and heat over medium-high heat until the oil shimmers. Add the breaded eggplant slices to the hot oil, a few pieces at a time, and fry on the first side until golden brown, about 2 minutes. Turn the eggplant and continue to fry until golden and crisp on the second side, 2 minutes. Transfer to a plate lined with paper towels; continue until all of the eggplant is fried.

4. Preheat the oven to 350°F.

5. Spread some of tomato sauce in a rectangular baking dish or individual casseroles. Spread 2 or 3 tablespoons of the filling mixture over a slice of fried eggplant and roll the slice up lengthwise. Place the roll into the baking dish seam side down. Continue until all of the eggplant slices are filled and rolled. Spoon the remaining tomato sauce over the rolls, top with the remaining mozzarella. Cover the baking dish loosely with foil and bake until the ricotta mixture is very hot and the mozzarella cheese has melted, about 20 minutes. Remove the cover and continue to bake until the cheese is golden brown, another 10 minutes. Serve directly from the baking dish or casserole on heated plates.

CAPELLINI WITH GRILLED VEGETABLES

T**HE TASTE** and texture of grilled vegetables with pasta are always a marvelous combination. You can use your broiler if you prefer. We offer a colorful mix of red onion, zucchini, yellow squash, and fennel, plus a handful of herbs tossed in. You can grill the vegetables ahead if you wish and let them stand at room temperature.

SERVES 8

1. Preheat the grill and bring a large pot of salted water to a boil for the pasta.
2. Combine the vinegar, ⅔ cup olive oil, salt, and pepper to make a vinaigrette. Toss the onions, zucchinis, squash, and fennel with the vinaigrette and grill until tender, 8 to 12 minutes. When the vegetables are cool enough to handle, cut them into 1½-inch dice.
3. Cook the capellini in the boiling water until al dente, about 6 to 8 minutes. Drain well.
4. Heat the remaining tablespoon of oil in a sauté pan. Add the shallot and garlic. Sauté until aromatic, about 1 minute. Add the grilled vegetables, tomatoes, and wine. Heat thoroughly. Season with the herbs and additional salt and pepper as needed. Adjust the consistency with the broth, if necessary.
5. Toss the capellini with about half of the Gorgonzola cheese, and top with the vegetable mixture. Garnish with the remaining Gorgonzola.

½ cup balsamic vinegar

⅔ cup plus 1 tbsp olive oil

Salt and pepper as needed

2 red onions, cut into ½-inch rings

2 zucchinis, cut into ½-inch thick slices

2 yellow squash, cut into ½-inch thick slices

1 fennel bulb, cut into ½-inch rings

1 pound capellini

1 shallot, minced

2 garlic cloves, minced

2 lb grape tomatoes, halved lengthwise

½ cup white wine

1 tbsp chopped parsley

1 tbsp chopped basil

½ cup Vegetable Broth (page 82), optional

6 oz Gorgonzola, broken into
    small pieces

PASTA DISHES

Pasta shapes like bowties, as well as long shapes like cappellini, add substance and visual appeal, as well as a wonderful texture, to vegetable main dishes. Restaurant kitchens sometimes prepare both the pasta and the vegetables in advance and then quickly finish them once the customer has ordered a dish. You can use some of the same techniques to streamline your work. There is a noticeable difference in flavor when you cook and serve the pasta all in one step, however. In addition, you'll have the benefit of some pasta cooking water to make any last minute adjustments to the consistency of your sauce; this common practice does more than just thin the sauce, it also adds a bit of body, since the starch from the pasta is in the cooking water.

ASPARAGUS WITH SHIITAKES, BOWTIE PASTA, AND SPRING PEAS

THE APPEARANCE of peas at the farmer's market signifies the arrival of spring, and this dish takes advantage of three different varieties of peas.

SERVES 8

1. Bring a medium saucepan of salted water to a boil to blanch the peas and a large pot of salted water to boil to cook the pasta. Preheat the broiler.

2. Toss the asparagus with the oil and 1 teaspoon of salt. Place in a baking pan under the broiler, turning occasionally, until tender and lightly browned, about 8 minutes. Slice the asparagus on a diagonal into 1-inch pieces and reserve.

3. Cook each type of pea separately in the boiling water until almost tender, about 2 minutes each. Remove them from the water using a slotted spoon or small strainer and rinse with cold water to stop the cooking. Drain well and reserve. (The vegetables can be prepared in advance and held in covered containers in the refrigerator for up to 12 hours.)

4. Cook the pasta in boiling water until tender to the bite, about 10 to 12 minutes. Drain well, reserving some of the pasta water to adjust the consistency of the dish.

5. Heat the butter in a sauté pan until it begins to turn brown. Add the shiitakes and shallots and sauté until the shallots and mushrooms are light brown, 2 to 3 minutes. Add the asparagus, green peas, snow peas, sugar snap peas, marjoram, 1 teaspoon salt, and a pinch of pepper. Sauté, stirring or tossing, until the vegetables are thoroughly heated, about 3 minutes. Add the hot pasta and toss the pasta with the cooked vegetables and scallions until evenly blended. Add a little of the pasta water to moisten the dish if necessary. Serve on heated plates and top with shaved Parmesan.

3 lb asparagus, peeled and trimmed

3 tbsp olive oil

Salt and pepper as needed

1 cup snow peas

1 cup sugar snap peas

2 cups frozen green peas

2 cups dried bowtie pasta

1 tbsp butter

3 cups sliced shiitakes

3 tbsp minced shallots

3 tbsp chopped marjoram

2 bunches scallions, split lengthwise, thinly sliced

Parmesan, shaved, to taste

TORTELLI WITH BITTER GREENS AND RICOTTA

FRESH PASTA DOUGH

3 cups all-purpose flour

1 tsp salt

5 eggs

4 tbsp olive oil

1 cup dandelion greens, leaves only

1 cup beet greens, leaves only

1 cup mustard greens, leaves only

2 tbsp olive oil

½ cup minced onions

¼ cup minced garlic

1½ cups whole milk or part-skim ricotta

1 cup grated mozzarella

Salt and pepper as needed

¼ cup butter

Grated Parmesan to pass on the side

THIS RECIPE uses just the leaves from a selection of cooking greens: beet greens, dandelion greens, and mustard greens are used here, but we like to change the combination, or feature just one, depending on what the market is featuring.

SERVES 8

1. To make the pasta dough in a food processor, place the flour and salt in the bowl and turn the food processor on. Add the eggs and olive oil through the feed tube with the processor running and continue to mix just until the mixture is evenly blended. It will look like a damp, coarse meal. If the mixture forms a ball that rides on top of the blade, it is too wet. In that case, add a few teaspoons of flour and continue to process briefly. If the dough will not hold together when you press it in your hand, add more water a teaspoon at a time. Remove the dough from the processor, knead it once or twice to make a smooth ball, and wrap in plastic wrap. Let the dough rest at room temperature for 1 hour before rolling it out.

2. Bring a large pot of salted water to a rolling boil over high heat. Add the dandelion, beet, and mustard greens, and cook until they are wilted and tender, about 3 minutes. Drain in a colander, rinse with cold water, and drain again. Gather the leaves into a ball, place them on a clean dish towel, and twist the towel to squeeze out the excess moisture. Chop the squeezed greens finely.

3. To make the filling, heat the olive oil in a sauté pan over medium-high heat. Add the onions and garlic and sauté, stirring frequently, until the onions are tender and translucent, 3 to 4 minutes. Transfer to a bowl and cool to room temperature. Stir in the chopped greens, ricotta, and mozzarella. Season generously with salt and pepper.

4. Divide the pasta dough in half. Working with one piece of dough at a time, roll out the dough using a pasta machine or a rolling pin. Cut each sheet of dough in half, so that you have two pieces of roughly the same dimensions. Drop generous tablespoons of the filling mixture onto one half of the dough sheet, spacing them about 3 inches apart. Gently lay the second half of the sheet over the filling, letting the dough drape over the filling. Use your fingers to gently press the dough around the filling and press out any air. Use a sharp knife or a rotary cutter (pizza wheel) to cut the tortelli apart. Use the tines of a fork to seal all around the edges. Transfer the filled tortelli to a sheet pan lined with parchment or waxed paper. Continue until you have filled all of the pasta.

5. Bring a large pot of salted water to a gentle boil over medium-high heat. Add the tortelli, working in batches so that you don't crowd the pot, and simmer until the pasta is cooked through and the filling is very hot, 4 to 8 minutes (the cooking time will vary depending on how dry the pasta is when it goes into the pot). Lift the tortelli from the water with a slotted spoon or spider, letting the water drain away. Continue until all the tortelli are cooked.

6. Heat the butter in a large sauté pan until it is very hot and is just starting to smell very nutty. Add the drained tortelli and toss or stir gently until they are evenly coated with the hot butter. Season with salt and pepper and serve in heated bowls or plates with grated Parmesan on the side.

FETTUCCINE WITH CORN, SQUASH, CHILES, CRÈME FRAÎCHE, AND CILANTRO

CREAMY, SWEET, and spicy, this pasta dish is a fresh alternative to the more commonly found dishes of Italian origin. Crème fraîche is a cultured cream that is very similar in flavor to sour cream. Its rich texture softens the spiciness of the chiles and provides a velvety sauce for this luscious dish.

SERVES 8

1. Bring a large pot of salted water to a boil for the pasta.

2. Heat the olive oil in a large saucepan or Dutch oven over medium heat until it shimmers. Add the onions and zucchini and sauté, stirring frequently, until the onions are translucent and the zucchini is tender, about 8 to 10 minutes. Add the corn, jalapeños, and garlic and sauté, stirring frequently, until the corn is very hot, another 5 minutes. Add the vegetable broth and season with the salt and pepper.

3. Cook the pasta until tender to the bite, about 8 to 10 minutes. Drain the pasta, add it to the sauté pan, and mix with the sauce.

4. Divide into pasta bowls and add a dollop of crème fraîche to each serving. Garnish with the cilantro.

2 tbsp olive oil

1 cup diced onions

1 cup diced zucchini

4 cups corn kernels, fresh or frozen

2 jalapeños, seeded and diced

2 tsp minced garlic

2 cups Vegetable Broth (page 82)

1 tbsp salt, or to taste

¼ tsp freshly ground black pepper

1 lb fettuccine noodles

½ cup crème fraîche

¼ cup chopped cilantro

CHICKEN AND VEGETABLE KEBABS

¼ cup lemon juice

¼ cup olive oil

2 tbsp chopped oregano

1 tbsp chopped mint

1 tbsp chopped parsley

Salt and pepper as needed

1½ lb skinless, boneless chicken breast, cut
   into 24 strips

18 slices zucchini or yellow squash,
   ½-inch-thick, optional

1 fennel bulb, cut into 12 wedges

1 red onion, cut into 12 wedges

12 large white mushroom caps,
   stems removed

A CLASSIC DISH. If you are using bamboo skewers, let them soak in cold water before stringing the ingredients on them. The soaking keeps the bamboo from scorching on the grill.

SERVES 4

1. Soak bamboo skewers in cool water for about 30 minutes before you begin to assemble the kebabs.

2. Combine the lemon juice, olive oil, oregano, mint, and parsley in a small bowl. Stir in salt and pepper. Place the chicken in a large zipper-close bag, add the marinade, and seal. Turn to coat the chicken with the marinade. Marinate in the refrigerator for about 20 minutes. Remove the chicken from the bag; discard the marinade.

3. Preheat a grill to medium-high.

4. Thread the ingredients on the skewers, alternating chicken, zucchini, fennel, red onion, and mushrooms. Season with a little additional salt and pepper, and grill until the vegetables are tender and the chicken is cooked through, turning as necessary, about 10 minutes total. Serve the kebabs immediately on a heated platter or plates.

VEGETABLE BURGERS

1 cup grated carrots

⅓ cup grated celery

¾ cup grated onions

¼ cup minced red pepper

¾ cup minced mushrooms

½ cup minced scallions

1 egg, lightly beaten

¼ cup chopped pecans

1 tsp chopped thyme

1 tbsp minced garlic

Salt and pepper as needed

1 tbsp olive oil

1½ cups matzo meal

¼ cup peanut oil, as needed for panfrying

6 slices Meunster or Cheddar cheese

6 sandwich rolls

½ cup baby spinach leaves

6 tomato slices

6 red onion slices

To make this recipe easier to prepare, grate and mince all the vegetables in a food processor. Add the matzo meal gradually and use just enough to help bind the vegetable mixture. It should hold together but still be moist.

SERVES 6

1. Combine the carrots, celery, onions, red pepper, mushrooms, scallions, egg, pecans, thyme, garlic, salt, pepper, and olive oil in a large bowl and mix together by hand with a wooden spoon until evenly blended. Add 1 cup of the matzo meal and mix until blended and sticky enough to hold together, adding more matzo meal, if necessary. Shape the mixture into patties using about ¾ cup of the mixture per patty.

2. Heat a fry pan over medium-high heat. Add enough of the oil to film the pan generously. Add the burgers and panfry on the first side until browned and crisp, 3 to 4 minutes. Turn the burgers over, and continue to panfry until crisp and golden on the second side, another 3 minutes. Top each burger with a slice of cheese, cover the pan, and cook just until the cheese melts, about 1 minute. (Prepare the burgers in batches if they don't fit easily into your pan, adding more oil to the pan between batches, if necessary.)

3. Serve the burgers on a roll or bun, topped with the spinach and slices of tomato and red onion.

EGGPLANT AND HAVARTI SANDWICHES

B ROILING THE eggplant for this sandwich gives it a crisp texture on the outside while the inside stays smooth and creamy. The red onion adds a crisp bite to the sandwich and a slightly sweet flavor. The ingredients come together to make a sandwich that pairs well with the Cream of Tomato Soup with Rice and Basil found on page 55.

SERVES 6

¼ cup olive oil

½ cup balsamic vinegar

1 tsp minced garlic

Salt and pepper as needed

Six ½-inch slices eggplant

6 hard rolls, sliced in half

½ cup roasted red pepper strips

12 slices Havarti

Six ¼-inch-thick slices red onion

1. Heat the broiler.

2. In a medium bowl, mix the olive oil, balsamic vinegar, garlic, salt, and black pepper together until thoroughly incorporated. Dip the eggplant slices into the oil and vinegar mixture to coat, and reserve the extra mixture. Place the eggplant slices on a broiling rack. Broil the eggplant for 6 to 7 minutes per side, or until lightly golden. Reserve.

2. Spoon the remaining oil and vinegar mixture generously on both sides of the rolls. Toast the rolls under the broiler until lightly golden, about 45 seconds.

3. Top half of each roll with a slice of eggplant, a piece of roasted red pepper, and 1 slice of cheese, and the other half with a slice of red onion and 1 slice of cheese. Season with salt and pepper as needed. Return to the broiler and heat until the cheese is melted, roughly 1 to 1½ minutes.

4. Assemble the sandwiches, cut in half, and serve.

MADEIRA-GLAZED PORTOBELLO STEAK SANDWICHES

PORTOBELLO MUSHROOMS are actually mature cremini mushrooms and have a dense, meaty texture when cooked. They can be prepared for this recipe a day ahead; cool the broiled mushroom caps completely and refrigerate until needed. Slice the mushrooms and allow them to return to room temperature before assembling the sandwiches.

SERVES 8

1. Preheat the broiler and place the oven rack in the upper third of the oven.

2. Remove the stems from the mushrooms and, using a sharp paring knife, cut away the gills. Combine the Madeira, 2 tablespoons of the olive oil, the garlic cloves, oregano, 1 teaspoon of salt, and ½ teaspoon of pepper in a large bowl; add the mushrooms and toss to coat. Set aside for 10 minutes to marinate.

3. Heat the remaining tablespoon of olive oil in a sauté pan set over medium-high heat. Add the onions and sauté until soft and translucent, about 5 to 6 minutes. Season with the remaining 1 teaspoon of salt and ½ teaspoon of pepper.

4. Place the mushrooms and onion slices on a baking sheet, brush with the marinade, and broil until browned and tender, about 4 minutes on each side. When cool enough to handle, thinly slice each mushroom. Fill the sandwich with slices of onion and mushroom and top with a slice of cheese.

5. Place the bottom half of each sandwich with the mushroom, onion, and cheese on a baking pan and place under the broiler until the cheese is melted, about 2 minutes.

6. Top each sandwich with the greens and a second slice of bread.

8 portobello mushrooms

¼ cup Madeira

3 tbsp olive oil

2 garlic cloves, bruised

½ tsp dried oregano

2 tsp salt

1 tsp black pepper

8 onion slices

16 slices rye or pumpernickel bread

8 slices Muenster or Havarti

4 cups mixed baby greens

CHICKPEA AND VEGETABLE TAGINE

2 tbsp olive oil

2 cups cippolini onions, peeled and halved

2 tbsp minced garlic

1 tbsp minced gingerroot

1½ tsp ground cumin

1 tsp ground coriander

½ tsp ground anise seed

¼ tsp cayenne

Salt and pepper as needed

⅛ tsp ground cinnamon

2 cups chicken or Vegetable Broth (page 82)

3½ cups medium-dice butternut squash,
    peeled and seeded

1½ cups medium-dice carrots, peeled

3 cups cooked chickpeas, drained and rinsed

2 cups diced tomatoes in juice (no salt
    added)

2¼ cups medium-dice sweet potatoes,
    peeled

1½ cups medium-dice parsnips, peeled

1 bay leaf

2 tbsp minced preserved lemon (or 2 tsp
    grated lemon zest)

2 tbsp coarsely chopped parsley

2 tbsp coarsely chopped cilantro

THIS TAGINE recipe includes a complex blend of spices and a generous assortment of vegetables. Cut the vegetables so that each type has a consistent size. You may need to adjust the cooking times slightly, depending on the maturity of your vegetables. If you can't find the preserved lemon we call for here, substitute a teaspoon of grated lemon zest instead.

SERVES 8

1. Heat the oil in a tagine or a flame-proof casserole over medium heat. Add the onions and sauté until they soften and become light golden, about 8 to 10 minutes. Stir occasionally as you cook the onions. The halves should fall apart into their separate layers as they cook. Add the garlic and ginger and sauté until aromatic, about 30 seconds. Add the cumin, coriander, anise, cayenne, salt, pepper, and cinnamon. Cook, stirring constantly, until the spices are toasted and thoroughly coat the onions, about 1 minute.

2. Add the broth, butternut squash, carrots, and chickpeas; bring to a boil over medium-high heat. Reduce the heat to low and simmer, partially covered, until the vegetables are just beginning to get tender, about 15 minutes.

3. Add the tomatoes, sweet potatoes, parsnips, and bay leaf and simmer until the vegetables are nearly tender, about 30 minutes. Add the preserved lemon and simmer for 20 minutes or until all of the vegetables are tender and cooked through. Remove and discard the bay leaf. Season to taste with salt and pepper. Sprinkle with the parsley and cilantro, and serve directly from the tagine or casserole onto heated plates.

PAELLA CON VERDURAS

3 tbsp extra-virgin olive oil

2 cups small-dice onions

2 cups thinly sliced leeks, white part only

2 cups chopped plum tomatoes, peeled and seeded

2 tbsp minced garlic

1½ cups medium-grain rice

2 cups cauliflower florets

1 cup sliced or quartered cooked artichoke hearts

1 cup fresh or frozen green peas

4 cups Vegetable Broth (page 82)

Salt and pepper as needed

1 cup roasted red peppers strips

¼ cup chopped parsley

THERE ARE several versions of paella enjoyed throughout Spain. This one takes advantage of a variety of fresh vegetables. Feel free to add whatever vegetables inspire you: green beans, chunks of zucchini or yellow squash, or cubes of pumpkin or Hubbard squash.

SERVES 6

1. Heat the oil in a paella pan or a wide skillet. Add the onions, leeks, tomatoes, and garlic. Cook, stirring frequently, until the juices from the tomatoes have cooked away and the onions are tender, about 5 minutes.

2. Add the rice and stir to coat well. Continue to sauté until lightly toasted, 2 to 3 minutes.

3. Add the cauliflower, artichoke hearts, peas, and enough broth to cover the rice and vegetables. Season with salt and pepper and bring to a boil. Reduce the heat to low, cover the paella pan or skillet, and cook until the rice has absorbed most of the broth, about 20 minutes.

4. Add the remaining broth, cover the pan, and continue to cook until the rice is very tender. Season to taste with additional salt and pepper.

5. Serve the paella directly from the pan garnished with the roasted pepper strips and chopped parsley.

ARTICHOKE AND SPINACH RISOTTO

FROZEN ARTICHOKES work nicely in this risotto, but most tinned artichokes have an overly briny, and sometimes slightly metallic taste.

SERVES 8

1. Heat 1 tablespoon of olive oil in a medium sauté pan over medium-high heat. Add the garlic and sauté until fragrant, about 1 minute, add the artichokes and ½ cup of the wine. Cover the pan and cook until the artichokes are just tender, about 3 minutes. Remove from heat and set aside.

2. Heat the remaining 1 tablespoon of olive oil in a medium sauce pan over medium-high heat, add the onions, and sauté until they are transparent and tender, about 5 minutes. Add the rice and stir to coat well. Continue to sauté until lightly toasted, 2 to 3 minutes. Add the remaining 1 cup of wine and cook until dry, about 5 minutes.

3. Add about one-third of the hot vegetable broth and a generous pinch of salt and cook, stirring gently until dry. Repeat with the remaining stock, adding it in thirds, and cook until the risotto has absorbed the broth. Add the spinach and stir to incorporate. Add the reserved artichokes and remove the pan from heat.

4. Stir in the tomatoes, butter, and Parmesan. Season with additional salt and pepper, if needed. Serve immediately in heated bowls or plates.

2 tbsp olive oil

2 tbsp garlic

4 cups chopped cooked artichoke hearts

1½ cups white wine

2 cups small-dice onions

2½ cups Arborio rice

8 cups Vegetable Broth (page 82), heated

Salt and pepper as needed

10 cups baby spinach

2 cups cherry tomatoes, cut in half

1 cup butter, cut into 1-inch pieces

1¼ cups grated Parmesan

Artichoke

ROASTED VEGETABLE PIZZA

ROASTING THE vegetables removes some of their moisture, for a pizza topping full of flavor that won't weigh down the crust. Cooking the vegetables on a grill will give them a bit of extra texture and a wonderful smoky taste.

SERVES 4

1. Preheat the oven to 425°F or preheat a gas grill to medium-high.

2. Put the sliced vegetables in a large colander and sprinkle them generously with salt. Allow the vegetables to rest for 15 minutes to begin extracting water. Rinse the salt from the vegetables. Drain and blot the vegetables dry to remove excess water before roasting.

3. Arrange the vegetables on baking sheets in a single layer and drizzle with the olive oil and garlic, reserving about 2 tablespoons of the oil.

4. Roast the vegetables in the oven or grill them over direct heat until lightly charred and tender, about 15 to 20 minutes. When the vegetables are cool enough to handle, cut them into thin strips if desired. (This can be done in advance and the vegetables held in a covered container in the refrigerator for up to 2 days.)

5. When you are ready to assemble and bake the pizzas, preheat the oven to 425°F. Scatter a thin coating of cornmeal on baking sheets (or preheat pizza stones in the oven if they are available; see note Baking Pizza below). Stretch the pizza dough into either 1 large round or 4 individual rounds and place on the prepared baking sheet. Spread the ricotta on the pizza dough in a thin layer and top with the chopped or sliced roasted vegetables and the mozzarella. Drizzle with a little of the remaining olive oil and top with the parsley.

6. Bake the pizzas until the crust is crisp and golden brown and the cheese has melted, about 15 minutes. Cut into wedges and serve immediately.

BAKING PIZZA

A crisp crust depends upon a hot oven. Ovens in pizzerias can reach much higher temperature than home ovens, but there are steps you can take to mimic the effect. Use a pizza stone, which helps keep the bottom of the crust crisp and dry as it bakes. Another option is to line a baking rack with unglazed tiles. Tiles and stones should be allowed to preheat before you put the pizza on them. A peel, which looks like a large wooden paddle, is used to slide the pizza onto the stone or tile. (Some baking sheets have edges on only 2 or 3 sides, and can be used as a peel as well). Use a quick, jerking motion and a flick of the wrist to slide the bread from the pan onto the tiles.

---

2 small yellow squash, sliced ¼ inch thick on a diagonal

2 small zucchini, sliced ¼ inch thick on a diagonal

2 medium Vidalia onions, sliced ¼ inch thick

1 medium eggplant, sliced ¼ inch thick

Salt and pepper as needed

1 cup extra-virgin olive oil, or as needed

2 tbsp minced garlic

Cornmeal for dusting

Pizza Dough (page 192)

1 cup ricotta cheese

1½ cups shredded mozzarella

3 tbsp chopped parsley

Pizza Dough

2 tsp or 1 package active dry yeast

2 cups warm water

3½ cups all-purpose flour

1 cup semolina flour

1 tbsp salt

¼ cup olive oil

THIS BASIC dough is great to bake on its own, slathered with olive oil, and punctuated with fresh herbs or slivered garlic.

MAKES 1 LARGE PIZZA, SERVES 4 TO 6

1. Combine the yeast with the water in a bowl and stir to dissolve.

2. Add the flours and the salt to the yeast and mix by hand with a wooden spoon, or in an electric mixer on medium speed using the dough hook, until the dough is smooth and elastic.

3. Place the dough in a lightly oiled bowl. Cover, put in a warm place, and allow to rise until doubled in size, about 1½ hours. Gently fold the dough over and allow to rise a second time, about 45 minutes.

5. Roll or stretch the dough into a 12-inch round for pizza. (See page 191 for more about topping and baking a pizza.)

Mandarin Pancakes

2 cups all-purpose flour

¾ to 1 cup boiling water, as needed

3 tbsp sesame oil, or as needed

THESE SIMPLE pancakes can be served with the Mu Shu Vegetables on page 194, or used with other fillings in a similar fashion. They can be made ahead of time and frozen.

MAKES ABOUT 18 PANCAKES

1. Sift the flour into a large bowl, add ¾ cup boiling water to the flour, and begin stirring it in immediately, adding a little additional water if necessary to make a dough. Knead the warm dough until smooth. Wrap the dough and let it rest at room temperature for 30 minutes.

2. Turn the rested dough out onto a floured surface. Cut the dough in half. Use a lightly floured rolling pin to roll each half out until it is ¼-inch thick. Use a cookie cutter to cut out 3-inch circles of dough.

3. Brush ½ teaspoon of sesame oil over the tops of 2 dough circles. Lay one pancake on top of another, so that the oiled sides are together. (The edges don't have to line up perfectly.) Roll out the pancakes to form a 6-inch circle. Repeat with the remainder of the pancakes. Use a damp towel to cover the prepared pancakes, to keep them from drying out as you work.

4. Heat a skillet over low heat. Add one of the pancake pairs and cook until browned, about 2 minutes. Turn and cook on the second side until browned, another 1 to 2 minutes. Remove the paired pancakes from the pan and pull them apart. Repeat with the remainder of the pancakes. Serve immediately.

ENHANCE your vegetable main dishes by introducing some hearty garnishes, like the egg crêpe and mandarin pancakes shown here. These Asian-inspired additions help round out stirfries, stews, and noodle dishes. They may look complex, but they are actually quite simple to prepare.

EGG CRÊPES

An egg crêpe is nothing more than a thin omelet. A touch of sesame oil gives it a subtle flavor that works well with other Asian ingredients and flavors.

1. Use a very flat, well-seasoned (or liberally oiled) pan to make the egg crepe. Let the pan heat up over medium-high heat while you whisk and season the eggs. Pour in the egg mixture and tilt the pan so that the eggs coat the pan in an even layer.

2. Once the eggs are set and cooked, flip the crepe out of the pan by turning it upside down over a work surface. Fold or roll up the crepe and use a chef's knife to cut the crepe into thin ribbons.

MANDARIN PANCAKES

Mandarin pancakes are made from a simple batter of flour and boiling water. They are quick to mix and ready to roll out and cook in about 30 minutes.

1. Cut the ball of dough in half, roll it out into a thin sheet, and use a round cookie cutter, about 3 inches in diameter, to cut out as many pancakes as possible.

2. Brush half of the pancakes with oil (sesame oil adds flavor), and then make stacks of 2 pancakes. Roll the stacks with a rolling pin to seal them together and double their size. Cover the pancakes you've already rolled out with a lightly dampened cloth while you finish rolling the rest.

MU SHU VEGETABLES

4 large eggs, lightly beaten

2 tsp sesame oil

Salt and pepper as needed

1 tbsp peanut oil

½ oz dried wood ears (black fungus)

½ oz golden lily buds

3 tbsp rice wine or dry sherry wine

1 tbsp minced garlic

1 tbsp minced gingerroot

2 tbsp dark soy sauce

½ cup julienned celery

1 medium carrot, julienned

½ cup julienned fennel

1 cup shredded napa cabbage

1½ cups julienned red peppers

½ cup minced scallions

1 cup bean sprouts, rinsed and drained

12 Mandarin pancakes (page 192)

Hoisin sauce as needed

Plum sauce as needed

4 scallion fans, optional (see headnote)

A T A restaurant you may find Mu Shu served with scallion brushes—slices of scallion with slits into the white portion so that they open up like bristles—that are used to spread on the hoisin sauce. The mu shu-filled pancake is rolled up like a cigar, and then dipped in plum or hoisin sauce. One of the elements in this mu shu dish is a shredded egg omelet, cooked like a thin crêpe (see page 193).

SERVES 4

1. To make the egg crêpe, combine the beaten eggs with 1 teaspoon of the sesame oil and a pinch of salt and pepper in a small bowl.

2. Heat a frying pan or wok over moderate heat and add 1 teaspoon of the peanut oil. Pour in the egg mixture and spread it quickly over the surface of the pan until it forms a thin crêpe-like pancake. There is no need to turn it over. Remove from the heat; and when cool shred the egg pancake and set aside.

3. To make the filling: Soak the dried wood ears and lily buds in warm water for about 20 minutes until soft. Squeeze the excess liquid from the wood ears and lily buds. Finely shred the wood ears, discarding the stem, and snap off the hard ends of the lily buds.

4. Heat a wok or large frying pan over high heat and add the remaining peanut oil. When almost smoking, add the wood ears, lily buds, and rice wine and stirfry for 1 minute. Add the garlic, gingerroot, and dark soy sauce and stirfry for another minute. Add the celery, carrot, and fennel and stirfry until very hot, about 2 minutes. Add the cabbage and stirfry until hot, another 2 minutes. Then put in the shredded egg, red peppers, scallions, and bean sprouts and continue to stirfry for 3 minutes until the ingredients are thoroughly mixed. Stir in the remaining sesame oil, and turn onto a large platter. Serve with the Mandarin pancakes, hoisin sauce, and plum sauce.

PORK CUTLETS WITH A WILD MUSHROOM RAGOUT

Dishes from the classic French culinary repertoire that feature mushrooms were often named *forestière,* or of the forest, because they were made from the seasonal mushrooms foraged from local woods and fields. In fact, many wild mushrooms suggested here actually are cultivated, making them available year-round instead of only in their natural season. Wavy-capped, apricot-colored chanterelle mushrooms are an exception, because they still usually are foraged rather than cultivated. Look for them at farmers' markets in the autumn and spring.

SERVES 4

1. Season the pork cutlets with salt and pepper. Dredge in the flour, shaking off any excess.

2. Pour oil into a large sauté pan to a depth of ⅛ inch and heat over high heat until the surface of the oil shimmers. Add the pork cutlets and pan fry on the first side until deep golden brown, 3 to 4 minutes. Turn the pork cutlets and continue cooking on the second side until the pork is cooked through and the exterior is golden brown, 3 to 4 minutes more. Transfer to a warmed platter and cover to keep warm while completing the ragout.

3. Pour off all but 2 tablespoons of oil, add the shallot to the pan, and sauté over medium heat until limp, about 1 minute. Increase the heat to high, add the mushrooms and thyme, and sauté until the mushrooms are lightly browned, about 2 minutes.

4. Add the wine and stir to deglaze the pan, scraping up any browned bits from the pan bottom. Add the broth and any juices released by the pork chops. Simmer over high heat until the liquid has reduced by about half, 6 to 7 minutes. Swirl in the butter to thicken the sauce slightly. Serve the pork chops immediately with the sauce.

Four 6-oz pork cutlets

Salt and pepper as needed

Flour for dredging

Olive oil, as needed

1 small shallot, minced

2 cups sliced assorted mushrooms (oyster, cremini, stemmed shiitake, chanterelle, and/or white)

1 tsp chopped thyme leaves

¼ cup dry white wine

¼ cup Chicken Broth (page 83)

2 tbsp unsalted butter

STIRFRIED GARDEN VEGETABLES WITH MARINATED TOFU

MARINATED TOFU

1¼ lb firm tofu

⅓ cup soy sauce

4 tsp minced gingerroot

4 tsp minced garlic

3 tbsp all-purpose flour

VEGETABLE STIRFRY

2 tbsp peanut oil

1½ bunches scallions, thinly sliced

4 tsp ginger, peeled, minced

3 tbsp minced garlic

3 carrots, sliced thin on the diagonal

2 lb broccoli florets

½ lb snow peas

5 tbsp soy sauce

½ tsp sesame oil

5 tbsp toasted sesame seeds

I T IS difficult to achieve the cooking temperatures your favorite Chinese restaurant does when stirfrying, but you can adapt by adding foods in batches and not filling up the wok with too many ingredients at once. Simply remove the vegetables from the wok as they get hot and allow the wok some time to reheat before you add the next batch.

SERVES 6

1. To marinate the tofu, drain the tofu, cut into 1-inch cubes, and place in a zipper-lock plastic bag. Add the soy sauce, ginger, and garlic. Seal the bag, pressing out any air (or place these ingredients all in a container). Marinate the tofu in the refrigerator, turning the bag occasionally, for at least 20 minutes and up to 12 hours.

2. Drain the tofu and discard the marinade. Blot the tofu dry with paper towels. Dust with flour, shaking off the excess.

3. Heat a wok or skillet over high heat. Add the oil and swirl to coat the bottom and sides of the wok or skillet. Add the tofu cubes (the tofu should be in a single layer and not touching; if necessary, work in batches). Stirfry until the tofu is lightly browned, about 2 minutes. Transfer the tofu to a plate.

4. Add the scallions, ginger, and garlic to the wok or skillet and stirfry just until aromatic, about 30 seconds. Add the remaining vegetables in sequence: first the carrots, followed by the broccoli, then the snow peas. Stirfry each addition until tender, about 2 minutes, before adding the next vegetable. Add the tofu and soy sauce; toss to combine. Stir in the sesame oil. Sprinkle with the toasted sesame seeds and serve at once on a heated platter or plates.

TOFU AND PEAS WITH CILANTRO IN A RED CURRY SAUCE

THAI RED curry paste, a mixture of hot red chiles, garlic, lemongrass, galangal (a ginger-like rhizome), and salt, adds a robust glow to this creamy stew of chicken, coconut milk, and fresh herbs. Green curry paste, made with fresh green chiles, lemongrass, and wild lime leaves, has a milder, tangier flavor and is often paired with vegetables or fish. Prepared curry pastes can be found in jars in the Asian foods section of many supermarkets, or in specialty food shops and Asian markets.

MAKES 4 SERVINGS

1. Heat the oil in a large sauté pan over medium heat. Add the onions and sauté until translucent, 5 to 7 minutes. Add the garlic and cook until aromatic, about 2 minutes. Add the red curry paste, 1 teaspoon of salt, and ½ teaspoon of white pepper. Stir to coat the onions and garlic evenly with the curry paste. Add the potatoes and stir to coat evenly with the curry paste.

2. Add the broth and bring to a simmer. Simmer until the potatoes are nearly tender, 15 to 20 minutes. Add the tofu and peas and continue to simmer until the peas are hot and tender, 5 to 6 minutes.

3. Meanwhile, toast the shredded coconut. Preheat the oven to 350°F. Spread the coconut on a baking sheet and bake until golden, about 5 minutes. Transfer to a bowl and set aside.

4. Using a slotted spoon, transfer the tofu, peas, and potatoes to a warmed bowl and cover to keep warm while completing the sauce. Add the coconut milk, brown sugar, and lemon zest to the pan the tofu was in and bring to a simmer, stirring constantly. Season the sauce with salt and pepper. If needed, add just enough of the cornstarch slurry while stirring to thicken the sauce slightly. Add the cilantro, basil, and mint.

5. Return the tofu and the potatoes to the pan and stir to coat them thoroughly with the sauce. Serve the curry over a bed of rice. Garnish each plate with about 2 tablespoons scallions and 1 tablespoon toasted coconut.

3 tbsp vegetable oil

1 cup diced onions

3 cloves garlic, minced

1 tbsp prepared red curry paste

Salt and freshly ground white pepper

6 small red potatoes, scrubbed, each cut into 6 pieces

1½ cups Vegetable Broth (page 82)

1 pound firm tofu, drained and cut into large cubes

1½ cups green peas, fresh or frozen

¼ cup shredded dried coconut

½ cup coconut milk

2 tbsp brown sugar

1 tsp grated lemon zest

Cornstarch slurry: 1 tbsp cornstarch blended with 4 tsp cold water (optional)

2 tbsp coarsely chopped cilantro

1 tbsp coarsely chopped fresh basil

1 tbsp coarsely chopped fresh mint

4 cups steamed white rice

4 scallions, white and green parts, sliced on the bias

GRILLED HALIBUT WITH ROASTED RED AND YELLOW PEPPER SALAD

2 red bell peppers, or 1 cup of prepared roasted peppers

2 yellow bell peppers, or 1 cup of prepared roasted peppers

¼ cup olive oil

½ onion, thinly sliced

3 tbsp garlic, thinly sliced

2 tbsp capers, chopped

1 tbsp sherry vinegar

½ tsp ground cumin

¼ tsp red pepper flakes

⅛ tsp ground coriander

1 tsp salt, or to taste

½ tsp freshly ground black pepper, or to taste

3 lb halibut fillet

YOU CAN skip a few steps in this recipe by using prepared roasted red and yellow peppers. At certain times of the year you may find peppers at a great price. Take advantage of the bounty by preparing double or triple batches of the salad to have on hand. You can add the peppers to omelets, salads, sandwiches, stews, and soups.

MAKES 8 SERVINGS

1. Preheat oven to 350°F.

2. Rub the peppers with 2 tablespoons of the olive oil and roast them in the oven for 25 to 30 minutes, or until the skins start to fall off. Place the peppers in a bowl, cover with a piece of plastic wrap, and allow them to steam for 5 minutes.

3. Peel the skin off of the peppers and remove the stems and seeds. Slice the peppers into thin strips.

4. Heat the remaining olive oil in a large sauté pan over medium-high heat. Add the onion and cook until lightly caramelized, about 8 to 10 minutes. Add the garlic and cook until aromatic, about 30 seconds.

5. Add the capers, vinegar, cumin, red pepper flakes, and coriander. Season with about ¼ teaspoon salt and a pinch of black pepper. Add the onion mixture to the peppers and keep warm.

6. Preheat a grill to medium-high. Cut the halibut into eight 6-ounce portions and season with salt and pepper. Grill the halibut until just cooked through, about 2 to 3 minutes per side. Serve each portion with ¼ cup of the roasted pepper salad.

SPINACH AND GOAT CHEESE QUICHE

2 tbsp vegetable oil

½ cup minced onions

4 cups spinach leaves, blanched, squeezed dry, and chopped

Salt and pepper as needed

¾ cup heavy cream

2 large eggs

½ cup crumbled fresh goat cheese

¼ cup grated Parmesan cheese

2 tbsp chopped sun-dried tomatoes (about 4)

One 9-inch Pie Crust (recipe follows), prebaked in a quiche or pie pan

WHEN USING fresh spinach, cut away the stems and rinse the spinach in several changes of cold water until you can't feel any traces of sand or grit in the rinse water. Packaged spinach should be rinsed and dried as well.

MAKES ONE 9-INCH QUICHE, SERVES 6 TO 8

1. Preheat the oven to 350°F.

2. Heat the oil in a large skillet over medium heat until it shimmers. Add the onions and sauté, stirring frequently, until translucent, 3 to 4 minutes. Add the spinach and sauté until very hot, about 4 minutes. Remove from the heat. Season with ¼ teapoon salt and a pinch of pepper. Transfer to a colander and let the spinach drain and cool while preparing the custard.

3. Whisk together the cream and eggs. Stir in the goat cheese, Parmesan, sun-dried tomatoes, and reserved spinach. Season to taste with salt and pepper. Spread the egg-spinach mixture evenly over the pie crust.

4. Set the quiche pan on a baking sheet and bake until a knife blade inserted in the center comes out clean, 40 to 45 minutes. If the pie crust begins to over brown, cover the edges of the crust with strips of aluminum foil or with pie shields. Remove the quiche from the oven and cool on a wire rack. Let the quiche rest at least 20 minutes before cutting. Serve hot, warm, or at room temperature.

Pie Crust Dough

MAKES ENOUGH FOR 1 DOUBLE-CRUST OR 2 SINGLE-CRUST PIES (9-INCH PANS)

2¾ cups all-purpose flour, plus extra as needed

1 tsp salt

1 cup cold diced butter (or ½ cup diced cold butter and ½ cup diced cold shortening)

½ cup ice cold water

1. Combine the flour and salt in a bowl and stir with a fork to blend the salt evenly with the flour.

2. Cut the shortening into the flour using a food processor, pastry cutter, or 2 knives until the mixture looks like coarse meal. Drizzle a few tablespoons of the cold water over the flour mixture and quickly rub the water into the flour. Continue to add the water, a few tablespoons at a time, until the dough is evenly moist, although not wet, and shaggy or rough in appearance. It should just hold together when you press a handful of it into a ball.

3. Turn the dough out onto a lightly floured work surface. Gather and press the dough into a ball. Divide the dough into 2 equal pieces for a double crust or 2 single crust pies. Pat each piece into an even disk, wrap well, and let chill in the refrigerator for 20 minutes before rolling and baking.

CARAMELIZED ONION TART

COOKING ONIONS until they are soft, tender, and golden brown gives them a rich, caramel color, and a surprisingly sweet flavor. Keep the heat low and stir frequently so that they develop a good, even color with no scorching.

MAKES ONE 9-INCH TART, SERVES 6 TO 8

1. Preheat oven to 350°F.

2. Heat the olive oil in a sauté pan over medium heat until it shimmers. Add the onions and sauté, stirring frequently, until golden and very soft (caramelized), about 15 minutes. Reduce the heat to low to prevent the onions from scorching. Remove the onions from the heat and reserve.

3. Whisk together the heavy cream, milk, eggs, salt, and pepper in medium bowl. Stir the reserved caramelized onions and 1 cup of the cheese into the egg mixture. Pour the egg mixture evenly into the pie crust. Sprinkle the remaining cheese evenly over the top of the tart.

4. Set the tart pan on a baking sheet and bake until a knife blade inserted in the center comes out clean, 40 to 45 minutes. If the crust begins to over brown, cover the edges with strips of aluminum foil or with pie shields. Remove the tart from the oven and cool on a wire rack. Let the tart rest at least 10 minutes before cutting. Serve hot, warm, or at room temperature.

2 tbsp extra virgin olive oil

2½ cups thin sliced yellow onions

¾ cup heavy cream

¾ cup milk

3 large eggs

Salt and pepper as needed

1¼ cups grated provolone cheese, divided use

One 9-inch Pie Crust (page 202), prebaked in a tart pan

WORKING WITH PIE DOUGH

You can improvise a wide array of appetizers and entrees that feature vegetables baked in a crust, including quiches and tarts.

BAKING BLIND

This technique is used to partially or completely bake the crust before you add the filling. To prebake the crust, preheat the oven to 400°F. Prick the dough evenly over the bottom and sides with the tines of a table fork. For quiche crusts, line the dough with a piece of parchment or waxed paper and fill about half-full with pie weights, dry beans, or rice. For tartlet molds, either line with paper and weights or set a second pan on top of the filled pan, and place the shells on a baking sheet upside down. Bake just until the edges of the dough appear dry, but have not taken on any color, 12 to 15 minutes. Remove the weights and paper. If baking completely, return the crust to the oven and bake until the crust is completely dry and light golden brown, about 8 minutes. When finished baking the crust, place the pan on a wire rack, cool to room temperature, and then fill and bake as directed in the recipe.

STORING DOUGH TO USE LATER

To store any leftover dough, pat the dough into flat disks or blocks and put them in a zip-close bag, pressing out as much air as possible before sealing the bag. It will hold 3 to 4 days in the refrigerator or up to 2 months in the freezer.

VEGETARIAN SHEPHERD'S PIE

PACKED WITH colorful vegetables, this hearty and warming shepherd's pie is full of slightly sweet and spicy flavors and topped with an unusual parsnip and potato puree. If you prefer, enjoy the stew on its own, without the topping.

SERVES 8

1. Preheat the oven to 350°F. Put the flour in a dry sauté pan. Toast, stirring over low heat, until it has a nutty aroma and is a light brown. Transfer the flour to a food processor or blender. With the machine running, pour in the vegetable broth.

2. Pour the broth mixture into a saucepan. Bring it to a simmer over medium heat, stirring frequently. Simmer the sauce for 10 minutes, or until thickened and smooth. Season with salt. The sauce is ready to use now or it may be cooled and stored in the refrigerator for up to 3 days.

3. Line an 8-inch springform pan or 2-quart casserole with three-quarters of the potato mixture; reserve the rest for the crust. Preheat a grill to low heat. Preheat the oven to 350°F.

4. Heat 2 tablespoons of the olive oil in a sauté pan over medium heat until it shimmers. Add the shiitake caps and sauté until tender, about 3 to 4 minutes. Season with salt and pepper. Using tongs, transfer the mushroom caps to the casserole, arranging them in a layer on the bottom of the casserole.

5. Toss the zucchini, carrots, fennel, and celery in the remaining 4 tablespoons of olive oil. Season the vegetables with salt and pepper. Grill the vegetables until tender. Cut the grilled vegetables into bite-sized pieces.

6. Return the vegetable sauce to a simmer. Add the grilled vegetables and the tomato and simmer over low heat until the vegetables are heated through. Add the herbs and vinegar. Adjust the seasoning with additional salt and pepper if needed. Spoon the mixture into the prepared pan or casserole. Put the remaining potato mixture into a pastry bag and pipe a lattice on top of the filling.

7. Bake for 30 to 35 minutes, or until the crust is golden brown. Let the pie settle for 10 minutes before serving.

½ cup all-purpose flour

1½ cups Vegetable Broth (page 82)

4 cups Parsnip and Potato Puree (page 206)

6 tbsp olive oil

2 cups shiitake mushrooms, stemmed

Salt and pepper as needed

1 zucchini, cut lengthwise into strips

3 carrots, peeled and cut lengthwise into strips

1 fennel bulb, trimmed and cut into sixths

4 celery stalks, peeled

1 tomato, peeled, seeded, and chopped

¼ cup chopped fresh herbs (parsley, chives, tarragon, etc)

¼ cup aged sweet wine vinegar

Parsnip and Potato Puree

MAKES 4 CUPS

3 cups large dice potatoes (preferably Idaho
or russet)

1½ cups thickly sliced parsnips

4 egg yolks, lightly beaten

3 tbsp butter, room temperature

Salt as needed

1. Bring a large pot of salted water to a boil. Add the potatoes and parsnips and simmer over low heat until they are tender enough to mash easily with a fork, about 12 to 15 minutes.

2. Drain the potatoes and parsnips. Return them to the pot and dry them over low heat for 2 to 3 minutes, shaking the pot occasionally so they don't stick.

3. Immediately purée the potatoes and parsnips through a food mill or ricer into a bowl. Stir in the egg yolks, butter, and salt. The purée is now ready to use to top the shepherd's pie.

SPAGHETTI SQUASH WITH VEGETABLE RAGOUT

One 4-lb spaghetti squash

1 tbsp olive oil

2½ cups sliced leeks, white and
light-green portions

3 tbsp minced garlic

2 cups small-dice zucchini

1 cup small-dice carrots

¾ cup small-dice celery

1 cup Vegetable Broth (page 82)

1 cup diced tomatoes, peeled and seeded

1 cup tomato purée

3 tbsp chopped basil

2 tbsp chopped parsley

2 tsp chopped oregano

Salt and pepper as needed

½ cup grated Parmesan

THE FLESH of spaghetti squash separates into fine strands, but retains a bit of crunch and a distinct flavor of squash.

SERVES 4 TO 6

1. Preheat the oven to 350°F. Set the whole squash in a baking pan and use a kitchen fork to pierce a few holes in the skin. Bake until the skin is golden brown and the flesh is tender, about 1 hour. Remove from the oven and let the squash cool enough for you to handle it easily. Cut the squash in half, scoop out and discard the seeds, then pull out the flesh with a fork to separate the strands; set aside.

2. To make the vegetable ragout, heat the oil in a large pot. Add the leeks and garlic and sauté until translucent, 3 to 5 minutes. Stir in the zucchini, carrots, and celery and sauté until evenly coated with the oil. Add the broth, diced tomatoes, and tomato purée and simmer until the vegetables are tender, about 20 minutes. (The ragout is ready to finish and serve now, or it can be made ahead, cooled, and stored in a covered container in the refrigerator for up to 3 days.) Add the basil, parsley, and oregano. Season to taste with salt and pepper.

3. Layer the spaghetti squash in a lightly greased baking dish or casserole. Spoon the ragout over the top of the spaghetti squash and sprinkle with the Parmesan. Bake in a 350°F oven until the ingredients are very hot, about 30 minutes. Serve directly from the baking dish or casserole on heated plates.

CRÊPES are the perfect wrapper to fill with a variety of vegetable fillings. They are also an excellent option for do-ahead meals. Make the crêpes and filling up to three days ahead of time, or stuff the crepes and hold in the baking dish up to one day ahead. You can keep them frozen, also, for up to one month.

PREPARING CRÊPES

A standard crêpe pan is about 9 inches in diameter. For a thin crepe, you'll use about 1/4 cup batter. The batter should flow easily, almost like heavy cream. Tilt and swirl the pan to coat with a thin layer. As you can see in the accompanying photograph, the crêpe should be thin enough to let some light through. This crêpe is set enough to remove from the pan after about 1 minute. For a bit more color, turn the crêpe once and cook for about 15 or 20 seconds more. (You should plan on making one or two "test" crêpes, so you can adjust the heat or the batter if necessary.)

FILLING AND BAKING CRÊPES

If you have made the crêpes ahead of time and frozen them, let them thaw at room temperature so they are flexible enough to roll. Place a crêpe flat on a work surface and spoon in the filling, about ⅓ cup or a mounded serving spoon, placing it in the center of the crêpe. Fold the crêpe in half over the filling. Use your fingertips to pull the edge into to the center, trapping the filling and pressing it to make a stuffed cylinder shape. Place the filled crêpes in a lightly buttered baking dish, seam side down, so they can't unroll as they bake.

CRÊPES WITH SPICY MUSHROOMS
AND CHILE CREAM SAUCE

SPICY MUSHROOM FILLING

2 tbsp olive oil

½ cup minced onions

1½ tsp minced garlic

4 cups sliced mushrooms

2 tsp minced serrano chile

2 tbsp lime juice

¾ tsp epazote

Salt and pepper as needed

CHILE CREAM SAUCE

2 cups heavy cream

2 dry poblano chiles, toasted and chopped

1 dry chipotle chile, toasted and chopped

12 Crêpes (page 210)

¾ cup crumbled queso fresco

WE LIKE the tender texture of crêpes in this dish, but the dish would be equally delicious made with regular or whole wheat flour tortillas.

SERVES 4

1. To make the filling, heat the olive oil in a sauté pan over medium-high heat. Add the onion and garlic to the oil and sauté, stirring frequently, until the onions are tender and translucent, 2 to 3 minutes. Increase the heat to high. Add the mushrooms and chile. Sauté the mushrooms without stirring until they are browned on one side, 3 to 4 minutes. Stir the mixture and continue to cook over medium heat until the liquid given off by the mushrooms cooks away, about 5 minutes. Add the lime juice and epazote. Season with salt and pepper. (This filling can be prepared in advance, cooled, and kept in a covered container in the refrigerator for up to 2 days.)

2. To make the chile cream sauce, combine the heavy cream and chiles in a small sauce pan. Simmer over very low heat until the cream is reduced and thickened and the sauce is very flavorful, 20 to 30 minutes. Strain the sauce and season with salt and pepper if needed. The sauce is ready to use now, or it can be stored in a covered container in the refrigerator for up to 6 days.

3. Preheat the oven to 375°F. Reheat the filling and the chile cream sauce separately over low heat, if needed, stirring occasionally, about 5 minutes.

4. To assemble the crêpes, lay one crêpe flat on a work surface. Place 2 tablespoons of the warm filling in the center of each of the crêpes and top with the crumbled queso fresco. Roll up the crêpe. Place the crêpes seam side down in a baking dish. Ladle the sauce over the crêpes and bake until the crêpes and the sauce are very hot, about 15 minutes. Serve at once on heated plates.

Crêpes

MAKES 12 CRÊPES

1½ cups all-purpose flour

¼ tsp salt

2 cups whole milk

2 large eggs

2 tbsp unsalted butter, melted and cooled

1. Sift the flour and salt together into a bowl. In another bowl, whisk together the milk, eggs, and butter until evenly blended. Add all at once to the dry ingredients. Stir just enough to make a smooth batter. Let the batter rest, refrigerated, for at least 2 hours or up to overnight. If the batter has lumps, strain through a sieve before preparing the crêpes.

2. Heat a crêpe pan or small nonstick skillet over medium-high heat and brush liberally with oil. Ladle about ⅓ cup of the batter into the crêpe pan. Lift the pan from the heat and tilt and swirl to completely coat the pan with a thin layer of batter. Cook on the first side until set and lightly browned, about 1½ minutes. Turn or flip the crêpe and finish cooking on the second side, 30 to 45 seconds more.

3. Flip the crêpe out of the pan onto a plate lined with parchment or waxed paper. Repeat with remaining batter to make 12 crêpes in all.

MAKING CRÊPES

The thinner the crêpe, the better. With each new batch of crêpes that you make, practice until you find the right amount of batter and level of heat for your pan.

MAKING THE BATTER

Crêpe batters have a more liquid consistency than other pancake batters. Whisk well to remove any lumps, then let the batter rest for 30 to 60 minutes to ensure tender crêpes.

PREPARING THE PAN

Crêpes are typically prepared in a small, flat, round pan with short, sloped sides. Small nonstick skillets also work well. Heat the pan over medium heat and grease with butter or oil to prevent sticking (or, in the case of nonstick pans, to add flavor).

COOKING THE CRÊPES

With a ladle or small measuring cup, quickly pour a small amount of batter into the pan. Immediately tilt and swirl the pan to spread the batter in a thin, even layer that just covers the bottom of the pan. Cook for a few minutes, then check the doneness of a crêpe by carefully lifting one edge and looking underneath it for a golden color with specks of light brown. With a metal spatula, loosen the edge of the crêpe from the pan, turn, and cook on the other side until golden.

Crêpes are easily made in advance. Cool them completely on baking sheets lined with parchment or waxed paper, then stack the crêpes, with parchment or waxed paper between each one. They can be wrapped well and refrigerated or stored in the freezer for later use.

CHILES RELLENOS

U SE A long, narrow chile for this dish. The chiles must be peeled for the batter to stick to them. You can use canned whole green chiles instead of fresh.

SERVES 6

1. Roast the chiles over a gas flame or under a broiler until the skin blisters and loosens; place the roasted chiles in a plastic or paper bag and let them cool and steam for 10 minutes. Scrape away the skin. Make a small slit through the side of the chile just under the stem, and pull out the seeds and ribs. Reserve.

2. Heat 2 tablespoons olive oil in a sauté pan until it shimmers. Add the onions and sauté until tender and translucent, but not browned, about 3 minutes. Transfer the onions to a mixing bowl and cool. Add the grated cheese to the cooled onions and season with salt and pepper. Stuff the chiles with the cheese and onion mixture until well filled. (The chiles can be stuffed up to 2 hours in advance and kept in a covered container in the refrigerator until you are ready to panfry them.)

3. To panfry the chiles, put enough oil in a deep skillet to come to a depth of ½ inch. Heat the oil to 350°F. Whip the egg whites by hand or with an electric mixer until they hold stiff peaks but are not dry. In a separate mixing bowl, stir together the egg yolks, flour, and salt until a thick batter forms. As soon as the batter is blended, spread about ½ cup flour in a shallow bowl or plate. Dredge the peppers in the flour, shake off any excess, and then dip the chile into the batter to cover on all sides. Place the chile into the hot oil and panfry on the first side until the batter is crisp and golden, 3 to 4 minutes. Turn the chiles over and continue to fry until the second side is crisp and the cheese is melted, another 3 minutes.

4. Serve the chiles with sour cream, fried tortilla strips, and cilantro sprigs.

6 fresh Anaheim or poblano chiles

½ cup olive oil, or as needed

2 cups medium-dice onions

2½ cups grated Monterey Jack

Salt and pepper as needed

BATTER

4 egg whites

4 egg yolks

¼ cup sifted flour, plus about 1 cup additional flour for dredging

½ tsp salt

1 cup sour cream

1 cup Fried Tortilla Strips (recipe follows)

6 cilantro sprigs

TO TEST the oil to see if it is the right temperature to fry the chiles rellenos, use a deep fat thermometer or use the classic bread cube test: A 1-inch cube of bread will turn golden brown after 1 minute in oil that is 350°F.

Fried Tortilla Strips

MAKES ABOUT 2 CUPS

1. Add the oil to a skillet to a depth of ½ inch. Heat until the oil shimmers (about 350°F). Add the tortilla strips (work in batches to avoid overcrowding the pan) and fry, stirring carefully once or twice to brown evenly, until crisp, about 2 minutes.

2. Remove the strips from the hot oil with a slotted spoon, transfer to absorbent paper to drain. Season with salt and cayenne pepper while the strips are still hot. The strips can be used now or held in a covered container at room temperature for up to 8 hours.

8 blue or yellow corn tortillas, cut into thin matchsticks

1 cup vegetable oil or as needed for frying

Salt and cayenne pepper as needed

CHAYOTE AND PINEAPPLE FILLING

2 tbsp olive oil

2 cups small-dice onions

1 tbsp minced garlic

1 tbsp minced jalapeño

¾ cup small-dice red peppers

1⅓ cups small-dice yellow peppers

½ cup small-dice roasted poblanos

3 cups small-dice chayote (peeled and seeded)

1 cup small-dice jícama, peeled

1 cup corn kernels, fresh or frozen

1 cup small-dice fresh pineapple

1 tbsp ground cumin

1 tsp coriander

1 tsp ground cinnamon

¼ tsp ground cayenne pepper

¼ cup chopped cilantro

¼ cup chopped flat-leaf parsley

Salt and pepper as needed

1 recipe Chimichanga Dough (page 214)

4 cups grated Monterey Jack or Cheddar cheese

1 cup peanut oil, plus more as needed for frying

Guacamole as needed (page 88)

Tomato Salsa as needed (page 265)

W HILE THIS might seem like an unusual combination, the flavors are perfect together. Read the note on page 266 for details on peeling both chayote and jícama.

SERVES 8

1. Preheat oven to 200°F; place an ovenproof platter in to warm.

2. Heat the olive oil in a large sauté pan over medium-high heat. Add the onions and garlic and sauté until translucent, about 2 minutes. Add the jalapeño and red and yellow peppers; sauté just until they begin to soften, about 3 minutes. Add the poblanos, chayote, and jícama and sauté until tender, about 5 minutes. Add the corn, pineapple, ground cumin, coriander, and cayenne; sauté until heated through, about 3 minutes. Remove pan from heat, and mix in the cilantro. Season to taste with salt and pepper.

3. Divide the chimichanga dough into 16 equal pieces and roll each piece into a ball. Cover the dough balls with a towel to prevent them from drying out as you work. Working with one ball of dough at a time, flatten the dough into a disk with the palm of your hand and then use a rolling pin to roll it into a 10-inch tortilla. Repeat until all of the dough is rolled out into 10-inch tortillas.

4. To fill the chimichangas, mound about ⅓ cup of the filling and 2 tablespoons Cheddar in the center of the tortilla. Fold in the sides of the tortilla and then roll up the chimichanga from the top down. Transfer the filled chimichanga to a platter or baking sheet, seam side down. Continue until all the chimichangas are filled and rolled.

5. Add enough peanut oil to skillet to come to a depth of ½ inch. Heat the oil over medium-high heat until it shimmers. Place four chimichangas in the pan at a time and panfry, seam side down, until the undersides are golden, about 2 minutes. Turn over with tongs and panfry until all sides are golden brown and crisp, about 6 minutes more. Transfer to paper towels to drain briefly; keep warm on platter in oven. Panfry the remaining chimichangas in the same manner.

6. Serve the chimichangas with guacamole and pico de gallo.

Chimichanga Dough

5 cups all-purpose flour

2 cups masa harina or fine cornmeal

1 tbsp salt

½ cup vegetable oil

2 cups water

CHIMICHANGA DOUGH is a pleasure to use and very easy to handle. It works well with a variety of fillings because of its neutral flavor. This dough fries up easily—nice and crisp!

MAKES ENOUGH FOR 8 CHIMICHANGAS

1. Whisk together the flour, masa harina, and salt in the bowl of a mixer.
2. Using the paddle attachment, mix in the oil. Add the water and mix until it forms into a ball, about 5 minutes.
3. Use immediately or refrigerate overnight, tightly wrapped in plastic.

BREAD CRUMBS

Bread crumbs can be either dry or fresh. You can find dried bread crumbs that are plain, seasoned, or Japanese-style (panko). For some dishes, only soft, fresh bread crumbs will do. Toasted bread crumbs, both fresh and dried, are often added to pasta dishes for additional texture. You can also use them for a little added crunch in phyllo dishes (page 124).

MAKING THE FRESH BREAD CRUMBS

The bread you choose should have a good firm texture and while it should still have some give when you press it, it shouldn't be perfectly fresh either. Cut the crust away from the bread and then slice it into 1-inch cubes. Put the bread into a food processor and pulse the machine on and off a few times until the bread is shredded into fine crumbs.

TOASTING BREAD CRUMBS

To toast bread crumbs, heat a little oil or butter in a small sauté pan over medium heat. When the oil or butter is hot, but not smoking, add a layer of bread crumbs, no more than ¼ inch thick. Stir or toss the bread crumbs to blend in the hot oil and continue to sauté, stirring or swirling the pan frequently, until the bread crumbs are lightly toasted, about 2 minutes. Immediately pour the bread crumbs out of the pan onto a cool plate so the heat of the pan doesn't keep toasting them.

SPRING GREENS AND CANNELLINI GRATIN

Y OU CAN used canned beans in this gratin as we do here, but if you have the time, cooking up a pot of beans means that you'll have some of the savory broth from the beans to replace the vegetable broth for a more intensely "beany" taste. Feel free to experiment with other cooking greens, such as escarole, tat soi (flat black cabbage), turnip, dandelion, or beet greens, but note that your cooking times may vary from those we give here.

SERVES 4 TO 6

1. Combine the beans, broth, tomatoes, and a generous pinch of salt and pepper in a saucepan and cook over medium heat, stirring occasionally, until the beans are completely tender and very flavorful, about 20 minutes. Season with additional salt and pepper and reserve.

2. Preheat the oven to 350°F.

3. Trim the stems of the chard or collard greens. Cut the stems away from the leaves and keep the stems and leaves separate. Chop the stems and greens into ½-inch pieces, and reserve.

4. Heat the olive oil in a large sauté pan over medium heat. Add the red pepper flakes and garlic and sauté until the aroma of the garlic is released, about 1 minute. Add the chard or collard green stems to the pan first and cook until they are wilted, about 4 minutes. Add the leaves to the sauté pan and season with salt and pepper. Continue to sauté, tossing occasionally, until the greens are tender, 10 to 12 minutes. Combine the greens with the beans and tomatoes and mix thoroughly. Season with additional salt and pepper if needed.

5. Put the greens and beans in a 9 × 13-inch baking dish or a 1½-quart ceramic casserole. Make an even layer over the top of the casserole with the bread crumbs. Bake until the crumbs are golden brown and the entire dish is very hot, about 45 minutes. If the crumbs begin to brown before the cooking time is complete, cover the pan loosely with aluminum foil. Serve hot directly from the baking dish or casserole on heated plates.

4 cups cooked cannellini, white kidney, or Great Northern beans, rinsed and drained

1 cup Vegetable Broth (page 82)

1 cup tomatoes (peeled, chopped, and seeded; see note on page 258)

Salt and pepper as needed

2 lb chard or collard greens, rinsed and drained

2 tbsp olive oil

1 tsp red pepper flakes, or to taste

1 tbsp minced garlic

2 cups lightly toasted bread crumbs (see note on page 214)

Side Dishes

T ISN'T ALWAYS easy to determine when a vegetable dish is something to serve "on the side" and when it is the main attraction. Think about a typical Thanksgiving table: At the center, a large, glossy, brown turkey, but ranged all around, a banquet of vegetable sides: Brussels sprouts with chestnuts, green beans flavored with nuts or bacon, creamed corn or spinach, baked squash drizzled with honey. Adding a variety of vegetable dishes to your meals means you have done more than fill up the empty space on your dinner plate, of course. A judicious selection livens up any main dish, even main dishes that feature vegetables.

THE MAIN DISH

The ingredients and cooking technique used for a main dish can help guide you toward the best side dish. Simply prepared foods, whether grilled, roasted, poached, sautéed or baked, can accommodate a more elaborate side dish. Stewed or braised vegetables, or a vegetable served with a sauce or a topping, are possibilities.

The intensity of flavor of the main item also should be taken into consideration. If you are serving a main dish of jerked chicken or a seafood curry, then your side dishes can be simply prepared.

Some main dishes have traditional sides. Apart from Thanksgiving traditions, we have come to expect certain vegetables with specific dishes: lightly steamed new peas with salmon for a New England Fourth of July, corn-on-the-cob with burgers and dogs for a backyard barbecue, glazed carrots with pot roast. It is up to you to decide if you like the tradition or want to turn it on its head by trying something unexpected, like parsnips with roast chicken instead of broccoli or green beans, or collard greens with meatloaf instead of creamed spinach or corn.

THE SEASONS

One of the greatest pleasures of shopping at farmstands and local markets is seeing the parade of seasonal vegetables. Whenever something is at its peak, you get more than the best buy. You also get the best flavor and nutrition. Sometimes, you may find it more appealing to let the side dishes you want to make from those fat, juicy asparagus or tender romano beans help you decide what main dish to make, instead of letting the main dish dictate the sides.

FLAVORS

Vegetables have distinct, and in some cases, assertive flavors. Think about how all the flavors will work together on a single plate. Vegetables that are somewhat sweet or starchy may taste too dull or bland if you pair them with a creamy or delicately flavored main dish, but those same vegetable side dishes take on a different character when paired with a more intensely flavored main dish.

COLORS

Too much of any color on a plate can be boring. Vegetables can add vibrant colors—deep greens, soft yellows, reds that range from pink to burgundy, and oranges. A plate of sliced roasted chicken is more attractive when bold colors are added, but less appealing when that same chicken is paired with only white or pale yellow vegetables.

TEXTURES

Just as the texture of a chicken changes depending upon the cooking technique you use, so will the texture of your vegetable side dishes. Zucchini is tender when stewed as part of a ratatouille, but takes on a whole different character when it is turned into crisp pancakes.

MAPLE-GLAZED BRUSSELS SPROUTS WITH CHESTNUTS

1¼ lb Brussels sprouts (two 10-oz containers), trimmed

Salt and pepper as needed

⅓ cup maple syrup

2 tbsp butter

¾ cup fresh or canned chestnuts (drain canned chestnuts)

B RUSSELS SPROUTS and chestnuts are a time-honored combination. If loose or bulk Brussels sprouts are available in your market, choose tiny sprouts of approximately the same size. If you buy the 10-ounce containers, separate the sprouts so that you can add the larger sprouts to the boiling water first. Cutting an X in the stem of large sprouts helps them cook evenly. Fresh chestnuts are delicious, but canned chestnuts are equally good with a lot less fuss.

MAKES 6 SERVINGS

1. Bring a large pot of salted water to a boil. Add the Brussels sprouts and cook until they are tender enough to pierce easily with a paring knife, 5 to 7 minutes. Using a slotted spoon, transfer the sprouts to a large bowl of ice water. When the sprouts are completely cooled, drain them thoroughly and cut the sprouts in half.

2. Combine the maple syrup, butter, and pepper in a large skillet over high heat and cook, stirring constantly, until the butter is melted and the maple syrup is boiling. Add the Brussels sprouts and chestnuts. Stir or toss until the Brussels sprouts and chestnuts are very hot, about 3 minutes.

BRUSSELS SPROUTS shine in simple dishes that make the most of their nutty taste. If you can find them sold on the stalk, you may be surprised at the difference in flavor and texture, compared to those sold in small round cartons. These darling vegetables are best after the first hard frost in fall.

TRIMMING BRUSSELS SPROUTS

Use a paring knife to trim away the end of the Brussels sprout that was attached to the stem. Next, pull away any very small or withered outer leaves. Once the leaves and stem are trimmed, cut into the stem.

Hold the sprouts, one at a time, with the stem end facing up. Press the blade of your paring knife into the stem, making a cut about ¼ inch deep. This will help the dense core of the Brussels sprouts to cook quickly. The faster you cook the sprouts, the sweeter they will taste.

FINISHING BRUSSELS SPROUTS

You can see by the change in color from the top photo to the bottom one, these sprouts have been cooked until they have a good color and are nearly tender. The final step adds more flavor and a beautiful sheen.

Heat the ingredients for a glaze or sauce. (Here, we've used maple syrup, but honey or molasses are good options, too.) Add the pre-cooked sprouts to the pan and keep them in motion, stirring or rolling them in the glaze, until they are evenly coated. They should be firm enough to hold together when you serve them, but tender enough to slice easily with a table knife.

BRUSSELS SPROUTS WITH MUSTARD GLAZE

3 cups Brussels sprouts

¾ cup Vegetable Broth (page 82)

1 tbsp whole-grain mustard

Salt and pepper as needed

BRUSSELS SPROUTS, a member of the cabbage family, are usually available fresh from late summer to late winter. Select small, bright-green sprouts with closed leaves. The smaller Brussels sprouts are more tender than the larger ones. If the Brussels sprouts are to be served with a meat dish, like turkey or pork roast, replace the vegetable broth with a jus or defatted pan juices from the meat.

SERVES 4

1. Rinse the Brussels sprouts, drain, and trim the stem ends by cutting away a thin slice with a paring knife. Cut a shallow X into each stem. Pull away any loose or yellowed leaves.

2. Bring a large pot of salted water to a rolling boil over high heat. Add the Brussels sprouts and cook until the tip of a paring knife goes into the stem end of the largest Brussels sprout easily, 10 to 12 minutes. Drain in a colander and reserve.

3. Return the pot to high heat. Add the vegetable broth and the mustard, whisking until the mustard is evenly blended into the broth. Simmer until the mixture is lightly thickened, about 2 minutes. Return the Brussels sprouts to the pot; stir or toss until evenly coated. Season to taste with salt and pepper. Serve at once in a heated bowl or on heated plates.

ASPARAGUS A LA PARRILLA

1 lb asparagus

6 tbsp extra-virgin olive oil, or as needed

Salt and pepper, as needed

½ cup fine-dice Serrano ham

1 tbsp minced garlic

¼ cup Chicken Broth (page 83)

¼ cup chopped flat-leaf parsley

1 tbsp lemon juice

2 hard-cooked eggs, chopped

THE SPANISH word "parrilla" refers to a grill that is set over an open fire. This dish pairs thick spears of grilled asparagus with a ham, parsley, and olive oil sauce.

SERVES 4 TO 6

1. Preheat a broiler or grill. Trim and peel the asparagus. Brush liberally with 2 tablespoons olive oil (or as needed) and season with salt and pepper. Broil or grill the asparagus until it is lightly charred and cooked through, turning to cook evenly, about 5 minutes. Transfer to heated plates or a platter.

2. Heat ¼ cup olive oil in a sauté pan over medium heat until it shimmers. Add the ham and garlic and sauté, stirring constantly, until the garlic is aromatic, about 1 minute. Add the broth and parsley and cook an additional minute. Whisk in the lemon juice; the sauce will thicken as the lemon juice is worked into the sauce. Season to taste with salt and pepper.

3. Pour the ham and olive oil sauce over the asparagus. Garnish with chopped, hard-cooked eggs.

Asparagus

When you are at the market, look for plump stalks of asparagus with tightly closed "buds" on the tip. Although the bottom of the spear may appear dry and woody, it should not be split or shriveled. To trim asparagus, simply cut away the bottom few inches of the spears, or bend the spear and let it snap into two pieces; fresh asparagus will snap and not bend.

To be sure that the stem and the tip cook evenly, gently peel the skin away from the stem end. If you apply too much pressure to the stalk, however, it can snap. Putting the spear flat on a work surface with the tip hanging over the edge makes it easier to peel without snapping it into pieces. Another option is to use a special tool for peeling asparagus. Instead of running the peeler over the asparagus, you pull or push the asparagus through the handle and against the blade.

PARMESAN-ROASTED WHITE ASPARAGUS WITH WHITE TRUFFLE OIL

ROASTING ASPARAGUS is an unexpected and surprisingly delicious alternative to steaming. We've suggested white asparagus in this recipe, but green asparagus is equally delicious.

MAKES 4 SERVINGS

1. Preheat the oven to 425°F.
2. Place the asparagus on a baking sheet and drizzle with the oil, Parmesan, thyme, salt, and pepper. Roast, turning the asparagus once or twice as it roasts, until the asparagus is tender with a crisp coating of Parmesan, 12 to 15 minutes. Serve warm or at room temperature. Drizzle with a little truffle oil just before serving if desired.

2 bunches white asparagus, trimmed

2 tbsp walnut or extra-virgin olive oil

1 tbsp grated Parmesan cheese

½ tsp chopped thyme

Salt and pepper as needed

Truffle oil, optional

Asparagus

BELGIAN ENDIVE À LA MEUNIÈRE

BELGIAN ENDIVES are deliberately protected from light as they grow to produce pale, satiny heads. Choose tight heads that show no scars or other blemishes. The leaves should be closed into a tight point and should have a pale ivory color, shading to a light yellowish green (or sometimes violet) at the tips.

SERVES 4

4 heads Belgian endive

2 tsp sugar

Salt and pepper as needed

2 tbsp fresh lemon juice

1 cup whole milk, or as needed

All-purpose flour for dredging

¼ cup vegetable oil

3 tbsp unsalted butter

2 tbsp minced flat-leaf parsley

1. Split each endive in half lengthwise and remove any bruised or damaged outer leaves. Bring a large pot of water to a boil and season with the sugar, 1 tsp salt, and 1 tsp of the lemon juice. Add the endives and boil, covered, until tender, 3 to 4 minutes. Transfer to a colander and drain, cut side down. When just cool enough to handle, press and drain on absorbent towels.

2. Transfer the endives to a cutting board and flatten each piece slightly by pressing down on it with the palm of your hand. Season the endives with salt and pepper. Put the milk and flour in separate bowls. Dip each endive half in the milk and then dredge in the flour.

3. Heat the oil in a large skillet over medium-high heat. Add the endives, in batches if necessary, and fry on the first side until golden brown, 2 to 3 minutes. Turn and fry on the second side until crisp and brown, 2 minutes more. Transfer the endives to a serving dish and cover to keep warm.

4. Pour off any excess oil from the pan and wipe out the browned flour with a paper towel. Add the butter and cook over medium heat until the butter begins to brown and take on a nutty aroma, about 30 seconds. Add the remaining lemon juice and the parsley and swirl it until the mixture thickens slightly. Pour the pan sauce over the endives and serve immediately.

MAPLE-GLAZED TURNIPS

2 lb purple-top turnips

2 tbsp unsalted butter

3 tbsp maple syrup

¼ tsp ground cinnamon

1 pinch freshly grated nutmeg

Salt and pepper as needed

Water as needed

1 tbsp chopped flat-leaf parsley

2 tsp fresh lemon juice

P AN-STEAMING, AN excellent technique for cooking vegetables, uses a small amount of flavorful liquid in a covered pan. There are two benefits: a quick cooking time that helps retain nutrients and color, and a flavorful liquid you can reduce to make a simple sauce.

SERVES 4

1. Peel the turnips and cut into even 1-inch cubes. Heat 1 tablespoon of butter in a sauté pan over medium heat. Add the maple syrup, cinnamon, nutmeg, and salt and pepper to taste. Add the turnips and then enough water to reach a depth of ¼ inch. Bring to a boil over high heat. Reduce the heat to a simmer, cover, and pan steam until the turnips are tender, 7 to 8 minutes.

2. Remove the cover from the pan, and continue to cook the turnips until the water has cooked away and the syrup has glazed each piece evenly, about 3 minutes. Add the remaining butter to the pan with the parsley and lemon juice. Shake the pan until the butter is melted and the turnips are evenly coated. Season to taste with additional salt and pepper. Serve immediately.

CREAMED SWISS CHARD
WITH PROSCIUTTO

2 tbsp olive oil

¼ cup diced prosciutto

¼ cup minced yellow onion

1 tbsp minced garlic

8 cups chopped Swiss chard leaves

⅓ cup heavy cream

Salt and pepper as needed

¼ cup grated Parmesan cheese

¼ tsp grated nutmeg

A s this dish proves, creamed vegetable dishes don't have to be bland. The assertive taste of chard paired with prosciutto is enhanced, not masked, by the addition of a touch of heavy cream.

SERVES 4

1. Heat the olive oil in a large sauté pan over medium heat. Add the prosciutto and sauté until aromatic, about 1 minute. Increase the heat to high, and add the onion and garlic. Sauté, stirring constantly, until the garlic is aromatic, about 1 minute more.

2. Add the Swiss chard, sautéing just until the leaves wilt, about 5 minutes. Add the heavy cream and bring to a simmer. Cook the Swiss chard until it is tender, about 5 minutes.

3. Season generously with salt and pepper. Remove from the heat, and stir in the Parmesan and nutmeg. Serve immediately in a heated bowl or on heated plates.

BRAISED KALE

3 cups Chicken Broth (page 83)

1 ham hock

2 lb kale

2 tbsp olive oil

1 slice bacon, chopped

1 cup chopped onions

½ cup minced garlic

½ cup white wine

Salt and pepper, as needed

T HE ADDITION of white wine to this dish gives it a subtle flavor boost. Another way you can introduce a bit more flavor is to simmer the ham hock in chicken broth while you clean the kale, as we do here.

SERVES 6 TO 8

1. Preheat the oven to 350°F.

2. Simmer the broth and ham hock together until the broth is very flavorful, about 20 minutes, while you prepare the kale.

3. Bring a large pot of salted water to a rolling boil. Trim the stems from the kale. Thoroughly rinse the leaves and drain well, then tear the leaves into bite-size pieces. Add the torn kale to the boiling water and cook, stirring once or twice, until the kale is bright green, 3 to 4 minutes. Drain in a colander, pressing on the kale to remove as much water as possible.

4. Heat the olive oil in a Dutch oven or casserole over medium heat until it shimmers. Add the bacon and cook, stirring frequently, until the fat is released from the bacon and the bacon bits are crisp, about 2 minutes.

5. Add the onions and garlic and sauté, stirring frequently, until the onions are tender and translucent, 3 to 4 minutes. Add the blanched kale and stir to coat thoroughly with the oil. Add the wine and simmer until the liquid is reduced by half.

6. Add the broth and ham hock, pushing the hock down into the kale. Bring the broth to a simmer, cover the pan, and braise in the oven until tender, 30 to 45 minutes. Using a slotted spoon, lift the kale from the Dutch oven or casserole and keep it warm while finishing the sauce.

7. Return the casserole or Dutch oven to high heat on the stovetop. Simmer the liquid until it is slightly thickened and very flavorful, about 5 minutes. Season to taste with salt and pepper. Return the kale to the casserole or Dutch oven, reheating the kale completely. Serve at once in a in a heated bowl or on heated plates.

BRAISED RED CABBAGE

This German-inspired dish mixes sweet and tart flavors to create a fine side dish for chops or game. Although red cabbage is traditional (the acid of the vinegar helps set the bright magenta color), you also can use green cabbage or a crinkly-leaved savoy cabbage.

SERVES 6 TO 8

1. Heat the oil in a Dutch oven over medium-low heat. Add the sliced onion and sauté until translucent, 6 to 8 minutes. Stir in the cabbage and cook until limp, 3 minutes.

2. Add the apple, broth, vinegar, cinnamon, cloves, sugar, salt, and pepper. Raise the heat to high and bring to a boil. Cover the pan, reduce the heat to low, and braise. Stir occasionally until the cabbage is tender, about 30 minutes.

3. Remove from the heat and stir in the jelly and lemon juice. Taste and season with additional salt, pepper, and lemon juice, if needed. Remove the cinnamon stick before serving.

2 tbsp vegetable oil

1 cup thinly sliced onion (halved before slicing)

4 cups shredded red cabbage

½ cup thinly sliced tart green apple (peeled and cored)

1½ cups Chicken Broth (page 83)

2 tbsp red wine vinegar

1 cinnamon stick

1 pinch ground cloves

2 tsp sugar

2 tsp salt

Freshly ground pepper, to taste

2 tbsp currant jelly

1 tsp lemon juice, or to taste

BROCCOLI IN GARLIC SAUCE

6 cups broccoli florets

3 tbsp soy sauce

2 tbsp Chinese rice wine or dry sherry wine

2 tbsp rice vinegar

2 tbsp Chicken Broth (page 83)

1 tbsp cornstarch

2 tsp chili paste

1 tsp sugar

2 tbsp peanut oil

1 scallion, white and green parts, sliced thin on the diagonal

1 tbsp minced gingerroot

2 tbsp minced garlic

½ red pepper julienne

Salt, as needed

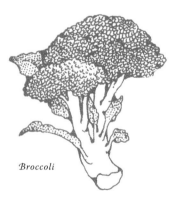

Broccoli

B LANCHING, OR cooking briefly in boiling salted water, helps the broccoli hold its bright color. Precooking also ensures that it will cook through in the rapid final stirfry. This also would make a great main course served on a bed of steamed rice.

SERVES 6 TO 8

1. Bring a pot of water to a boil and blanch the broccoli for 2 minutes, until a vivid green but still firm. Drain. (If the broccoli is cooked in advance, refresh it in ice water and drain again. Refrigerate until ready to stirfry.)

2. Combine the soy sauce, wine, rice vinegar, broth, cornstarch, chili paste, and sugar in a small bowl. Set aside.

3. Heat the oil in a wok over medium-high heat. Add the scallion, ginger, and garlic and stirfry until aromatic, about 1 minute. Raise the heat to high, add the red pepper, and stirfry for 1 minute more. Add the broccoli and stirfry until the broccoli is hot, about 1 minute. Whisk the soy sauce mixture to recombine, and then add it to the broccoli. Bring to a boil without stirring, about 30 seconds; stir just until the sauce coats the vegetables. Taste and season with salt, if needed. Serve immediately on heated plates.

BEET GREENS AND WHITE BEANS SAUTÉ

I f you can't find beet greens, substitute broccoli raab, kale, escarole, collard greens, or turnip greens. Use cannellini beans, Great Northern, or navy beans in this dish.

SERVES 6

1. Heat a large sauté pan over medium-high heat. Add the olive oil and heat until the oil shimmers. Add the garlic and sauté, stirring frequently, until it is tender and aromatic, about 1 minute. Add the red pepper flakes, if using, and sauté until aromatic, 20 to 30 seconds.

2. Add the beet greens and cook, stirring and tossing briskly with a wooden spoon to coat the greens evenly with the oil. When the greens have cooked down and are a vivid green color, about 5 minutes, add the broth. Season to taste with salt and pepper.

3. Bring the broth to a simmer, and then add the beans and cook, stirring frequently, until the greens are fully wilted and the dish is very hot. Season to taste with the malt vinegar.

2 tbsp olive oil

2 tbsp minced garlic

¼ tsp crushed red pepper flakes, optional

10 cups coarsely chopped beet greens

½ cup Chicken Broth (page 83)

1 tsp salt, or to taste

½ tsp ground black pepper, or to taste

2 cups cooked white beans, drained and rinsed

2 tsp malt vinegar, or to taste

ZUCCHINI PANCAKES

T HESE PANCAKES feature feta cheese and chopped walnuts to punctuate the relatively mild taste of zucchini in these crunchy fritters.

SERVES 6 TO 8

1. Place the grated zucchini in colander. Sprinkle with salt and let stand for 30 minutes. Squeeze the zucchini to remove as much liquid as possible. Dry the zucchini by pressing it between several layers of paper towels.

2. In a large bowl, combine the zucchini, scallions, eggs, flour, dill, parsley, tarragon, salt, and pepper until evenly blended. Fold in the feta cheese. (The pancake mixture can be prepared to this point up to 3 hours ahead. Cover tightly and refrigerate. Stir to blend before continuing.) Fold the walnuts into the zucchini mixture.

3. Preheat the oven to 300°F to keep the pancakes warm as you work. Place a baking sheet in the oven.

4. Add enough oil to a skillet to come to a depth of about ⅛ inch, and heat the oil over medium-high heat until the surface of the oil shimmers. Working in batches, drop heaping tablespoons of the zucchini mixture into the hot oil, leaving enough room for the pancakes to spread as they cook. Fry until the pancakes are golden brown and cooked through, about 3 minutes per side. Transfer each batch of pancakes to the baking sheet in the oven to keep warm. Serve immediately with the tzatziki sauce.

3 cups coarsely grated zucchini

Salt and pepper as needed

2 cups chopped scallions

4 eggs, lightly beaten

½ cup flour

⅓ cup chopped dill

⅓ cup chopped parsley

2 tbsp chopped tarragon

½ cup crumbled feta cheese

⅔ cup chopped walnuts

Olive oil for pan frying

1 cup Tzatziki Sauce (page 278)

OKRA STEWED WITH TOMATOES

1 lb fresh small okra pods

2 strips smoked bacon, diced

½ cup Vegetable Broth (page 82) or water

1 cup onion julienne

3 to 4 plum tomatoes, peeled, seeded,
 and chopped

Salt and freshly ground black pepper to taste

OKRA, A member of the hibiscus family, has not been welcomed with open arms in most parts of the country. Its most familiar "home" is in gumbo. Actually, the term "gumbo" is a transliteration of the Angolan term for okra: "ngombo." Okra is itself a variant of the term used for it by natives from Ghana, "nkruma."

MAKES 4 SERVINGS

1. Rinse the okra, trim away the caps, and slice about ½ inch thick. Reserve.
2. Combine the diced bacon with ¼ cup of the broth or water in a skillet and set the skillet over medium-high heat. Cook, stirring from time to time, until the water has cooked away and the bacon has released some of its fat, about 2 minutes.
3. Add the onion to the skillet, and reduce the heat to low. Continue to sauté, stirring frequently, until the onion is a deep golden brown, 12 to 15 minutes.
4. Add the sliced okra, the remaining broth or water, and the tomatoes. Cover the skillet and reduce the heat to low. Cook gently, stirring from time to time and adding a little additional broth or water, if necessary, for about 15 minutes (or longer if you prefer the okra quite soft).
5. Season generously with pepper. Add salt to taste.

RATATOUILLE

THIS CLASSIC Provençal dish hails from the south of France, where it makes the most of the Mediterranean bounty of late summer. On a hot day, it can be served cool for a light supper or lunch dish.

SERVES 4 TO 6

1. Heat the olive oil in a sauté pan over medium heat. Add the garlic and sauté until aromatic, about 1 minute. Add the onions and sauté until translucent, 4 to 5 minutes.

2. Add the tomato paste and cook over medium heat until it deepens in color and gives off a sweet aroma, about 1 minute. Add the broth and stir to deglaze the pan, scraping up any browned bits from the pan bottom.

3. Add the eggplant, zucchini, mushrooms, and green pepper and simmer until the vegetables are tender but not falling apart, 10 to 12 minutes. Stir in the tomatoes and continue to simmer until the tomatoes are heated through, 2 to 3 minutes. Add the parsley and basil. Taste, season with salt and pepper, and then serve.

2 tbsp olive oil

3 tbsp minced garlic

2 cups diced yellow onions

1 tbsp tomato paste

¾ cup Chicken Broth (page 83)

4 cups diced eggplant

1⅓ cups sliced zucchini (quartered lengthwise before slicing)

1 cup quartered mushrooms

1 cup diced green pepper

2 cups chopped tomatoes (peeled and seeded)

¼ cup chopped flat-leaf parsley

¼ cup chopped basil

Salt and pepper as needed

ROASTED CORN SUCCOTASH

YOU CAN roast or grill the corn for this dish. Dampen the husks before you begin to add a bit of moisture for steam. To check the corn for doneness, pull back some of the husk and look at the kernels. They should be plump and moist, and should "pop" easily when pressed with the tines of a table fork.

SERVES 6 TO 8

1. Preheat the oven to 400°F. Dampen the husks with cold water and place the corn directly on the oven rack. Roast the corn until the kernels are tender and cooked through, 10 to 15 minutes. When the corn is cool enough to handle, pull away the husk and the silk. Cut the kernels from the cob and reserve.

2. Heat the olive oil in a large sauté pan over medium-high heat until it shimmers. Add the corn and zucchini and sauté, stirring occasionally, until the zucchini is tender, about 3 minutes. Add the tomato, lima beans, scallions, and broth, and continue to sauté until all of the ingredients are very hot, about 4 minutes. Remove the pan from the heat and stir in the parsley, tarragon, and cardamom. Season to taste with salt and pepper. Serve at once in a heated bowl or on heated plates.

4 ears corn in the husk

1 tbsp extra-virgin olive oil

1 cup diced zucchini

1 cup chopped tomato, peeled and seeded

1 cup cooked lima beans

½ cup scallions, thinly sliced on a diagonal

¾ cup Vegetable Broth (page 82)

1 tbsp chopped parsley

2 tsp chopped tarragon

¼ tsp ground cardamom

Salt and pepper as needed

ZUCCHINI SQUASH WITH TOMATOES AND ANDOUILLE

1 lb zucchini (about 2 medium or 3 small)

1 tbsp olive oil or vegetable oil

½ cup crumbled smoked andouille sausage

½ cup red pepper julienne

2 tbsp minced shallot

2 finely minced garlic cloves

2 tomatoes (peeled, seeded, and chopped; juices reserved)

2 tbsp minced cilantro or flat-leaf parsley

2 tsp fresh lemon juice

Grated zest of ½ lemon

Salt and freshly ground pepper, as needed

INSTEAD OF zucchini, try other types of summer squash, such as yellow squash, flat, oval sunburst squash, or the delectable round, green *rond de Nice* squash. When choosing any summer squash, look for specimens that are firm, slightly shiny, and smooth skinned.

SERVES 4

1. Trim the zucchini and quarter them lengthwise. Cut the zucchini crosswise into slices about ½ inch thick.

2. Heat the oil in a skillet over medium heat. Add the andouille and cook, stirring occasionally, until it starts to brown and crisp, 2 to 3 minutes. Add the red pepper, shallot, and garlic, and cook, stirring occasionally, until softened, 2 to 3 minutes.

3. Add the zucchini with the tomatoes and their juices. (Add about 2 tablespoons water if the tomatoes are not juicy.) Cover and pan steam over high heat until the zucchini is very tender, about 5 minutes. Add the cilantro or parsley, lemon juice, and zest, and toss to blend evenly. Season to taste with salt and pepper. Serve immediately.

SAUTÉED BROCCOLI RAAB WITH GARLIC AND CRUSHED PEPPER

3 lb broccoli raab

¼ cup olive oil

3 tbsp thinly sliced garlic

1 or 2 anchovy fillets, optional

¼ to ½ tsp crushed red pepper flakes

Salt and pepper, as needed

THE BITTER and pungent flavor of broccoli raab is made less bitter and strong by blanching it first. The flavors in this dish also work beautifully with blanched, chopped spinach, green beans, or cauliflower florets.

SERVES 6

1. Bring a large pot of salted water to a boil. Wash the broccoli raab and remove any tough stems and very large leaves. Blanch the broccoli raab in the boiling water until it is bright green, about 3 minutes. Drain and rinse the broccoli raab to stop the cooking. Squeeze dry and chop, if desired.

2. In a sauté pan, heat the oil over low heat. Add the garlic and cook gently, stirring frequently, until the garlic is limp and barely golden, about 2 minutes. (Keep the heat very low to avoid scorching the garlic.)

3. Add the anchovy fillets, if using, and smash them into the olive oil with the back of a spoon. Cook until the anchovy is dissolved, about 1 minute. Add the red pepper flakes and stir into the oil. Increase the heat to high, add the broccoli raab, and sauté quickly until the broccoli raab is very hot, about 3 minutes. Season to taste with salt and pepper. Serve immediately on heated plates or in a heated serving bowl.

SICILIAN-STYLE SPINACH

1 tbsp olive oil

2 tbsp diced pancetta or 1 slice bacon, diced

1 anchovy fillet, chopped

¼ cup minced yellow onion

1 tbsp minced garlic

8 cups spinach leaves

Salt and pepper as needed

2 tbsp dark or golden raisins

1 tbsp toasted pine nuts

THE ADDITION of raisins to this spinach dish reflects the influence of the Ottoman Empire throughout the Mediterranean region. They introduced combinations that called for a touch of dry fruit for sweetness, to highlight the briny taste of the anchovy and the heat of the garlic.

SERVES 4 TO 6

1. Heat the olive oil in a large sauté pan over medium heat. Add the pancetta and sauté until the fat renders and the pancetta is translucent, about 1 minute. Raise the heat to high and add the anchovy, onion, and garlic. Sauté until the garlic is aromatic and the anchovy has dissolved into the oil, about 1 minute more. Add the spinach and sauté until deep green, tender, and softened, 3 to 4 minutes more.

2. Drain the mixture, if necessary, and season generously with salt and pepper. Remove from the heat and stir in the raisins and pine nuts. Serve immediately.

CITRUS-ROASTED BEETS

For a truly eye-catching dish, try combining several different colors of beets such as red, golden, or the candy-striped Chioggia beets, which when cut reveal a pattern of pink and white concentric rings.

MAKES 4 SERVINGS

1 lb beets (about 6 small beets)

Zest of 1 orange

1 tsp salt, plus additional to taste

½ tsp freshly ground pepper, plus additional
    to taste

2 tbsp olive oil

2 tbsp fresh orange juice

3 tbsp chopped fresh cilantro, flat-leaf
    parsley, or mint

1. Preheat the oven to 350°F. Trim the stem ends of the beets, leaving about 1 inch intact; leave the root ends untouched. Place the beets in a small baking dish with water to a depth of ¼ inch. Scatter half of the orange zest, the salt, and the pepper over the top. Cover the pan tightly with aluminum foil and bake until the beets are tender enough to pierce easily with the tip of a paring knife, about 1 hour.

2. When the beets are cool enough to handle, trim the ends and slip off the skins. Quarter each beet lengthwise and cut each quarter into ½-inch-thick slices.

3. Whisk together the olive oil, remaining orange zest, orange juice, and cilantro in a serving bowl. Add the roasted beets and toss well. Season to taste with additional salt and pepper. Serve warm.

HOISIN-CARAMELIZED ROOT VEGETABLES

T HE HOISIN adds a rich flavor and color to this simple vegetable dish. The larger the vegetable cut, the longer the cooking time.

SERVES 6

1. Preheat the oven to 350°F. Combine the oil and hoisin and heat in a roasting pan, add the vegetables, and toss until coated evenly. Season generously with salt and pepper. Pour the water over the vegetables.

2. Cover the pan with a lid or aluminum foil and place in the preheated oven. Roast the vegetables until nearly tender, about 30 minutes. Remove the cover and finish roasting, turning the vegetables so that they cook evenly, another 10 to 15 minutes. Season to taste with additional salt and pepper. Serve at once in a heated bowl or on heated plates.

2 tbsp peanut oil

2 tbsp hoisin

2 cups thickly sliced carrots

2 cups yellow turnip wedges

2 cups thickly sliced parsnips

1 fennel bulb, wedge cut

1 cup pearl onions, peeled, optional

Salt and pepper as needed

¼ cup water

SWEET AND SOUR GREEN BEANS
WITH WATER CHESTNUTS

1 lb green beans, trimmed, cut into
   2-inch lengths

2 tbsp soy sauce

2 tbsp hoisin sauce

2 tbsp rice wine vinegar

1 tsp (or to taste) hot pepper sauce

2 tsp peanut oil

1 garlic clove, minced

One 8-oz can sliced water chestnuts,
   drained

1 tsp dark sesame oil

THESE BEANS are easy to prepare and feature a refreshing Asian flavor profile that is a quick and easy complement to your favorite Asian-inspired entrée. They are also delicious served cold as a vegetable salad.

SERVES 8

1. Trim the stem ends from the green beans, rinse well with cold running water, and drain. Cut the beans into pieces about 2 inches long. Place the green beans in a steamer basket and set in a saucepan over 1 inch of boiling water. Cover and steam until just tender, about 5 minutes; drain.

2. Combine the soy sauce, hoisin sauce, vinegar, and hot pepper sauce in a small bowl. Reserve.

3. Heat a wok over high heat. Add the peanut oil and heat until the oil shimmers. Add the green beans and garlic. Stirfry the beans until they are bright green and hot, about 2 minutes. Add the soy sauce mixture and continue to stirfry, tossing the beans until they are coated with the sauce. Add the water chestnuts and drizzle with the sesame oil. Serve at once in a heated bowl or on heated plates.

WINTER SQUASH, a popular denizen of holiday tables, typically is baked and topped with brown sugar and nuts. If you don't want to bake your squash whole, you can use the techniques shown here to make delicious sautés, or simply cut squash into dice that you can add to soups and stews.

PEELING WINTER SQUASH

Acorn, pumpkin, butternut, and Hubbard squashes have a hard thick rind. The rind protects the squash and keeps it from spoiling for long periods, but makes your job a challenge if you want to remove the rind before you cook the squash.

1. Make some initial cuts that give you a flat surface. Cut through a butternut squash at the point where the "neck" meets the rounded "body." Cut through a round squash like acorn squash from stem end to blossom end.

2. Use a spoon to scoop out the seeds and any filaments in the center of the squash. Then, set your squash, flat side down, on a work surface and use a chef's knife to cut away the skin.

COMBINING VARIETIES

Squashes come in varying colors and textures. Some are a deep vibrant orange, while others are a creamy light yellow. Although each variety of squash has a distinct taste, it can get lost if you don't take some steps to bring it out.

1. Instead of boiling or steaming cut squashes, pan-steam them in some broth. You can add a sprig or two of thyme, or a bay leaf while the squash cooks. Once the squash is tender, remove the cover and let the broth reduce.

2. Add plenty of seasoning ingredients. Dried fruits, like the cranberries shown here, add tartness as well as color and texture. Nuts are a perfect foil for the rich taste of a classic winter vegetable.

WINTER SQUASHES SAUTÉED WITH CRANBERRIES AND TOASTED PECANS

¼ cup pecans

1 tbsp dried cranberries

½ cup boiling water

1 cup Vegetable or Chicken Broth
(pages 82–83)

1 cup diced or julienned butternut squash

1 cup diced or julienned acorn squash

1 cup diced or julienned pumpkin

2 tbsp butter

Juice of 1 lemon

Salt and pepper as needed

REMOVING THE rind from a hard-skin squash can be a challenge. Give yourself plenty of room to work, and be sure to cut a thin slice from the bottom or side of the squash to help it stay flat on the cutting board. Or you can opt to use frozen cubed squashes instead.

SERVES 4

1. Preheat the oven to 300°F. Place the pecans on a shallow baking pan and toast the pecans approximately 10 minutes, stirring occasionally, until brown. Set aside.

2. Combine the dried cranberries with boiling water. Allow them to plump for 10 to 15 minutes. Chop them coarsely and set aside.

3. Bring the broth to a boil over high heat in a skillet. Add the squash and pumpkin. Cover the skillet and simmer over low heat until tender, about 10 to 12 minutes. Remove the cover, increase the heat to high, and allow any excess moisture to cook away, about 2 to 3 minutes.

4. Drain the cranberries and add them to the skillet along with the pecans, butter, lemon juice, salt, and pepper. Continue to cook for another 2 minutes, stirring gently to distribute all of the ingredients evenly. Serve immediately.

Sauces & Relishes

AUCES AND RELISHES are more than just an afterthought. Properly chosen to suit the dish you are serving, they can be the little extra that elevates a dish from the ordinary to the sublime. They can add moisture, eye appeal, and flavor. They can enhance a particular flavor or texture, or provide a delightful contrast. In this chapter, we've collected recipes for a variety of sauces and relishes that feature vegetables, as well as some classic sauces that are perfect to serve with vegetables.

CONDIMENTS

Condiments are assertive, sauce-like creations, typically served on the side and added at the diner's discretion. However, condiments also can be found as spreads or dips, adding a little extra to sandwiches, dressings, and salads. Some people actually do make their own mustards, mayonnaise, and chutney. They are not difficult to make, and are always more interesting when made by hand. That said, the quality and variety of condiments in any well-stocked market makes them a wonderful boon to a time-strapped cook.

MAYONNAISE

Used as a spread, a binder for salads, or a sauce, mayonnaise is one of the classic sauces that all chefs learn to master. Handmade versions have a richer color, since they include a greater percentage of egg yolk than commercial varieties. (For more about making and seasoning mayonnaise, see page 282.)

MUSTARD

Plain and flavored mustards have a wonderful aroma and a complex flavor that pairs beautifully with meats, cheeses, and poultry. Mustard can even be served as a dip. It is frequently added to vinaigrettes and other dressings and is also used to glaze meats as they roast. Special mustards from around the

world have their own unique qualities. Some are very hot, others are mild; some are very smooth, others are grainy.

CHUTNEY

Chutneys are sweet-and-sour condiments, often fruit-based (though vegetable-based versions exist as well) and generally highly spiced, favored in Indian cuisines. Chutneys may be cooked, similar to a pickle or relish, or they may be raw, making them similar to other cold raw sauces such as salsa.

Mango chutney is probably most familiar worldwide, but tomatoes, eggplant, melons, apples, and pineapples are also commonly used to prepare chutneys.

SALSA

A salsa can be raw or cooked. It may include familiar ingredients (tomatoes, onions, chiles or peppers, and a touch of lime juice) or more exotic items, like jícama, chayote, or green papaya. Serve salsas as either a condiment or as a dip or topping for a variety of foods, ranging from chips to grilled fish, meats, or poultry.

RELISH

A relish may be as simple as a mound of sliced cucumbers or radishes, or as complex as a curried onion relish, cooked in a pickle or brine, highly seasoned, and garnished with dried fruits. Relishes are served cold to act as a foil to hot or spicy foods, or to liven up dishes that need some extra kick.

PICKLES

Pickles encompass any food that has been brined. They can be made from vegetables, fruit, or eggs. The brine often contains vinegar, although a salt brine also can be used to make special pickles. Pickles may be extremely tart, such as half sours, or sweet, like the sweet pickle chips (both recipes are on page 269).

017664. VEGETABLE STANDS IN MERCADO TOCON, HAVANA, CUBA. COPYRIGHT 1904 BY DETROIT PHOTOGRAPHIC

Tomatoes

Tomatoes lend a special flavor to dishes that include them, whether they have been simply chopped and combined with other ingredients in a salsa, briefly cooked into a coulis, or simmered into a rich sauce. There are a number of advance preparation techniques you can use with tomatoes.

SLICED TOMATOES

Larger tomatoes, sometimes referred to as slicing tomatoes, are easiest to cut into even slices, with smooth, clean surfaces, when you use a knife with a thin blade that has a serrated edge. If your knife is at all dull, it will have a hard time cutting through the skin. You may press down too hard to force it through the skin, and end up crushing or bursting the tomato. Before you slice tomatoes, cut away the blossom end, the small dark spot on the bottom of the tomato. Use a paring knife or a tomato corer to remove the stem and core. The first slice at the core end may not be as attractive as the rest of the slices. Tomatoes are also commonly cut into wedges. Make a cut from the stem end to the blossom end. If you haven't already removed the core, use the tip of a paring knife to cut it away. Cut each half into wedges of the size you like. Cherry tomatoes also can be cut into wedges or halves.

CHOPPED TOMATOES

If you are planning to cook the tomatoes, you'll find that most recipes call for the tomatoes to be peeled and seeded before they go into the pot. Chefs call tomatoes prepared this way tomato concassé. Use the following technique:

1. *Prepare the tomatoes by cutting a shallow X in the blossom end (the bottom of the tomato). You also can cut out the core at this point if you wish.*

2. *Bring a pot of water to a rolling boil. Partially fill a bowl with ice water. Lower the tomatoes, two or three at a time, into the boiling water using a slotted spoon. After 10 to 30 seconds (depending on the age and ripeness of the tomatoes), take them out and plunge them into ice water.*

3. *When the tomatoes feel cool to the touch, take them out of the water and pull away the skin, starting at the X at the bottom.*

4. *To remove the seeds from peeled tomatoes or from canned whole tomatoes, cut the round tomatoes in half at their widest point. Plum tomatoes are more easily seeded by cutting lengthwise. Gently squeeze out the seeds in a bowl. Use a clean fingertip to help get them out.*

4. *Cut or chop the tomato to the size and shape required.*

MAKING TOMATO COULIS

A coulis is a sauce that is essentially just a puree of an ingredient. Tomato coulis is lightly cooked to bring out more of the tomato flavor. The sauce is pureed by pushing it through a sieve so that the natural fibers in the tomato give the coulis some body and texture. Let the coulis cool after you remove it from the stove, then pour it into a sieve that you've set over a bowl and use a spoon to push the coulis through the sieve, being sure to scrape the bottom of the sieve as you finish. Stir the coulis. It is now ready to reheat, to finish with cream or fresh herbs, or to store in the refrigerator for up to 4 days.

DEVELOPING FLAVOR IN TOMATO SAUCE

Simmering tomatoes until they take on a deep rusty color does more than change the sauce's appearance. It also changes the sauce's taste and texture. Keep the heat low and stir the sauce often. As the tomatoes cook, their natural sugars begin to caramelize, giving the tomatoes a characteristic rusty or brick red appearance. This also sweetens the sauce, so you may need to adjust the flavor by adding bit of water or salt. At the same time, the moisture in the tomatoes is cooking away and thickening the sauce.

TOMATOES fill many roles in the kitchen, from the main ingredient in a dish to an important supporting aromatic ingredient in others. One of the most popular uses of tomatoes is as an ingredient in a sauce, such as our basic tomato sauce, tomato coulis, or pomorola, or uncooked sauces like a salsa or a relish.

FRESH TOMATOES IN A COULIS

A coulis is described on page 258. To make this style of sauce from fresh tomatoes, choose tomatoes that are more meaty than juicy. Roma or plum tomatoes are a good choice. Taste the tomato before you cook it into a coulis. Then, you can decide what adjustments you want to make to improve the sauce's flavor.

A standard kitchen sieve is perfect for straining and pureeing a coulis. Food mills are also useful. These tools result in a light sauce that still has enough texture to cling.

CANNED TOMATOES FOR A SAUCE

When fresh tomatoes are out of season or don't have much flavor, you may want to use canned tomatoes, alone or in combination with fresh tomatoes. To learn more about how to work with canned tomatoes, read the note on page 261. Remember to taste your canned tomatoes before you start cooking. Some varieties are noticeably sweet, while others are slightly acidic.

You can add aromatic herbs and spices as your sauce cooks. We've added basil here. If you like to make large batches of sauce, you may prefer to omit seasonings and herbs from the main batch so you can customize smaller amounts throughout the week.

BASIC TOMATO SAUCE

MAKES 4 CUPS

2 tbsp olive oil

¼ cup minced garlic

6 cups chopped plum tomatoes, peeled and seeded, juices reserved

3 or 4 sprigs basil

1 tbsp chopped basil

Salt and pepper as needed

1. Heat the olive oil in a 2-quart sauce pot over medium heat until it shimmers. Add the garlic and sauté, stirring constantly, until its aroma is apparent, about 30 seconds. Add the tomatoes and reserved juices, along with the basil sprigs, to the pot, and bring the sauce to a boil. Reduce the heat to low, and simmer the sauce 20 to 25 minutes. Remove and discard the basil sprigs.

2. Add the chopped basil and simmer until very flavorful, about 5 minutes. Taste the sauce and adjust the seasoning to taste with salt and pepper.

TOMATO COULIS

MAKES 3 CUPS

3 lb plum tomatoes

2 tbsp olive oil

1 tsp minced garlic

5 basil leaves

Salt and pepper as needed

1. Peel, seed, and chop the tomatoes as explained on page 258.

2. Heat the olive oil in a saucepan over medium heat. Add the garlic and sauté it until aromatic, about 30 seconds. Add the chopped tomatoes and basil leaves. Bring the sauce to a simmer and cook gently, stirring frequently, until the liquid released by the tomatoes has cooked away, about 15 minutes.

3. Remove and discard the basil leaves. Puree the coulis through a food mill fitted with the coarse disk or with a handheld blender. Simmer the coulis a little longer over medium heat if it is too thin. Season to taste with salt and pepper.

4. The sauce is ready to serve now, or it may be rapidly cooled and stored under refrigeration for later use.

POMAROLA TOMATO SAUCE

THIS IS the recipe for the signature tomato sauce of Tuscany. It is a nice take on a basic tomato sauce, with the addition of extra basil and hot peppers. If you use red pepper flakes instead of dried chiles, remember that the whole chile is removed from the sauce, while the red pepper flakes stay in the sauce, so start with a small amount and add more as the sauce simmers until it has the heat level you like. This is supposed to be a hearty, chunky sauce, but if you like a smoother sauce, puree it through a food mill.

MAKES 4 CUPS

2 tbsp olive oil

½ cup minced onions

4 tsp minced garlic

6 cups chopped plum tomatoes, peeled and seeded

2 or 3 dried red chile peppers (or ½ tsp red pepper flakes)

¼ cup chopped fresh basil

Salt and pepper as needed

1. Heat the olive oil in a large saucepan over medium-high heat. Add the onions and sauté until translucent, about 6 minutes. Add the garlic and sauté until fragrant, about 1 minute.

2. Add the tomatoes and dried chile or red pepper flakes, and bring the sauce to a boil. Reduce the heat to low, and simmer for 20 to 25 minutes.

3. Add the basil and simmer for 5 minutes more. Remove and discard the dried chiles. Season to taste with salt and pepper.

USING CANNED TOMATOES FOR SAUCES

You can replace the fresh tomatoes in any of these recipes with canned whole tomatoes that have been seeded and coarsely chopped. (Reserve the juices to add to the pot as well.) Be sure to taste the tomatoes before starting the sauce. If the tomatoes need extra body or flavor, sauté ¼ to ⅓ cup tomato paste with the onions after the onions are translucent. Another option is to replace half of the whole tomatoes with tomato purée.

TOMATO-GINGER COULIS

1 cup vegetable oil

¼ pound peeled and grated gingerroot

4 tomatoes, chopped

Salt and pepper as needed

1 tbsp vinegar, or to taste

SERVE THIS sauce with grilled fish such as swordfish, or with pasta and vegetables.

MAKES 2 CUPS

1. Heat the oil in a small saucepan over medium heat and add the ginger. Remove from the heat and set aside to steep for at least 15 minutes.

2. Puree the tomatoes, salt, pepper, and vinegar in a blender. Add the infused oil and blend until emulsified.

ROASTED RED PEPPER PUREE

4 red bell peppers, roasted, peeled, seeded, and chopped

½ cup Vegetable or Chicken Broth (pages 82–83), or as needed

¼ cup heavy cream, optional

Salt and pepper as needed

ROASTING PEPPERS gives them a whole new flavor—smoky, rich, and surprisingly sweet. If you have a lot of peppers to peel, try grilling them on a gas or charcoal grill for an extra level of flavor. This coulis is finished with heavy cream, but if you are doubling or tripling the recipe to freeze for later, it is best to add the cream after you've thawed and reheated the coulis.

MAKES ABOUT 2 CUPS

1. Puree the peppers in a food processor or blender. Add the broth and continue to puree until the sauce is quite smooth and thin enough to pour easily.

2. Strain the mixture into a mixing bowl; add the heavy cream, if using, and salt and pepper to taste.

3. The coulis either can be used immediately or stored in the refrigerator, covered, for up to 1 week.

TO ROAST PEPPERS

- *Use tongs or a fork to hold a whole pepper in the flame of a gas burner, turning the pepper until all of its sides are blackened, or*

- *Cut the peppers in half, pull away the seeds, and rub the outsides lightly with oil. Place them, cut side down, on a baking sheet and broil until blackened.*

Once the peppers are blackened (by either method), place them in a plastic bag and let them rest until they are cool enough to handle. Then pull away the charred skin, using a paring knife or your fingers to loosen the skin. Discard the seeds, ribs, and stems.

TOMATILLO SALSA

A TOMATILLO IS a fruit that looks like a small, unripe tomato with a papery husk. Tomatillos have a tart and lemony flavor and commonly are used in Southwestern and Mexican cuisines. This easy salsa is an excellent complement to grilled meats.

MAKES 2 CUPS

1. Remove the husks from the tomatillos. Place the tomatillos and the jalapeño in a pot and cover them with water. Boil until the tomatillos are fully cooked and have become a dull olive green color, about 10 minutes.

2. Strain the tomatillos from the water and place them directly into a food processor fitted with a metal chopping blade. Add the jalapeño and garlic cloves. Process the mixture until completely smooth. Add the cilantro to the food processor and pulse to chop and incorporate. Season to taste with salt and pepper. Serve warm or chilled.

10 tomatillos

1 jalapeño, stemmed, seeded, and ribs removed

2 garlic cloves

1 bunch cilantro

Salt and pepper as needed

TO MAKE a hotter salsa, do not remove the seeds and veins from the jalapeño.

BLACKENED TOMATO SALSA

"BLACKENING" THE tomatoes gives them a smoky taste, as well as making it easy to peel the tomatoes.

SERVES 6; MAKES ABOUT 3 CUPS

1. Place the tomatoes on a wire rack directly over a gas burner or on a medium-high grill. Turn them frequently until they are blackened over their entire surface. Set aside.

2. Heat the oil in a large sauté pan over medium heat. Add the onion slices and cook on both sides until they are a very deep brown, about 15 to 20 minutes total cooking time.

3. Coarsely chop the tomatoes and onions. Combine the tomatoes, onions, chili, and salt in a blender or food processor. Puree the mixture in short pulses to make a chunky salsa. Serve warm or at room temperature.

5 plum tomatoes

1 tbsp olive oil

1 Spanish onion, cut into ¼-inch-thick slices

½ dried chipotle chile

Salt to taste

TOMATO SALSA

COMMON TO the cuisines of the Southwest and Mexico, the variations of tomato salsa are endless. Serve Tomato Salsa with tortilla chips as an appetizer or as an accompaniment to a variety of Southwestern and Tex-Mex dishes, such as fajitas, burritos, and enchiladas; or enjoy it with grilled meats, fish, and poultry.

SERVES 8

Combine all of the ingredients in a bowl. Let the salsa rest for at least 15 minutes before serving in order to develop flavor. Adjust the seasoning with salt and pepper to taste.

4 plum tomatoes, chopped

4 scallions, sliced thin

½ cup minced onions

1 tsp minced garlic

2 tbsp chopped cilantro

1 jalapeño, seeded, chopped fine

2 tbsp lemon juice

ADD ADDITIONAL jalapeño peppers, Tabasco sauce, or cayenne pepper for a hotter salsa. A small amount of white wine or sherry vinegar may be added to adjust the flavor. Other additions include parsley, chopped celery, jícama, celeriac, and sweet bell peppers.

GREEN PAPAYA SALSA

THIS REFRESHING salsa has a surprisingly rich flavor and makes the perfect cooling counterpart to spicy stews and curries. If papayas are hard to find, make the salsa with a diced firm-ripe mango or fresh pineapple.

MAKES 8 SERVINGS

Using the largest openings on a box grater, grate the papaya and carrot into a large bowl. Add the lime juice, cilantro, vinegar, molasses, ginger, garlic, salt, and pepper; toss to coat. Let the salsa rest at room temperature for 30 minutes before serving.

1 green papaya, peeled and seeded

1 carrot, peeled

Juice of 1 lime

2 tbsp chopped fresh cilantro

2 tsp red wine vinegar

2 tsp molasses

1 tsp grated peeled fresh ginger

1 garlic clove, minced

Salt and pepper as needed

CHAYOTE-JÍCAMA SALSA

1 chayote squash, peeled and sliced

1 jícama, peeled and julienned

2 tomatoes, peeled, seeded, and diced

1 jalapeño, minced fine

½ cup diced red onion

1 tbsp cider vinegar

Salt and pepper as needed

Dash of Tabasco to taste

TO PEEL chayote, use a vegetable peeler to remove the outer skin. Jícama is easier to peel with a sharp paring knife. First halve or quarter the jícama lengthwise, then pull and slice away the skin and the fibrous layer just below the skin.

THIS QUICKLY prepared salsa incorporates two vegetables that originated in South America and Mexico. However, it was not until recently that they made a noticeable appearance in markets throughout the United States. If you are unfamiliar with these vegetables, be sure to read the preparation instructions found in the note at left.

MAKES 6 TO 8 SERVINGS

1. Bring about 1 inch of water to a rolling boil over high heat in a sauté pan. Add the sliced chayote and cover the pan. Pan-steam the squash for about 12 minutes, or until the chayote is very tender. Drain it, and rinse with cool water to stop the cooking.

2. Combine the chayote slices with all of the remaining ingredients in a bowl.

3. Chill the salsa for at least 2 to 3 hours or overnight. Taste the salsa and adjust the seasonings with additional vinegar, salt, pepper, or Tabasco, as needed.

HALF-SOUR PICKLES

Pickling cucumbers, also known as Kirby cucumbers, can be found in many green grocers and farm stands from the middle to the end of summer. They are smaller, and more "warty" than the slicing cucumbers used in salads.

MAKES 25 PICKLES

1. Combine the pickling spice, vinegar, water, salt, garlic, and cucumbers in a stockpot and bring to a boil.
2. Remove the pan from the heat. Remove the garlic and add the fresh dill.
3. Allow the pickles to marinate in the brine overnight before serving. Pickles can be held in the refrigerator for up to 2 weeks. To jar the pickles for longer storage, see the sidebar on page 270.

1 tbsp pickling spice

½ cup cider vinegar

1½ quarts water

¼ cup kosher salt

12 garlic cloves, peeled and crushed

25 pickling cucumbers, washed

3 sprigs fresh dill

SWEET PICKLE CHIPS

Pickle chips are delicious as part of a sandwich or served on the side, chopped and added to salads and salad dressings, or on their own as part of a traditional relish tray that includes olives, celery and carrots sticks, and radishes.

MAKES 8 CUPS

1. Wash the cucumbers and slice ¼ inch thick. Slice the onions ¼ inch thick. Combine the cucumbers and onions with cider vinegar, salt, mustard seeds, 2 tablespoons of the sugar, and the water in a large pot. Bring the liquid to a simmer over high heat; immediately reduce the heat to low and simmer for 10 minutes. Drain, discard the liquid, and set aside.
3. Bring the white vinegar, celery seed, allspice, turmeric, and remaining sugar to a boil. Pour the pickling mixture over the cucumbers and onions. Let rest under refrigeration for 3 to 4 days before serving. Hold under refrigeration for up to 4 weeks.

4 lb Kirby cucumbers

2 large onions

3 cups cider vinegar

1 tbsp salt

1 tsp whole mustard seed

4 cups sugar

8 cups water

2½ cups white vinegar

2 tbsp celery seed

1 tbsp crushed allspice berries

2 tsp ground turmeric

PICKLED BEETS AND ONIONS

16 baby beets, tops trimmed

2 medium red onions, julienned

2 tbsp sugar

⅓ cup white vinegar

2 tsp salt

⅔ cup water

THIS IS a classic relish that makes the most of the sweet taste of baby beets and the heat of red onions.

MAKES 4 SERVINGS

1. Bring a large pot of salted water to a rolling boil. Add the beets, reduce the heat, and simmer the beets until tender, 12 to 15 minutes. Drain them well. When cool enough to handle, slip off the skin. Place the beets in a bowl and set aside.

2. To make the marinade, combine the onions, sugar, vinegar, salt, and ⅔ cup water in a saucepan and bring to a boil over high heat. Simmer for 5 minutes.

3. Pour the hot marinade over the beets, and cool to room temperature. Cover the beets well and refrigerate for several hours or overnight before serving.

SAFE PICKLING AND CANNING

Every fall, legions of home cooks process cucumbers, green beans, and a host of other vegetables into pickles. And every year, some of those foods go bad. Low acid foods can develop *clostridium botulinum* which could result in botulism in canned foods—a deadly form of food poisoning.

The pickle recipes we have included here are meant to be eaten within a few weeks and make a relatively small batch. If you are interested in pickling, there are many excellent resources available that can help. If you are new at pickles and preserves, you can get a great education in how to properly clean and sterilize jars, use the cold or hot pack method, and process the pickles by consulting the USDA's publication, *Complete Guide to Home Canning*. Using the right tools, having reliable recipes, and understanding how to keep foods safe and wholesome is imperative.

The National Center for Home Food Preservation is a source for current research-based recommendations for most methods of home food preservation, including fermented, smoked, and dried foods made at home. Information and publications can be found at their website (http://www.uga.edu/nchfp/how/general.html). The Center was established with funding from the Cooperative State Research, Education and Extension Service, U.S. Department of Agriculture (CSREES-USDA) to address food safety concerns for those who practice and teach home food preservation and processing methods.

RED ONION MARMALADE

2 medium red onions, sliced thin

2 tbsp dry red wine

2 tsp sugar

2 tsp Grenadine

2 tsp cider vinegar

Salt and pepper as needed

1 tsp chopped fresh thyme (or ½ tsp dried leaves)

MARMALADES ARE similar to jams and jellies. The difference lies in the way that the food is handled. Jellies are made from the juice of fruits and vegetables, jams from the whole food. Conserves and marmalades usually leave the food whole or thinly sliced. This marmalade could be made with Vidalia or other sweet onions. Use a white wine instead of red wine for the best appearance, or try a dry sherry or vermouth.

MAKES 1 CUP

1. Mix all of the ingredients except the fresh thyme in a saucepan; simmer over medium-low heat until almost all of the liquid has evaporated.
2. Remove from the heat and add the thyme.
3. The marmalade may be served now, or properly cooled and stored as follows: Transfer the room-temperature marmalade to a clean jar or bowl. Cover tightly and refrigerate. The marmalade can be held under refrigeration for up to 10 days.

ROASTED RED PEPPER AND APRICOT RELISH

1 tbsp olive oil

½ cup minced red onions

½ tsp minced garlic

¾ cup minced roasted red bell peppers

½ cup Vegetable Broth (page 82)

¼ cup minced dried apricots

1 tbsp red wine vinegar, plus as needed

1 tsp honey mustard

2 to 3 drops hot sauce, as needed

Salt and pepper as needed

1 tbsp chopped fresh parsley

THE FLAVOR and color combinations in this vibrant relish are so wonderful, you'll want to double the recipe and have plenty on hand to spread on whole wheat crackers or to liven up a simple roast turkey sandwich. To hold the relish, pour it into perfectly clean jars or other containers, seal tight, and keep refrigerated for up to 2 weeks.

MAKES 2 CUPS

1. Heat a sauté pan over medium heat. Add the oil and heat until the surface ripples. Add the onions and garlic and sauté, stirring frequently, until tender and translucent, about 2 minutes.
2. Add the peppers, broth, apricots, 1 tablespoon vinegar, and the mustard; bring to a boil. Reduce the heat and simmer until most of the liquid has cooked away, about 15 minutes. Season to taste with the hot sauce, additional vinegar, salt, and pepper. Add the parsley just before serving. Serve at room temperature or chilled.

CORN RELISH

2 ears corn, husked

¼ cup diced red pepper

1 small jalapeño, seeded and chopped fine

1 scallion, sliced thin

2 tbsp tightly packed brown sugar

3 tbsp cider vinegar

2 tsp powdered dry mustard

Dash of Tabasco sauce

1 tsp Worcestershire sauce, or to taste

½ tsp salt, or to taste

THIS LIGHTLY spiced, sweet and sour relish is a classic choice to accompany such American favorites as grilled hamburgers or steaks, hot dogs, or as an accompaniment to a variety of sandwiches. It also can be served on a bed of lettuce along with a variety of other sliced, shredded, or diced vegetables to make a more substantial salad that can stand on its own as a main course.

MAKES 5 TO 6 SERVINGS

1. Bring a large pot of water to a boil. Add the corn and cook until the kernels are just barely tender, about 5 minutes. Remove the corn from the water. When it is cool enough to handle, cut the kernels from the cob into a mixing bowl. Add the red pepper, jalapeño, and scallion. Reserve until needed.

2. Heat the remaining ingredients in a skillet over high heat and bring to a boil. Remove from the heat and add the corn mixture. Toss until evenly coated.

3. Serve the relish warm, or allow it to cool to room temperature, place it in a clean bowl or jar, cover tightly, and store in the refrigerator for up to 10 days.

SPICY MANGO CHUTNEY

Some stores offer peeled and sliced mango in the produce section, which makes putting this delicious chutney together very quick. If you are choosing a fresh mango for this recipe at the market, look for a firm, heavy fruit with some yellow and orange, but the flesh should be relatively firm.

MAKES ABOUT 2 CUPS

Combine the mango and brown sugar in a saucepan. Add the vinegar, raisins, jalapeños, garlic, ginger, salt, and pepper. Bring to a boil, reduce the heat to low, and simmer 15 minutes. Transfer to a clean storage container. Cover and refrigerate for at least 24 hours to allow the flavor to mellow. The chutney can be held for up to 2 weeks.

2 cups chopped mango

⅔ cup packed dark brown sugar

2 tbsp cider vinegar

⅓ cup dark raisins

1 tbsp minced jalapeños, or to taste

2 tbsp minced garlic

1 tbsp minced ginger

Salt and pepper as needed

HANDLING HOT CHILES

Scotch bonnets, along with the closely related (and equally potent) Jamaican hots and habaneros, are small, fiery-hot chiles that are irregularly shaped and range in color from yellow to orange to red. Use gloves when handling hot chiles to prevent irritation, and be sure not to inadvertently rub your eyes or face.

HAZELNUT ROMESCO SAUCE

THIS RICH sauce is the perfect accompaniment to grilled and broiled vegetables or to accompany savory vegetable entrees.

MAKES 2 CUPS

1. Put the ancho chiles in a small saucepan and cover with cold water. Bring to a boil over high heat, then immediately remove the pan from the heat. Let the chiles steep for 20 minutes. Strain the chiles from the water. Reserve some of the soaking liquid to adjust the consistency of the sauce.

2. Put the roasted red pepper, hazelnuts, olive oil, tomato paste, vinegar, garlic, paprika, and cayenne in a blender. Puree to a smooth consistency, adding a bit of the chile soaking liquid, if necessary, to puree the sauce and reach a soft, sauce-like consistency (about the same consistency as mayonnaise). Place in a covered container, refrigerate, and allow to rest overnight to develop the best flavor. Adjust the seasoning with salt before serving.

2 ancho chiles (dry)

Cold water as needed

2 cups chopped roasted red bell pepper

2 cups chopped hazelnuts, skinned

⅔ cup olive oil

2 tbsp tomato paste

2 tbsp red wine vinegar

1 tbsp minced garlic

1½ tsp Spanish paprika

¼ tsp cayenne pepper

Salt as needed

HARISSA

HARISSA IS a spicy-hot Tunisian condiment that traditionally accompanies couscous. It frequently is used to flavor soups and stews. For the best flavor, grind caraway, coriander, and cumin seeds yourself just before making the harissa (a spice or coffee grinder will give you the finest grind). Covered tightly, harissa will keep in the refrigerator for several months.

MAKES ABOUT ⅔ CUP

1. Stem, seed, and break up the chiles. Soak them in cold water for 15 minutes. Drain well, wrap in cheesecloth or place in a strainer, and press out any excess moisture.

2. Chop the garlic, sprinkle with the salt, and mash to a paste using the side of a knife.

3. Grind the chiles, garlic, caraway, coriander, and cumin in a mortar and pestle. (A spice grinder also may be used, but it may smell like harissa forever after.)

4. Place the harissa in a small jar or other suitable container and drizzle it with the oil to make a thin layer. Cover tightly and store in the refrigerator.

9 dried New Mexico or other large, hot red chiles

1 garlic clove, peeled

Salt and pepper as needed

¾ tsp ground caraway

¼ tsp ground coriander

¼ tsp ground cumin

1 tbsp extra-virgin olive oil

TZATZIKI SAUCE

½ cup plain yogurt

½ cup sour cream

½ cup grated cucumber, squeezed dry

1 tsp minced garlic

1 tbsp extra-virgin olive oil

1 tbsp minced fresh mint or dill

1 tsp lemon juice, or as needed

½ tsp grated lemon zest

Salt and pepper as needed

THIS YOGURT-AND-CUCUMBER sauce cools the heat from fiery curries, and adds richness to Zucchini Pancakes (page 237). You also can serve it on its own as a salad.

MAKES 1½ CUPS

Combine the yogurt, sour cream, cucumber, and garlic in a food processor and puree until smooth. Transfer to a bowl and fold in the olive oil, mint or dill, lemon juice, and zest. Stir until combined and season to taste with salt and pepper. Keep refrigerated until ready to serve.

MUSTARD

⅓ cup dry mustard

1 tbsp sugar

¾ tsp salt

3 large eggs

⅔ cup malt vinegar

1 tsp honey

¼ tsp Tabasco sauce

USE THIS mustard whenever you would normally serve a prepared mustard. It has a wonderfully sharp taste and a creamy texture that make it a good choice to serve with roasted or grilled foods. Include it in salad dressings and dips, or as a spread for sandwiches.

YOU MAY not have thought of making your own mustard, but this recipe is easy to make. To vary the flavor of this mustard, add ingredients such as mashed and chopped green peppercorns, chopped fresh tarragon or chives, a little honey to taste, grated orange or lemon zest, or maple syrup. Double the recipe so you can take half along as a house gift the next time you are invited to dinner.

MAKES APPROXIMATELY 1 CUP

1. Bring about 2 inches of water to a boil in a saucepan, and reduce heat to low.

2. Whisk the mustard, sugar, salt, and eggs together in a metal bowl until smooth. Add the malt vinegar and mix well.

3. Place the bowl over the simmering water and cook, whisking constantly, until thickened. The mustard should fall from the whisk in ribbons that remain visible on the surface for several seconds. Remove the mustard from the heat, and stir in the honey and Tabasco sauce. Cool to room temperature, then place in a clean bowl or jar; cover tightly and chill thoroughly before serving. The mustard may be stored in the refrigerator for up to 2 weeks.

PESTO

½ cup lightly packed chopped basil leaves

¼ cup grated Parmesan cheese

¼ cup toasted pine nuts

1 garlic clove, minced

3 tbsp extra-virgin olive oil, plus as needed

Salt and pepper as needed

I F YOU have a mortar and pestle, use it for your pesto. This pesto recipe doubles or triples easily. If you are making a big batch, leave the Parmesan out of the portion you want to store, transfer to a clean jar, and cover with a thin layer of olive oil to prevent the sauce from darkening and drying out.

MAKES 1 CUP

1. Put the basil in a food processor and process until the basil is evenly chopped. Add the Parmesan, pine nuts, and garlic, and scrape down the sides and bottom of the bowl.

2. With the processor running, gradually add the olive oil until a thick, heavy paste forms. It should have a distinctly coarse texture, but should not appear oily. Transfer the pesto to a bowl. Taste it and add salt and pepper as needed.

3. The pesto is ready to use now. To hold the pesto for later use, pour a thin layer of olive oil over the surface and store it in a covered container in the refrigerator for up to 2 weeks, or in the freezer for up to 2 months.

CREAM SAUCE

2 tbsp unsalted butter

7 tbsp all-purpose flour

2 cups whole milk

1 cup heavy cream

Salt and pepper as needed

⅛ tsp freshly grated nutmeg, optional

U SE THIS cream sauce to make perfect creamed vegetable dishes. You can add grated or crumbled cheeses to turn this into a cheese sauce, the ideal topping for vegetable gratins and binder for vegetable casseroles.

MAKES ABOUT 2½ CUPS

Melt the butter in a saucepan over medium heat. Add the flour and cook, stirring frequently, to make a blond roux, about 5 minutes. Whisk the milk and cream into the roux. Bring the cream sauce back to a boil. Add ½ teaspoon salt, ¼ teaspoon pepper, and the nutmeg, if using. Reduce the heat to low and allow the sauce to simmer, stirring frequently, until it is thickened and no longer tastes floury, about 20 minutes. Remove from the heat and cover to keep warm, or cool the sauce and store in a covered container in the refrigerator for up to 3 days.

MAYONNAISE is an important basic sauce. If you make it yourself you can control not only the way it tastes, but also its thickness. It is per-fect to serve as an accompaniment to a num-ber of recipes. The oil you choose makes a sig-nificant difference in the flavor of the sauce.

ADDING THE OIL

Unless you have an extra pair of hands in the kitchen, you will need a strategy to keep your bowl still. You'll need one hand to pour the oil and the other to whisk as you pour, so in lieu of that extra hand, set your mixing bowl on a cloth towel to keep it still.

When you start to add the oil to your egg yolks, pour it very slowly, almost one drop at a time. When you've added enough oil to begin to thicken the sauce, you can add it a little more rapidly, as shown here.

FLAVORED MAYONNAISE

On its own, mayonnaise has an almost bland taste. To add in-terest to the sauce, stir in ingredients that are pungent and fla-vorful. Some additions, like the red pepper puree shown here, give mayonnaise a beautiful color. Others, like the chopped spinach and herbs for Sauce Verte (page 282), add flavor, color, and texture. Fold in lots of garlic or shallots (minced or roasted and pureed), diced pickled vegetables, or capers for extra punch.

MAYONNAISE

2 egg yolks

1 tbsp white vinegar

2 tbsp cold water, as needed

½ tsp dry mustard

Salt and pepper as needed

1½ cups olive oil (or a combination of olive and canola oil)

Lemon juice as needed

SOMETIMES REFERRED to as the mother sauce of the cold kitchen, mayonnaise can be seasoned to fit many needs. Variations can be made by adding purées of herbs, peppers, or tomatoes. Saffron can be infused in some of the oil to lend brilliant color. Diced or chopped pickles, capers, or olives may be added to increase flavor and texture.

MAKES 2 CUPS

1. Whisk together the egg yolks, vinegar, 1 tablespoon of water, mustard, and ½ teaspoon of salt until slightly foamy.

2. Add the oil gradually in a thin stream, whisking constantly, until all the oil is incorporated and the mayonnaise is thick. Adjust the consistency with a few drops of water if it becomes too thick as you whisk it.

3. Season the mayonnaise to taste with salt, pepper, and lemon juice, as needed. Refrigerate immediately.

Green Mayonnaise (Sauce Verte)

Add ⅓ cup chopped cooked spinach after the oil is incorporated and the mayonnaise is thick. (Remember to squeeze cooked or thawed frozen spinach well before chopping. Reserve the juice to give the mayonnaise more color.) Add ¼ cup finely minced herbs (a combination of dill, tarragon, chives, and parsley is nice, but you can feel free to add other herbs to suit your taste). Stir the mayonnaise and refrigerate immediately.

Rouille

Prepare as for basic Mayonnaise (above), adding the 2 teaspoons of minced garlic to the egg yolk mixture along with the vinegar and water. Stir in ¼ cup Roasted Red Pepper Puree (page 262).

HOLLANDAISE SAUCE

½ tsp cracked peppercorns

¼ cup white wine or cider vinegar

¼ cup water, or as needed

4 large egg yolks, fresh or pasteurized

1½ cups melted or clarified butter

2 tsp lemon juice, or as needed

2 tsp salt, or as needed

Pinch ground white pepper

Pinch cayenne, optional

Hollandaise is a classic accompaniment to steamed vegetables, notably asparagus and artichokes. You can vary this sauce by folding in chopped tarragon and a bit of Dijon-style mustard.

MAKES 2 CUPS

1. Put 3 inches of water in a sauce pan and bring to a simmer.

2. In a small pan, combine the peppercorns and vinegar. Cook over medium heat and reduce until nearly dry, about 5 minutes. Add ¼ cup water to the vinegar reduction. Strain this liquid into a stainless steel bowl.

3. Add the egg yolks to the vinegar reduction and set the bowl over the pot of simmering water. Whisk constantly and cook the mixture until the yolks triple in volume and fall in ribbons from the whisk. Remove the bowl from the simmering water and set it on a clean kitchen towel to keep the bowl from slipping.

4. Gradually ladle the warm butter into the egg mixture, whisking constantly. As the butter is blended into the yolks, the sauce will thicken. If it becomes too thick and the butter is not blending in easily, add a little water or lemon juice to thin the egg mixture enough to whisk in the remaining butter. Season the hollandaise with lemon juice, salt, pepper, and cayenne, if desired.

5. The sauce is ready to serve at this point, or it may be finished as desired by adding a variety of additional ingredients (see the notes above). The sauce should be held warm over a hot water bath or it can be held sealed in a vacuum bottle.

INDEX

A

acorn squash, 6

appetizers, 86–124

about: artichokes, 8, 14, 90–91; crudités, 86; cutting tempura vegetables, 116; making crostini or canapés, 102

Artichoke Ceviche in Belgian Endive, 92–93

Artichoke Dip, 88

Avocado and Black Bean Crostini, 104, 105

Avocado with Marinated Fiddlehead Ferns, 95

Baked Tomatoes with Goat Cheese, 100

Baked Vidalia Onions, 101

Cheddar Corn Fritters, 120, 121

Chilled Asparagus with Mustard Herb Vinaigrette, 108–9

Garlic and Parsley Butter, 103

Greek Grilled Vegetables, 114

Grilled Vegetables with a Parsley Salad, 114

Guacamole, 88

Mixed Grill of Garden Vegetables with Charmoula, 114–15

Onion Dip, 89

Portobello with Tuscan Bean Salad and Celery Juice, 107

Red Pepper Mousse in Endive, 106

Spanakopita, 122–24

Spinach and Sausage Stuffed Mushrooms, 94

Spinach Dip, 89

Stuffed Cherry Tomatoes with Minted Barley Cucumber Salad, 96, 97

Stuffed Grape Leaves, 110–11

Tomato Sampler with Pan-Fried Calamari, 98–99

Vegetable Tempura, 118–19

Vietnamese Fried Spring Rolls, 112, 113

apples

Curried Squash and Apple Soup, 62

Frisée with Almonds, Apples, Grapes, and Goat Cheese, 142

aromatics

in soups, 32–33, 35

sweating or smothering, 35

artichokes

about, 8, 90–91; cooking, 90; cooking with, 91; Jerusalem artichokes, 8; preparing, 14, 90, 91; serving, 90; trimming, 90

Artichoke and Olive Salad, 162

Artichoke and Spinach Risotto, 189

Artichoke Ceviche in Belgian Endive, 92–93

Artichoke Dip, 88

Mixed Grill of Garden Vegetables with Charmoula, 114–15

arugula

about, 4; selecting, 2

Spinach and Arugula Salad with Strawberries, 144

Tomato, Arugula, and Mozzarella Salad, 152

asparagus

about, 8, 224; cutting for tempura, 116; preparing, 224; selecting, 224

Asparagus a la Parrilla, 224

Asparagus with Shitakes, Bowtie Pasta, and Spring Peas, 176, 177

Chilled Asparagus with Mustard Herb Vinaigrette, 108–9

Parmesan-Roasted White Asparagus with White Truffle Oil, 225

avocados

about, 8; potassium content, 1; salads with, 139; storing, 9

Avocado and Black Bean Crostini, 104, 105

Avocado with Marinated Fiddlehead Ferns, 95

Chilled Cream of Avocado Soup, 79

Guacamole, 88

Tomato, Avocado, and Roasted Corn Salad, 140–41

Two-Cabbage Slaw with Avocado and Red Onion, 158

B

bacon. See pork

Baked Tomatoes with Goat Cheese, 100

Baked Vidalia Onions, 101

baking and roasting vegetables, 20–21, 153

Balsamic Vinaigrette, 131

Basic Tomato Sauce, 260

basil

Cream of Tomato Soup with Rice and Basil, 55

Pesto, 280

batonnet cut, 12

beans

about: selecting, 2; stringing, 14; types of, 7

Avocado and Black Bean Crostini, 104, 105

Beet Greens and White Beans Sauté, 235

Chilled Infusion of Fresh Vegetables with Fava Beans, 80, 81

Chinese Long Bean Salad with Tangerines and Sherry-Mustard Vinaigrette, 163

H'Lelem (Tunisian Vegetable Soup), 44

Portobello with Tuscan Bean Salad and Celery Juice, 107

Spring Greens and Cannellini Gratin, 215

Beef, Vietnamese Water Spinach and, Soup, 48, 49

Beet Greens and White Beans Sauté, 235

beets

about, 8

Citrus-Roasted Beets, 247

Pickled Beets and Onions, 270–71

Roasted Beet and Orange Salad, 160, 161

Belgian endive. See endive

Blackened Tomato Salsa, 263

boiling vegetables, 18–19

bok choy, about, 2, 4

Borscht, Chilled, 72

Braised Kale, 232

Braised Red Cabbage, 233

braising and stewing, 26–27

bread crumbs, 214

breadings, applying, 25

broccoli

about, 4; selecting, 2; storing, 9

Broccoli in Garlic Sauce, 234

Cream of Broccoli Soup, 52–53

broccoli rabe

about, 4; selecting, 2

Sautéed Broccoli Raab with Garlic and
Crushed Pepper, 244–45

broiling and grilling, 25–26

brussells sprouts

about, 4, 220; finishing, 221; preparing,
221; selecting, 2; trimming, 221

Brussels Sprouts with Mustard Glaze,
222–23

Maple-Glazed Brussels Sprouts with
Chestnuts, 220

Burgers, Vegetable, 182

butter

about: finishing and reheating in,
16

Garlic and Parsley Butter, 103

Buttermilk-Chive Dressing, 138

butternut squash. *See* squash

buying vegetables, 1–3, 11

C

cabbage

about, 10; selecting, 2; storing, 9

Braised Red Cabbage, 233

Two-Cabbage Slaw with Avocado and Red
Onion, 158

Calamari, Pan-Fried, with Tomato Sampler,
98–99

canapés, making, 102

canning safety, 270–71

Capellini with Grilled Vegetables, 175

Caramelized Onion Tart, 203

Caraway Squash Bisque, Chilled, 78

carrots

about, 6; cutting for tempura, 116;
storing, 9

Cold Carrot Bisque, 76–77

Moroccan Carrot Salad, 164

cauliflower, about, 2, 10

celeriac, about, 8

celery

about, 10; celery juice, 107; storing, 9

Portobello with Tuscan Bean Salad and
Celery Juice, 107

chanterelle mushrooms, selecting, 2

chard. *See* Swiss chard

Charmoula, 114

Chayote

about: peeling, 266

Chayote and Pineapple Chimichangas,
212–14

Chayote-Jícama Salsa, 266–67

Cheddar Corn Fritters, 120, 121

cheese

Baked Tomatoes with Goat Cheese, 100

Cheddar Corn Fritters, 120, 121

Cheese Croutons, 34

Chopped Steakhouse Salad with Maytag
Blue Cheese and Red Wine Vinaigrette,
146, 147

Corn Chowder with Chiles and Monterey
Jack, 46

Cucumber, Tomato, and Feta Salad,
132

Eggplant and Havarti Sandwiches,
183

Frisée with Almonds, Apples, Grapes, and
Goat Cheese, 142

Goat Cheese or Cheddar Rusks, 34

Green Beans with Frizzled Prosciutto and
Gruyère, 148, 149

Spinach and Goat Cheese Quiche, 202

Tomato, Arugula, and Mozzarella Salad,
152

Tomato Salad with Warm Ricotta Cheese,
152

Warm Brie Dressing, 143

chicken

Chicken and Vegetable Kebabs, 180–81

Chicken Broth, 83

Chickpea and Vegetable Tagine, 186–87

chiffonade cut, 12

chiles

about: hot, handling, 275

Chile Cream Sauce, 208–9

Chiles Rellenos, 211

Corn Chowder with Chiles and Monterey
Jack, 46

Fettuccine with Corn, Squash, Chiles,
Crème Fraîche, and Cilantro, 179

Harissa, 277

Chilled Asparagus with Mustard Herb Vinaigrette, 108–9

chilled soups. *See* soups (cold)

chimichangas

Chayote and Pineapple Chimichangas,
212–14

Chimichanga Dough, 214

Chinese Long Bean Salad with Tangerines
and Sherry-Mustard Vinaigrette, 163

Chipotle-Sherry Vinaigrette, 140

chopping vegetables, 12

Chorizo and Vegetable Soup, 39

chutney, about, 256

Citrus-Roasted Beets, 247

Classic Vegetable Soup, 38

coatings, applying, 25

cold soups. *See* soups (cold)

collard greens, about, 2, 4, 9

colors, of vegetables, 1, 17, 218

condiments. *See* sauces and relishes

cooking techniques, 18–27

applying coatings and breadings, 25

boiling, 18–19

deep frying, 24

grilling and broiling, 25–26

microwaving, 16, 19–20

panfrying, 23–24

pureeing, 27, 47, 51

roasting and baking, 20–21

sautéing, 21–23

steaming and "pan-steaming", 19

stewing and braising, 26–27

cooking vegetables, 3–27

in advance, 16

color retention while, 17

dark green vegetables, 4–6

determining doneness, 15–16

evaluating quality, 15–16

flavor retention while, 17–18

general guidelines, 3–4, 11

handling and, 11

legumes, 6–7

nutrient retention while, 17

orange vegetables, 6

other vegetables, 8–10

A Note on the Type

This book was set in the OpenType version of Adobe Warnock.
Begun as a personal typeface for the co-founder of Adobe Systems, John
Warnock, by noted type designer Robert Slimbach, the project gradually grew
to include an italic and multiple weights, and it was decided to release the
typeface to the general public. A full-featured modern composition family
designed for versatility in a variety of mediums and printing situations,
Warnock synergizes classically derived letterforms of old style types
with elements of transitional and modern type design.

Art direction, design, and composition by Kevin Hanek

Printed in Singapore by Imago Worldwide Printing